COLONIAL CULHUACAN, 1580–1600

COLONIAL CULHUACAN, 1580–1600

A Social History of an Aztec Town

S. L. Cline

UNIVERSITY OF NEW MEXICO PRESS
Albuquerque

Library of Congress Cataloging-in-Publication Data

Cline, S. L., 1948–
  Colonial Culhuacan, 1580–1600.

  Bibliography: P.
  Includes index.
  1. Nahuas—Social conditions.   2. Culhuacán (Mexico)—
Social conditions.   3. Aztecs—Social conditions.   4. Indians
of Mexico—Social conditions.   I. Title.
F1221.N3C58   1986   972'.53   86–7114
ISBN 0-8263-0884-8

© 1986 by the University of New Mexico Press.
All rights reserved.
First edition.

Designed by Susan Gutnik

To Marvin Shinbrot, notlaçonamictzin

CONTENTS

Illustrations / ix
Preface / xi
1 / Background to Colonial Culhuacan / 1
2 / The Testaments of Culhuacan / 9
3 / Piety, Death, and Wills / 13
4 / Town Government / 35
5 / Family and Inheritance / 59
6 / Wealth / 87
7 / Gender and Status / 107
8 / Land / 125
9 / Conclusions / 161
Appendix 1 / Prices / 173
Appendix 2 / Spanish Loanwords / 177
Appendix 3 / Testaments of Cristina Tiacapan / 183
Appendix 4 / Division of doña Luisa Juana's Estate / 189
Notes / 213
Glossary / 235
Bibliography / 239
Index / 249

ILLUSTRATIONS

Figures

Fig. 1 Relación geográfica map of Culhuacan / 40
Fig. 2 A Culhuacan house plan / 52
Fig. 3 A Culhuacan genealogy / 67
Fig. 4 Cadastral of Juan de San Miguel's portion of doña Luisa Juana's estate / 128

Map

Lake Texcoco region / xviii

Tables

Table 1 Culhuacan rulers / 5
Table 2 Genealogy of Angelina Mocel's family / 10–11
Table 3 Wards of Culhuacan c. 1580 / 56–57
Table 4 Titled testators / 108
Table 5 Testators with titled kin / 109
Table 6 Numerical iconography / 131
Table 7 Toponyms associated with Chinampas / 136
Table 8 Toponyms associated with Tlalmilli / 138

PREFACE

This work is a portrait of life in the Indian town of Culhuacan in the late sixteenth century. Culhuacan was renowned in the prehispanic period as a refuge for the Toltecs after the fall of Tula (about A.D. 1100); but in the late sixteenth century, it was just another Indian town under Spanish rule. This study of a small but historically important Aztec town is unique because it is based primarily on documentation in the native language of Nahuatl, *The Testaments of Culhuacan* (Cline and León-Portilla, 1984). The wills of some of the men and women who died in Culhuacan provide a wealth of information about life and death in the late sixteenth century. The focus is on the *people* of Culhuacan, using the lives of individuals to create a social history of an Indian town.

Anthropologists have described life in present-day villages by living there themselves, by interviewing people, and by observing customs and practices. Historians attempting to reconstruct life in a community are forced to rely on the written records of those long dead.

Some types of documents, such as Inquisition records, lend themselves well to historical reconstruction of the lives of individuals. From a single case brought before the Inquisition, the Italian historian Carlo Ginzburg could reconstruct the cosmology of a sixteenth-century Italian miller (Ginzburg, 1980). More analogous for this study of Culhuacan is Emmanuel LeRoy Ladurie's recreation of life in the fourteenth-century Occitan community of Montaillou, using extensive Inquisition records (1979a).

Testaments and wills are also valuable to historians. A will is a window into someone's life. The men and women who made them listed their property, named their heirs, discharged their debts, made arrangements for the care of their children, and ordered masses. Although the assumption often is that wills were only made by the wealthy, historians of Europe have used testaments to discern patterns of peasant societies, including family structure, residence, and property holding (Goody et al., 1976). Others have used wills to probe changing attitudes toward religion and death (Ariès, 1981; Vovelle, 1978).

The principal source for this study of colonial Culhuacan is a book of wills written in Nahuatl, *The Testaments of Culhuacan*. A detailed description of it is given in Chapter 2. The Culhuacan wills were recorded by Indian notaries entirely in Nahuatl, the language of the Aztecs. In the sixteenth century, Spanish friars taught Indian notaries to write their languages in Latin letters. Records in Nahuatl exist in various archives, dating from the midsixteenth century through to the early nineteenth.

There are several different types of Nahuatl documents. Some were directed toward the Spanish colonial administration, such as petitions to the king to redress grievances. Other Nahuatl documents, such as testaments, were written for the Indians' own use. Essentially all Nahuatl documents are legal records. Except for a few letters exchanged by members of the Motecuhçoma family, which also concerned legal matters (Anderson et al., 1976), Nahuatl documents were public records, not private expressions of sentiment.

Wills are one of the few types of colonial Nahuatl documents which were *standardly* made by individual Indians concerning their families, their property, and their religious beliefs. For this reason, they are important for social historians. Some Nahuatl wills were ultimately introduced into evidence in property suits before Spanish courts, but initially they were simply the records of testators' final wishes. Wills were used to regulate transmission of property within the Indian community and were not primarily addressed to the Spanish world. The limitation of using just one type of historical source for this study—testaments—is offset by the richness of that source. The Culhuacan wills give detailed information on a variety of topics, allowing me to reconstruct a picture of the town and its people from the viewpoint of its Indian citizens.

There is a paucity of other sources for sixteenth-century Culhuacan. There exists a small number of printed sources such as the Relación geográfica (1580) (Gallegos, 1927; Monterrosa Prado, 1970) and a fragment of a baptismal register (1588) (Gorbea Trueba, n.d.).

In addition, there are a few scattered archival sources for the town during the period of study. These include a small cache of Nahuatl documents on an estate division of a Culhuacan noblewoman (1580–1594) (AGN–T–58–4); a lawsuit preserved in the Bibliothèque Nationale de Paris, which includes a Nahuatl will (1576–1594) (BNP 110); and finally, records of Culhuacan land sales to Spaniards (1585–1628) (AGN–T–1739–5).

For many years studies of Nahuatl-speaking peoples focused either on the Aztecs of the prehispanic and conquest eras or on modern-day peasants. The glory of the Aztec empire, the horror of massive human sacrifice, the vacillation of Motecuhçoma, the deeds of Malinche, and the tragedy of Cuauhtemoc captured both popular and scholarly attention. Anthropologists who studied twentieth-century Nahua-speaking villages concentrated on modern practices and attempted to relate them to the prehispanic past (Redfield, 1930). Oscar Lewis's restudy of the town of Tepoztlán, Morelos (1951), includes a section on the colonial history of the town, but only as background to a modern ethnography. There was a hiatus between the prehispanic past and the present. The colonial descendants of the Aztecs, the Indians who lived under Spanish rule, were neglected by scholars who were more interested in the prehispanic era or in modern cultural survivals than in the process of transformation during the colonial period to new cultural modes.

Beginning in the late 1940s a group of scholars emerged, trained mainly in history and anthropology, who were interested in *colonial* Indians. Any study of colonial Aztecs now undertaken builds on the work by this group who examined how the Indians were ruled, how many there were, and what effects they had on the shaping of colonial Mexico. For the purposes of this study of colonial Culhuacan, the classic works by Charles Gibson are the most valuable. *Tlaxcala in the Sixteenth Century* (1952) is one of the earliest and best modern studies of a single Mexican town. Gibson draws on Spanish political sources and native sources in Spanish to produce a detailed picture of Tlaxcala's institutions. His *Aztecs Under Spanish Rule* (1964) is an unsurpassed general account focusing on changes in Indian culture in the Valley of Mexico over the entire colonial period. Gibson's sources are mainly records in Spanish, many of which were produced by the colonial government in its efforts to rule the Indians.

As scholars begin to learn Indian languages, they can read the records produced by Indians for their own use, and a potentially different history of colonial Indians can be written. There are numerous sixteenth-century reports by Spaniards which should be modified in light of the new information from Nahuatl documentation. While there was no country-wide conspiracy of Indians to mislead Spaniards about their cultural patterns, nor were Spaniards merely fumbling toward an understanding of native culture, there are differences between Spaniards' reports and what is found in Nahuatl documentation. Some of this can be attributed to Spanish misunderstanding of Indian ways, but perhaps some of what is at variance can be attributed to regional variations (Borah, 1984:27). What was true for the Puebla-Tlaxcala regions might not hold for Morelos—or for Culhuacan. Thus scholars turn again to doing local and regional studies, clearly demarcated by time and place. Many of these are now classified as ethnohistory. Ethnohistory has become a respectable field in its own right, but integrating it with the vast amount known about the history of the Spanish world deepens our understanding of cultural change.

In this study I hope to reach not just the coterie of Mesoamerican ethnohistorians but scholars of other disciplines, as well as students, and the general public. I focus on the people of a typical Aztec town sixty years after the conquest, seeking to pinpoint the cultural continuities from the prehispanic period and the changes wrought by the conquest.

An introductory discussion describes the ecological and historical background of colonial Culhuacan, the town's prominence as the heir to the Toltecs, its political decline in the prehispanic era, and its role in the Spanish conquest. Since the Culhuacan wills are the principal source for information on the town, in Chapter 2 I provide a brief discussion of *The Testaments of Culhuacan*. In Chapter 3 I bring the reader to the deathbeds of some Culhuacan citizens. This chapter is a discussion of wills, death, and the religious sentiments that shaped people's final actions. Most studies of Indians' deaths have focused on Indians in the aggregate (the deaths of whole Indian populations from epidemic disease) or deaths of a few Aztec kings (Motecuhçoma and Cuauhtemoc). How individual colonial Indians confronted death is a complex interaction of prehispanic practices, newly introduced Christian beliefs, and Spanish legal practices. In Chapter 4 I outline the town government of Culhuacan and describe administration with special reference to estate division and resolution of disputes involving inheritance. The basic structures of town government were explicated by Gibson (1952, 1964), but estate division as a legal process is an area not previously explored in depth. In Chapter 5 I examine the family as a unit of social organization and as an institution for property holding. While we have known the ideals of kin behavior from the description by fray Bernardino de Sahagún, the Culhuacan wills provide examples of actual social behavior between kin. I discuss inheritance in this chapter because many of my inferences about social behavior are made from bequest patterns and comments of testators concerning bequests. In this chapter I also assess the effects of Spanish law and family patterns on colonial native society. In Chapter 6 I evaluate sources of wealth, such as land, money lending, and commerce; I also examine wage labor as a source of income. In addition, I discuss other forms of wealth, such as movable goods and houses. In Chapter 7 I analyze factors that shaped Culhuacan society: class, gender, and wealth. Since there are many Culhuacan wills by women as well as men, poor people as well as rich, commoners as well as nobility, it is possible to explore the dynamics of a colonial Indian society in its complexity. Very little has been written on colonial Aztec women as a group. In general, I have integrated my discussion of them in the text, and where I can illuminate some aspect of their role in colonial Indian society, I have done so. However, there are aspects of gender which merit explicit discussion. In Chapter 8 I discuss land tenure extensively. In a preindustial society such as that of Culhuacan, land tenure goes to the heart of economic and social structure. The changes in land tenure brought about by population decline, the erosion of native practices, and the activities of Spaniards buying land are examined.

Some historians have argued that the history of subordinate peoples will be reintegrated into general history only by "number and anonymity" through quantitative history (Furet quoted by Ginzburg, 1980:xx). As Ginzburg has remarked, historians with this view no longer ignore the lower classes, but condemn them to silence (Ginzburg, 1980:xx). In this study of Culhuacan, I have relied on the words of the dying to tell us about life there. One Culhuacan notary scribbled some notes after a will: "The son Nicolás of the Juan

Velázquez mentioned here died, and his wife Angelina, and his father-in-law Pablo Huitznahuatl. No one is left" (TC 206,207). Four centuries separate us from the people of Culhuacan, no one is left, but their voices still speak to us.

A note on usage and citations is in order. Some specialists will object to my use of the term "Aztec," saying that it properly refers to the Mexica of Tenochtitlan. Following Charles Gibson, I use *Aztec* in its inclusive sense. The term has endured despite attempts at modification or substitution and has the value of general recognition that the term *Nahua* lacks. Another note about usage: I prefer the spelling *Culhuacan* rather than the alternative *Colhuacan*. Quotations from the printed text of *The Testaments of Culhuacan* are given at the end of the quote with the notation, (TC) and two page numbers, indicating the pages in the Nahuatl text and the English translation. Citation of printed sources follows social science practice of author, year, and page number in parentheses in the main text. Footnotes are reserved for archival citations and further discussion.

Profound thanks go to Miguel León-Portilla for inviting me to join the project to edit *The Testaments of Culhuacan,* and for granting me permission to write this full-scale analysis of the wills on my own. Sincere thanks go to James Lockhart for his role in acquiring the documents and for help in translation. I greatly appreciate assistance by Edward E. Calnek, Anatole Joffe, David Marley, H. B. Nicholson and Jerome A. Offner in acquiring archival materials relating to this study. In addition, thanks go to Frances F. Berdan, Mary W. Cline, Charles Gibson, H. R. Harvey, Susan Kellogg, J. J. Rivaud, Susan Schroeder, Della Sprager, and Barbara J. Williams for help in various stages of this project. Harvard University granted me a leave, giving me time to complete this manuscript. I thank the University of Victoria for the use of its facilities while I was preparing the book. I acknowledge the Faculty of Arts and Science, Harvard University, and the Tinker Foundation for research funds for travel to Mexico; I also acknowledge the Newberry Library, Chicago for a Short Term Fellowship in aid of my research on Culhuacan. I acknowledge the Archivo General de la Nación, Mexico; the Bibliothèque Nationale de Paris; and the University of Texas library for permission to reproduce materials here. And my thanks go to my husband, Marvin Shinbrot, for his total support of my efforts.

Victoria, British Columbia
December 1984

Lake Texcoco region

1 / BACKGROUND TO COLONIAL CULHUACAN

"Place of those with ancestors"

Colonial Culhuacan was a small town with a long history.[1] The name Culhuacan means "the place of those with ancestors,"[2] and "by implication, Culhuacan is a city that stands for ancient traditions" (Davies, 1980:23). The town appears in native chronicles, most noted as a refuge for the Toltecs. Culhuacan was one of many Indian towns in Central Mexico. It was located in the Valley of Mexico[3] at the southern end of the Mesa Central. The Valley is surrounded by volcanic mountains, some as high as 5,000 meters, dividing it from other natural zones. To the west lies the highland Valley of Toluca; to the East, that of Puebla-Tlaxcala; to the south, the subtropical Valley of Morelos. The Valley covers some 8,000 square kilometers, nearly half of which are too steep for more than marginal use. Most of the Valley floor is around 2,200 meters above sea level. Although today much of it is dry and dusty, in the sixteenth century, a massive but shallow lake system (about 1,000 square kilometers) occupied the central area (Parsons et al., 1982:6–8).

From north to south the lake was about seventy kilometers. Three subsystems made up this inland sea. The central part, Lake Texcoco, was the largest and lowest. Lake Xaltocan-Zumpango to the north, and Lake Chalco-Xochimilco to the south were smaller and higher than Lake Texcoco, and they drained into it. While the waters of Lakes Texcoco and Xaltocan-Zumpango were saline, Lake Chalco-Xochimilco was freshwater. On the shores of Lake Chalco, at the western tip of the Ixtapalapa peninsula, Culhuacan was founded, perhaps as early as the seventh century.[4]

In the prehispanic and early colonial periods, before the lake level dropped, the Ixtapalapa peninsula jutted into the lake system, effectively dividing the waters. The peninsula still has rough terrain, composed of old volcanic massifs. Culhuacan grew up at the base of the farthest west of these, the Cerro de la Estrella (Blanton, 1970: 35–36). In the Aztec era, it was the most important mountain for all the peoples of the Valley, for it was the site of the New Fire ceremony (Linné, 1948:154). This ritual, according to Aztec belief, was a signal that the universe would continue for another fifty-two-year calendar cycle. At the end of every cycle, all the fires in the realm were extinguished for five days. From the top of this mountain, a new fire was kindled by the rays of the sun. The last New Fire ceremony before the arrival of the Spaniards was in 1507. The mountain, called Huixachtecatl in Aztec times, during floods might have been an island, with Culhuacan its only settlement (Linné, 1948).

Despite the problems of flooding, the lake system was vital to the Valley of Mexico. In a country with rough terrain, few roads, and no pack animals in the prehispanic era, the shallow lake linked towns by boat. Where it was necessary, canals were built. On the Ixtapalapa peninsula, a huge canal "like a large river" was the principal route from Culhuacan and neighboring Mexicatzinco to the capital Tenochtitlan (Paso y Troncoso, 1979:194). Market goods bound for the capital were carried "in long canoes, like little barques" (Vargas Rea, 1957:14). Even in the late sixteenth century, "three or four thousand passed through each day" (Paso y Troncoso, 1979:194). Great causeways spanning the water were another link between the island capital of Tenochtitlan and the mainland, the longest of which was to Ixtapalapa.

The lakes abounded with waterfowl and fish. From September to March there were wild cranes, geese, ducks, and herons (Vargas Rea, 1957:22). The lake people found many of these beautiful birds good tasting and savory (Sahagún, XI:27) Little lake fish were also part of the lake dwellers' diet (Gallegos, 1927:173).

Around Lake Chalco, the freshwater southern lake, cultivators built chinampas, mounds of land extending into the shallow lake waters. Ditches were left between them, allowing water to reach plants independent of the seasonal rainfall. Fresh vegetables could be grown year-round.[5] The lake towns of this region were the Chinampa Towns. The people of Culhuacan, according to archeological excavations, were the first to build chinampas, the earliest dated at about A.D. 1100 (Blanton, 1970:333-34).

Archeologists have long been interested in Culhuacan. Franz Boas first investigated it in 1911-12. Because of the large number of black-on-orange potsherds at the site, he gave this domestic ware the name "Culhuacan style." This pottery is contemporary with the building of the chinampas, about A.D. 1100 (Aztec I). Culhuacan was densely settled then, "perhaps the largest community in the Valley at that time" (Blanton, 1970:336). Evidence indicates that Culhuacan was the first town built deliberately on the lake (Blanton, 1970:333). Potsherds from Teotihuacan (Teotihuacan IV) found near Culhuacan indicate contacts and perhaps settlement from there (Blanton, 1970; Sejourné, 1970). Some of these potsherds were used in building the chinampas. On the slopes of the Cerro de la Estrella, a large classic and early Toltec site was found (Blanton, 1970:146-47, 165-66, 334).

Archeologists have placed the earliest date of settled village life in the Valley of Mexico at 1500 B.C. (Sanders et al., 1979:94). However, the earliest written historical accounts, which are semilegendary and semihistorical, only date to about the tenth century. Many of these are migration myths in pictorial form, revolving around the Toltec empire and ethnic groups entering the Valley of Mexico as the empire declined or collapsed. Scholars do not agree about the evidence.[6]

The peoples of the Valley had a strong historical sense, tracing their origins and ethnicity through migration narratives. The peoples can be divided into a number of separate groups. The Otomí were linguistically distinct and late arrivals in the Valley, often residing in political units controlled by speakers of Nahuatl, including Culhuacan (Gorbea Trueba, n.d.). Different groups of Nahuatl-speaking peoples often viewed themselves as ethnically distinct, such as the Xochimilca, Chalca, Tepaneca, Acolhuaque, Cuitlahuaca, Mexica, and the Culhuaque, the people of Culhuacan (Gibson, 1964:9ff).

The written historical record for Culhuacan is quite complicated. The town was not merely one of the oldest settlements in the southern Valley of Mexico, but important historically. Accounts of Culhuacan's prehispanic history are often conflicting on major points. While

Central Mexican peoples viewed the town as the legitimate heir to the Toltec heritage, native chronicles differ about Culhuacan's relation to Tollan, the Toltec center of power. Some sources have Culhuacan coming to importance only after the fall of Tollan (about A.D. 1100), while others indicate it was Tollan's partner and therefore well established by the time Tollan fell. According to Chimalpahin, Culhuacan, along with Otumpan, was Tollan's ally. He lists six towns subordinate to Culhuacan: Coyoacan, Cuitlahuac, Mizquic, Xochimilco, Malinalco, and Ocuilan (Chimalpahin, 1958:20). The first four are Chinampa Towns, just as Culhuacan was. Domination of the last two may indicate that Culhuacan extended Tollan's influence outside the Valley of Mexico into Toluca and Morelos (Davies, 1980:27–8).

Although "the books are filled with names of kings," for Culhuacan just who they were and when they ruled is a major puzzle. Nigel Davies has devoted considerable attention to these questions. Using the *Anales de Cuauhtitlan* (1975) and Chimalpahin's *Memorial breve* (1958) he has worked out a tentative chronology of Culhuacan's rulers and the dates of their reigns (Davies, 1977; 1980).

Culhuacan's time of political dominance was brief, possibly less than fifty years. But according to Davies,

> the role of Culhuacan as the bastion of Toltec culture in the Valley of Mexico is fundamental to the whole history of the period that separates the Toltec from the Aztec Empire. [Chichimecs, Acolhuas, Tepanecs, Chalcas and Mexica] were successive claimants to power [who] sought in turn to occupy Culhua land, while their leaders wooed the daughters of its ruler (Davies, 1980:41).

The defeat of Culhuacan in 1253 was accomplished by the Acolhua ruler of Coatlinchan, Huetzin. Despite its defeat, Culhuacan continued to be viewed as the legitimate heir of the Toltecs and was a major cultural center. The histories of Culhuacan and the militaristic Mexica became entwined. The Mexica in their migration to central Mexico from the semimythical Aztlan had settled at Chapultepec in 1299, only to be expelled from there by the Culhuaque in 1319. The Mexica then threw themselves on the mercy of Coxcox, the ruler of Culhuacan. According to Codex Acatitlan, the Mexica ruler Huitzilihuitl was sacrificed in Culhuacan, and the Mexica exiled to inhospitable Tizaapan. Another account describes the Culhuaque as being so impressed by the staying power and fortitude of the Mexica that they began trading and intermarrying with

Table 1 Culhuacan Rulers

1205–13 A.D. ?Chalchiuhtlatonac
1213–48 Nauhyotzin
1248–53 Cuauhtepexpetlatzin
1253–72 Huetzin
1272–95 Nonoalcatl
1295–1309 Xihuitltemoc
1309–1327 Coxcox
1324–1336 Huehue Acampichtli
1336–1371 Achitometl II*
1377–1413 Nauhyotzin II
1413–1430 Acoltzin

Source: Davies, 1980: 35, 372.
*When the first Achitometl reigned is unclear, the sources contradict each other. Davies suggests that Achitometl might be the same person as Coxcox (1980:367).

them. Ever after, the upstart Mexica called themselves the Culhua-Mexica, and claimed ties to the Toltec line.

The Mexica joined their Culhuaque masters in a war with Xochimilco, an important chinampa town, and their participation was crucial to the victory. Culhuacan became alarmed at their vassals' military strength, and after a particularly provocative incident in which a Culhua princess was sacrificed and flayed, the Mexica were forced out and were exiled to a barren island in the middle of Lake Texcoco where they built their city of Tenochtitlan (Berlin, 1948:42; Durán, 1967 II:41, 43; Tezozomoc, 1975:57).

Culhuacan was conquered by the Mexica in the fourteenth century; though the exact date is in dispute, it was after the Mexica's departure to Tenochtitlan. According to the *Anales de Cuauhtitlan,* Culhuacan was conquered in the year 2 Calli (calculated by Davies as 1377). After the conquest, Culhuacan was ruled by two men. The first was the Mexica Nauhyotzin, who was killed by the Tepanec ruler, Tezozomoc of Azcapotzalco. His successor was Acoltzin, killed by the Acolhua ruler, Nezahualcoyotl of Texcoco.

Culhuacan participated in the wars fomented by their conquerors, the Mexica of Tenochtitlan. The Relación geográfica of Culhuacan gives a thumbnail sketch of its role. "The natives of the town of Culhuacan had war by order of Motecuhçoma with those of Huexotzinco and Tlaxcala and other parts which were against... Motecuhçoma." In those wars, the Culhuaque were dressed in typical garb. "At that time they wore cloth for belts and all the rest in leather, without anything else. And their arms were bows and arrows and cudgels and bucklers" (Gallegos, 1927:172).

Culhuacan figures in Spanish conquest chronicles only in a minor way. The Mexica of Tenochtitlan, though, had apparently impressed upon Hernando Cortés their Culhua connection, for he consistently refers to the island dwellers as Culhua. At one point he says "the name Culua [Culhua] comprises all the lands and provinces subject to Temixtitlan [Tenochtitlan]" (Cortés, 1971:173). Ixtapalapa, the strategically located town neighboring Culhuacan, receives greater attention in Cortés's chronicle. The Spaniards first entered Tenochtitlan using the causeway from there. Lake towns, including Culhuacan, rallied to Tenochtitlan's cause, though Cortés avers that he did not attack them (Cortés, 1971:217, 231). The Spaniards' native allies from Chalco despoiled them, and they then submitted (Cortés, 1971:231).

The Spanish gained control of Central Mexico with the fall of Tenochtitlan in 1521. Following the pattern established in the Caribbean, the labor and tribute of the conquered peoples were granted to the victors in an arrangement called *encomienda*. The encomienda was the basic colonial institution of the early colonial period. In exchange for the tribute and labor of specific groups of Indians, the grantholders, called *encomenderos,* were to see that their Indians were Christianized and were to provide certain military services to maintain Spanish control. The encomienda utilized existing native rulers and tribute structures, the Spaniards being more concerned with the final tribute or labor than in how it was acquired or mobilized.

Cortés distributed practically all of Central Mexico in encomienda immediately after the conquest. He awarded the newly established Spanish capital, built on the ruins of Tenochtitlan, the tribute and labor from the Four Towns: Culhuacan, Ixtapalapa, Huitzilopochco, and Mexicatzinco, but Culhuacan was subsequently awarded to Cristóbal de Oñate.

The encomendero of Culhuacan was fairly typical. Cristóbal de Oñate, however, had not participated in the conquest of Mexico, arriving in New Spain (as Mexico was called in the colonial period) in 1524 at the age of twenty. Oñate acquired Culhuacan as an encomienda in 1525 when Cortés was on an expedition to Honduras. In addition, he received tribute from other towns, including Tacámbaro and income from four towns in New Galicia (now the Guadalajara area), as the result of his participation in the expedition of Nuño de Guzmán. When a major uprising of Indians, the Mixtón War, occurred in New Galicia, Oñate served under the first Spanish viceroy, don Antonio de Mendoza, to suppress it. Oñate was a cofounder (about 1547), with Diego de Ibarra, of the silvermining town of Zacatecas. Oñate married well, taking doña Catalina de Salazar, the daughter of New Spain's treasury officer, as his wife (Himmerich, 1984:402).

The encomienda of Culhuacan remained in Cristóbal Oñate's hands for over forty years. He met a bad end, getting involved in a conspiracy of encomenderos, and was taken to Spain and executed in 1568. However, his son, Hernando Oñate, was not barred from inheriting the encomienda, and it remained in the family until 1659, when the Crown took control of it (Gibson, 1964:418). In 1580, the family lived in Mexico City (González de Cosío, 1952:156), and probably only occasionally (if at all) visited Culhuacan which was nine miles south-southeast of the capital.

Spanish presence in Culhuacan in the late sixteenth century was minimal. In 1580 it had a royal administrator, the *corregidor* Gonzalo Gallegos.[7] In addition, the town had a resident Augustinian prior and perhaps two other friars at a given time. And in 1580, around thirty-six hundred Indians lived there.[8]

2 / THE TESTAMENTS OF CULHUACAN

"He hid many testaments that the deceased ordered"

To the Indian notary Miguel Jacobo de Maldonado, I believe we owe the existence of an important source of information on the colonial Aztecs, *The Testaments of Culhuacan*. For unknown reasons, "he hid many testaments that the deceased ordered." Because of that, the Indian town government took the book of wills away from him and took steps to preserve it (TC 222,223). That book of wills has survived; it is the principal source for this study of late sixteenth-century Culhuacan. Since the corpus of wills plays such an important role in this study, a brief description of it is provided here.[1]

The Testaments of Culhuacan is a unique source. It is the largest known collection of sixteenth-century Nahuatl wills. It is a parchment-bound book of sixty-five testaments and thirty-six related documents written on European paper. The documents date from 1572 to 1606, but the majority are from 1580 and 1581. The collection is large, consisting of fifty-two complete wills and thirteen fragments, totaling sixty-five. There are twenty-nine complete testaments by men, twenty-three by women; eight testament fragments by men, four by women, and one fragment of a testament in which the gender of the testator cannot be determined. The year 1581 has the largest number of dated wills, with twenty. Fourteen are dated 1580. Fourteen are undated, but many of them were undoubtedly composed in the years 1580 and 1581, since they are found between wills dated in that period, the notaries' hands are recognizable, and the testaments fall within the period for these notaries' terms of office. The earliest will is dated 1572, and the last document has a date of 1606.

The value of the testaments is partly due to the large number for a concentrated period. Comparisons between people are possible because we are dealing with them at the same point in time. The value of the testaments also lies partly in that many are by members of the same families. For this reason, a number of patterns can be traced through several generations. Not only can we see the wealth that some individuals controlled alone, but also the resources they could possibly draw on from other family members. Another virtue of this group of testaments is that it is a homogeneous *collection* of undisputed cases of inheritance, not various testaments scattered in separate lawsuits over inheritance for a given period.[2] Although the Culhuacan collection contains many testaments by elites, nonetheless many are by men and women who have little or no property.

Until recently the book formed part of the library of Dr. Ignacio Pérez Alonso of Mexico City. It is now in the collections of the Universidad Iberoamérica in Mexico. The wills originally belonged to the Augustinian convent of San Juan Evangelista Culhuacan, but at some point the manuscript fell into private hands, perhaps in the mideighteenth century when the Augustinians left,

Table 2 Genealogy of Angelina Mocel's Family

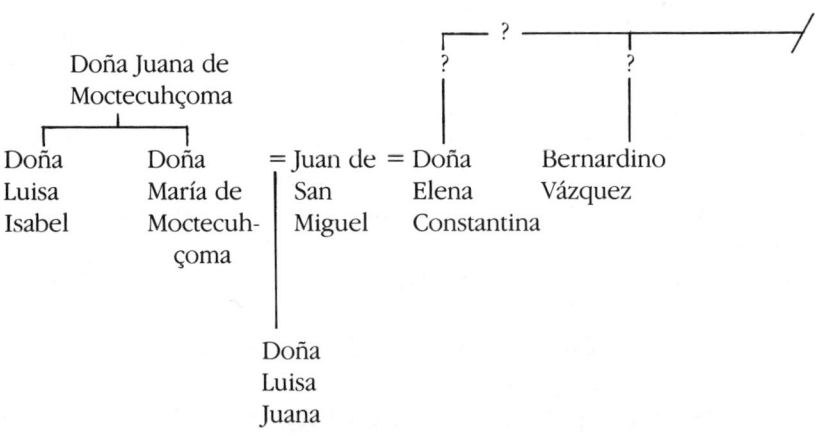

or when the church was demolished in 1892. The transcription and translation to English of *The Testaments of Culhuacan* is published by the UCLA Latin American Center (Cline and León-Portilla, 1984).

As a literary device to focus the narrative and to emphasize that we are dealing with individual people and not faceless numbers, throughout the volume I have followed the life and death of Angelina Mocel and her family. *The Testaments of Culhuacan* provides the most information on her family, containing wills by her; her father, Pablo de San Gabriel Huitznahuatl; her husband, Juan Velázquez; her cousin, Bernardino Vázquez; her mother's sister, María Tiacapan; and her mother's uncle, Antonio Tlemachica.[3] In addition, Angelina Mocel was connected by marriage to relatives of the Aztec ruler Motecuhçoma II.[4] Angelina's cousin doña Elena Constantina married the widower of doña María de Motecuhçoma and became the stepmother of doña Luisa Juana, who died in 1580. Doña Luisa Juana's testament is found outside the collection of Culhuacan wills; her will is included in documentation about the division of her estate.[5] In Table 2, the kinship information is summarized.

The testators were a cross-section of Culhuacan society. There were thirty-seven men and twenty-seven women, about equal representation. A higher percentage of widowed women (37%) than men

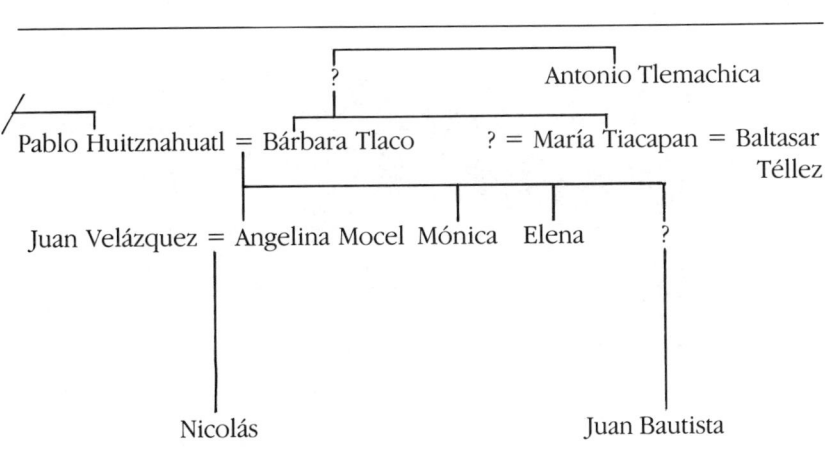

(20%) made testaments. More men (47%) were married at the time of their death than women (26%). There were a few testators who appear to have been single at the time of their deaths, listing no spouse and no lineal descendants which would indicate previous marriage (15% women, 11% men). These were likely young people, a supposition bolstered by the fact that most single people left their property to older relatives such as uncles. A third of the testators were clustered in a few residential wards, the greatest number coming from Santa María Cihuatecpan (eleven), Santa María Tezcacoac (nine)[6] and Eitlatocan ("Three Kings") Coatlan (eight). Two-thirds of the wills were by people resident in over twenty other wards. The collection includes wills of a number of elites, those with titles in Spanish or in Nahuatl which give clues to the testators' status. About a third of the wills are by people who have titles themselves or people who mentioned the names of titled relatives. About two-thirds of the testators have *no* known connections to elites. Some of the known elites were not wealthy, despite their status.

The Testaments of Culhuacan provides information about the families and property of a broad range of Indians living sixty years after the conquest. From the final words of the Culhuacan's citizens, we learn about their religious practices, town government, commercial networks, family relations, material culture, land tenure, and of course, bequest patterns—a picture of life in Culhuacan at the end of the sixteenth century.

3 / PIETY, DEATH, AND WILLS

"Now on the verge of my death"

The year was 1581, and Angelina Mocel lay dying. Gathered around her were some of her family—her mother, Bárbara Tlaco;[1] her uncle, Baltasar Téllez; her sister-in-law, María Salomé—and also the town officials who acted as executors for the will, Agustín Vázquez, Miguel Josef, and Diego Elías. The town notary, Miguel Jacobo de Maldonado, sat close and wrote the opening formulas of Angelina's final will and testament.

> Know all who see and read this document that I, Angelina Mocel of the ward of Santa María Magdalena Tezcacoac, even though I am sick, nonetheless my spirit and soul are undisturbed, and I very truly believe in the Most Holy Trinity, Father, Son, and God the Holy Spirit, just one true God omnipotent. I place my soul entirely in His hands, because He made it and redeemed it with His precious blood. And when I die, let our Lord come to take my spirit and soul. And my body I give to the earth because from earth it came (TC 180,181).

In recent years, Miguel Jacobo and the other notaries had had much occasion to record the final words of the dying. A great plague swept through the Valley of Mexico from 1576 to 1581, killing the Indians with a "rising of blood" (Gallegos, 1927:172), perhaps meaning nosebleed which was symptomatic of pulmonary plague (MacLeod, 1973:9; LeRoy Ladurie, 1981:32). Writing to the the king in 1581, Culhuacan's Spanish *corregidor* noted that the population was about 3,600, and added candidly, "in past times after the conquest, there were many more [Indians], and with the pestilence they have, especially the pestilence they call *cocoliste,* they have died" (Gallegos, 1927:172).[2]

As she sat by her daughter's deathbed, listening to the dictation of Angelina's final will, Bárbara Tlaco could recount firsthand the virulence of the plague. This was not the first time that she had acted as a witness to a loved one's final agony, nor would it be the last. In July of 1580, her uncle Antonio de San Francisco Tlemachica had died (TC 96ff), but he was an old man. Bárbara Tlaco herself had grandchildren, so her uncle's death did not catch him in his youth. But in February of 1581, her son-in-law, Angelina's husband, Juan Velázquez, died (TC 204ff), leaving her daughter widowed with a sickly child, Nicolás. Less than a month later, her own husband, Pablo de San Gabriel Huitznahuatl, also died (TC 164ff), leaving Bárbara herself widowed with two daughters who were still minors. And now, another daughter, Angelina dead that May. But Bárbara Tlaco's losses were not over that month. On the 20th, she again was a witness to a will, for her older sister, María Tiacapan (TC 174ff). And before long, Bárbara Tlaco's grandson, Nicolás, followed his parents, grandfather, great-aunt, and great-great-uncle to the grave (TC 206,207).

Catholic belief saw the last will and testament as a sacred act. Making a final testament was linked to making a final confession and was a necessary prerequisite to burial on sacred ground. Dying intestate did not pose a problem just for the potential heirs whose inheritance was in doubt, but was a horror, tantamount to dying in a state of sin (Pollock and Maitland, 1923:I,128). The religious invocations of wills, such as Angelina Mocel's, calling upon God's mercy, commending the soul to Him and the earthly body to an earthly resting place, were formula phrases. The phrases could change over time and from one place to another,[3] but the intent was the same. The will was a religious act as well as a civil document disposing of property.

Only sixty years after the Spanish conquest, Indians in small towns like Culhuacan had adopted many of the outward forms of Christianity. This chapter deals with these outward forms of piety found especially in last wills and testaments. Although Indians resisted some fundamental aspects of Christianity (Klor de Alva, 1982), in the sixteenth century the Church was a well-established institution in Indian towns, and individual Indians expressed Christian beliefs in public contexts such as wills.[4]

The mandate to Christianize the Indians was one of the justifications for the Spanish conquests in the New World. In Mexico the "spiritual conquest" was first undertaken by the Franciscans, with twelve friars arriving in 1524. Other Orders arrived later, including the Augustinians, who claimed Culhuacan as one of their parishes. In 1580 Culhuacan had two resident Augustinian friars based at the main church of San Juan Evangelista. The building had been under construction in 1552 (Gerhard, 1972:179) and doubtless was completed before 1580.

The spiritual conquest required the replacement of the native pantheon with the Christian God and a host of saints. How easily accepted and thorough the replacement was is open to question, as the friars themselves recognized. But the friars counted as early successes the baptism of thousands, replacement of the native calendar by the Christian, the construction of scores of churches, and the establishment of hospitals. A school for the sons of the native elite was established, to train them for the priesthood. However, the friars' initial hopes for a native priesthood were abandoned by the midsixteenth century. In 1555 the ordination of Indians was banned because they were not deemed qualified (Ricard, 1966:217ff). Spaniards were the intermediaries between the Indians and God.

Indian men did serve the Christian church, and a hierarchy of religious officials evolved in each Indian town. At the top Spaniards created the office of *fiscal*, a highly prestigious post held by a nobleman. "Nobody went into public office who was not noble. To such a degree was this the case that even after their conversion to Christianity they would not permit those whom they chose to serve in the monastery... to be commoners and *macehualtin;* rather [they chose them from among] noblemen, even the cooks and the gardeners" (Torquemada, 1975:II,347). In Culhuacan, there was an official in charge of the choir [*corotopile*], one in charge of sweeping the church [*teopan topille tlachpanqui*], and officials simply called *teopantlaca*, "church people," who carried out a number of duties connected with the church, such as conveying corpses to the church for funeral masses. Women served the Christian church as *cihuatepixque*, making sure women parishioners went to services.

Christianity is a salvationist religion, focusing on the actions of an individual in life and the soul after death. To be a good Christian in the sixteenth century required baptism, marriage in the church, the final rites, and a testament. Whether the Indians had a prehispanic testamentary tradition is unclear. An early report by the Franciscan friar Motolinia (1971:134–35) says there was none in the Cuernavaca region. Another early account, by Francisco López de Gómara (1943:222–23), indicates that there was a great diversity of patterns in Mexico as a whole, as well as between "peasants" (*villanos*) and nobles. Both concur that customary rules dictated how an estate was divided. However, if that had been uniformly the case, there would have been no need for testaments. The Aztecs did have a tradition of performing important transactions, such as the sale of land and slaves, in public. Perhaps before the conquest, Aztecs publicly bequeathed property through oral declarations (Durand-Forest, 1962).

Since Christianity was a religion based on written texts, the friars saw literacy as an important element in conversion of elites. Soon after the Spanish conquest, Spaniards taught select Indians to read and write Nahuatl. In the prehispanic period, a system of writing had developed in Mesoamerica. Though mainly pictographic, it was moving to representation of sounds near the time of the conquest. What was important for the development of literacy in the colonial era was a prehispanic tradition of recordkeeping. Pictorial elements persisted in native manuscripts in the colonial period, but native scribes recognized that alphabetic writing was a major breakthrough technologically. Aztec notaries literate in Nahuatl were operating in many Central Mexican towns by the midsixteenth century. One notary taught another and a self-perpetuating tradition existed on the local level until the end of the colonial period (Karttunen, 1982).

Literacy was not widespread, however, even among Indian elites. Although literacy was not restricted by law to notaries, in practice they were virtually the only fully literate natives. Frequently a notary would say, "the witnesses do not know how to write, for which reason they do not set down their signatures in their own hands" (TC 262,263). These notes fulfilled legal requirements establishing the validity of a will (Markov, 1983:442).

Being literate did not mean that a person would write a holograph will. The notary Miguel García ordered his testament before another notary (TC 100ff). Perhaps García was too ill to write, but more likely he viewed making a will as a public act necessitating a notary.

In Spain and also much of Europe, testamentary law derived

from the Roman Code of Justinian. The Roman principles were incorporated in the basic legal code of Spain, The *Siete partidas* of Alfonso X, which became the basis for Spanish law in the New World in 1555. The code defined two types of wills, oral (*testamentum nuncupatiuum*) and written (*testamentum in scriptis*), and established criteria for their validity (Markov, 1983:440ff).

Although Spanish wills derived from Roman law, which simply viewed a testament as a civil document for the transmission of property, the religious function of a will was important. Previous to the sixteenth century, ecclesiastics as well as notaries drafted and preserved wills, but it then became the province of the notary. Even though clerics no longer drew up wills, testaments came before ecclesiastical, not civil, courts (Ariès, 1980:189).

In New Spain, the formulas and rules for making written testaments were drawn up by ecclesiastics. The Franciscan friar Alonso de Molina included in his *Confessionario mayor en lengua mexicana y castellana,* published in Mexico City in 1565, an entire chapter devoted to the matter of testaments and the notary's role. A notary was to be asked:

> And when the invalid made a testament, signifying and declaring his final will, did you perform your office faithfully and without trickery? Do you know well all the things that you are obligated to do in order that the testament be good and firm? Think then now about what I will tell you and I will examine well, because you are obligated to do and carry out all the things I will tell you and declare (León-Portilla, 1976:18).

Molina outlines a series of directives that notaries should follow. These concern the qualities that witnesses should have, the necessity for the testator to know his or her rights and obligations, and to indicate if he or she has debts to pay, and to select freely the one who will carry out the dispositions. In addition, the notary was to read back the text dictated to him and obtain the approval of the testator and the attestation of the witnesses. Finally, Molina suggests how a testament should be written, specifying formulas which became standard (León-Portilla, 1976:18–19).

The phrasing of the religious invocations in Nahuatl follows invocations of Spanish testaments, essentially translations to Nahuatl. Some Spanish words had no Nahuatl equivalent or were deliberately untranslated and appeared in loanword form in the invocations. For example, the friars reinforced the difference between Christian and Aztec divinities by the use of the loanwords for the Most Holy Trinity (*santísima trinidad*) and the Holy Spirit (*espíritu santo*). Other Spanish loanwords stand out in Nahuatl testaments such as the words for testament (*testamento*), witness (*testigo*), and executor (*albacea*). These were concepts and roles introduced by the Europeans, and they are included in Molina's *Vocabulario en lengua castellana y mexicana y mexicana y castellana,* first published in 1555. This dictionary was compiled to aid the religious in their missionary efforts. The inclusion of these words and phrases in the *Vocabulario* was likely reflective of Molina's desire to facilitate expression of testamentary material (León-Portilla, 1976:17).

Angelina Mocel's testament is typical in its invocation of the Holy Trinity. Likely Miguel Jacobo de Maldonado, the notary for her will, merely used phrases he had written many times before. His predecessor in the office of notary, Juan de San Pedro, used many of the same phrases, but some wills he wrote included other wording. Juana Tiacapan of Aticpac's testament invoked the Holy Trinity, but she wanted "my guardian angel to carry me before God" (TC 66,67). An unknown notary recorded Ana Mocel's invocation, which was quite specific about what she hoped of God. "I ask Him to favor me by pardoning me all my sins, and to carry me to His home in heaven when my soul abandons my body." She was unique in one of her requests, asking "as a special aid to my soul, in order that it not stay long in Purgatory, I want a vigil and a mass when my body is buried" (TC 24,25). This might indicate Ana's particularly deep belief and concern for the afterlife, since no one else expressed belief in Purgatory, nor did anyone else request a vigil for the soul. The father of another testator paid for vigils for her and her dead mother.[5] Ana Mocel's will might have been expressing her own beliefs, but it might also have been merely a notarial turn of phrase. Invocations in testaments have been used as an index of changing religious beliefs in Europe (Vovelle, 1978).[6]

When Angelina Mocel's relative, the noblewoman doña Luisa Juana,[7] made her will, the official in charge of the choir [*corotopile*], Marcos Jorge, recorded it. Much of the invocation is typical of notarial style, but there are some special touches, indicating perhaps that the lady's words concerning her beliefs were being recorded verbatim. "I strongly vow that I will always live and die in the True Faith. Let our Lord not ordain that He should abandon me, so that the devil will not cloud my judgment."⁸ Formulas for invocations could accommodate additions or changes in wording requested by the dying. Testators could seemingly influence the wording of the opening formulas. Nevertheless, the majority of invocations are not verbatim statements.

Formulas were repetitious and boring to the notaries who had to write them over and over. In the closing formulas of a statement concerning Simón Moxixicoa's estate, Maldonado utilized one of the loanword phrases from Spanish dear to him, the all-encompassing *et cetera*. Referring to officials who executed an estate division and were validating it, Maldonado wrote "Here they put their signatures, etc. [sic]" (TC 160,161). In the will of Joaquín de Luna, Maldonado cut off the invocation "And I believe all that the Holy Church of Rome believes. Therefore now I make my testament, etc. [sic]" (TC 152, 153). What he had left out was probably the phrase "First I give my body to the earth because from earth it came." That omission seems to be due to laziness or impatience. On another occasion, Maldonado dutifully recorded the lengthy complaints of María Tiacapan of Coatlan concerning her good-for-nothing uncles. When she began praising her grandmother, also apparently at length, Maldonado lost patience with the longwinded testator and cut her short. "She has acquired merit in the whole time since we were left orphaned, etc. [sic]" (TC 132,133). Maldonado was probably irritated by the repetitive nature of the work; sometimes he omitted portions of formulas and speeches.

In Culhuacan, the procedure was the same for each of the wills. Someone would perceive that death was near, and the family would summon the notary. Said one man, "When our late sister-in-law was about to die I said to her 'let the notary come to write down all your property'" (TC 86,87). In another case, Diego Sánchez dictated his will in the town's hospital. A black man "cut me with a knife [causing injuries] from which I am about to die" (TC 220,221).

Violence was not the usual cause of death. Ana Tiacapan of the ward of Santa María Tezcacoac declared "that my illness is very grave, and for this reason I make my testament" (TC 56,57). When Miguel Oçoma spoke to those at his sickbed, he gave instructions that "if I die tomorrow or the next day, [you are] to speak promptly on behalf of my soul" (TC 244,245). Another testator, Luis Tlauhpotonqui, lay sick in a house that his late father had given him. He too thought his death was close, but asked that the house be "for me [in which to live] for however many days I yet lie sick." His end would be the end of the house too. "When I have died, the wood of the house will be burnt [as firewood]" (TC 139,141).

Sometimes an invalid, thinking death was imminent, prematurely made a will. The notary Alonso Dávila de Santiago drew up Juan Tezca's will on 15 January 1580, but it was a false alarm and Juan lived on. Santiago noted in the margin that "[the testator] from Santa María Magdalena has not yet died" (TC 30). Since death from the pestilence was a common event, people had to regard illnesses as life threatening. The formula-sounding phrase that the testament was made "now on the verge of my death" (TC 64,65), was usually close to the mark. Indeed, the witnesses for Ana Tiacapan of Tepanecapan "were called when the invalid fainted once" (TC 94,95). Perhaps because he was too far gone, Baltasar Nentequitl "declared when he was about to die 'I cannot make a testament'" (TC 56,57). An eighteenth-century will from Amecameca was not completed because the testator died midway through it (Karttunen and Lockhart, 1978:164–165).

Though people seemed to accept that illness was fatal, a natural though sad event, in Diego Sánchez's words, as he lay dying from stab wounds, we sense his feeling that his life was being cut short. "[It is not as] if I had just taken sick, because it is the moment of my death, nor was it my fault" (TC 220,221). Death came anyway.

Time was important when death was near. The notary Juan de San Pedro noted at the close of Ana Tiacapan of Tepanecapan's will that "this was written Sunday at noon" (TC 94,95).[9] Angelina Mocel's relative, doña Luisa Juana, made her will at "midnight, the day of the Holy Cross, the 3rd of the month of May of the year 1580."[10] She was not the only one to have a religious feast day noted, for Marcos Hernández's will was made "Thursday, the feast of Saint Catherine, the 21st day of November of the year 1599" (TC 278,279).[11] But more standardly the notary just recorded the day of the week and the date according to the Christian calendar.

Death usually found people at home, and they ordered their wills there. Antonio de San Francisco Tlemachica, Angelina Mocel's great uncle, ordered his will in "the house where I lie sick" (TC 96,97). In 1579, a friar in the nearby municipality of Huitzilopochco administered the sacrament of Extreme Unction, given only to the dying, in Indians' homes "because of the risk of bringing them to the church, so they shouldn't die in the road" (García Pimentel, 1897:12). On the other hand, the presence of Culhuacan's Augustinian friars is never once recorded at the deathbed, even in the testament of Diego Sánchez who died in the town's hospital which was run by the church (TC 214ff).

Although the friars were apparently not at the deathbeds, they took care of their parishioners' spiritual welfare after death, following the provisions in the wills by saying masses for the repose of their souls. Often the prior, fray Juan Núñez, or one of the others who served in succeeding years, like fray Juan Zimbrón, or fray Cristóbal de Agurto, noted on the testament that a certain number of masses had been said for the deceased.

The church might have been insistent on the making of wills because ecclesiastics received money for masses through testamentary bequests. The church likely saw itself as competing with heirs for a portion of the estate. In 1588, the Crown forbade wills in which Indians disinherited kin to pay for masses (Chevalier, 1952:311). Perhaps in the absence of heirs, the church did not look sternly on intestacy because it received the whole estate. One official said concerning Ana Xoco, whose property was sold after her death, that "she left no children and did not make a will; she just died" (TC 262,263). The six pesos from the sale of her movable goods went for masses. The Spanish friar, Sebastián de Castro, and a number of native church officials acted as witnesses to the sale. Another time, fray Juan Núñez noted he received money from town officials for masses, saying "these said deceased people did not make testaments but ordered orally that [the money] should be given to the church" (TC 30,31).

When the notary Miguel Jacobo finished writing the overtly religious section of Angelina Mocel's will, she was properly identified by name and place of residence, the Holy Trinity was invoked, and her competence to make a will "even though [her] body is sick" was established. Now came the listing of her earthly possessions and her wishes for their disposal. Foremost in her mind was a practical problem. "I have no assets at all with which to be buried," she said, ordering a house her father had willed her be sold to pay for the interment. And after that was paid for, "whatever money should be left of the proceeds from the house will be spent on me, for masses to be said for me." (TC 180,181).

Coming up with cash for burial by selling something of value happened even in the best families. Anything of value could be sold for burial. One noblewoman's relatives said they pawned an emerald [*chalchihuitl*]. "When doña Ana de Coronado was buried, the [money] for her burial was borrowed" (TC 72ff). Stone used in construction was valuable, and apparently it was easily converted to money for the imminent expense of burial. Juan Tezca had some stone; "what I have quarried will be used for me, and with it I will be buried" (TC 32,33). Juana Tiacapan of Aticpac also had stone at her disposal. "When I die, the stone that is still scattered here at the entrance [of my land] is to be sold. The proceeds in money are to be spent on my burial" (TC 68,69). Simón Moxixicoa also had stone for his burial, "a *quappantli* of porous stone [*tezontli*] brought from Santiago Tetla" (TC 158,159).

Land was sold for burial expenses. In addition to Juan Tezca's stone for burial he said "when I die, [the land] is to be sold; with half [of the proceeds] I will be buried, and with the other, a mass will be said for me." The land was important property, for Juan said it was "patrimonial land which my grandfather Francisco... left me" (TC 32,33). Miguel Chimaltecuhtli ordered that one chinampa "is to be sold when I die; [the proceeds] will be spent on my burial" (TC 48,49). Mateo Juárez had some idea how much his burial would cost. He declared "the hoe is also to be sold in order that I be buried; the price to be given you is a full five tomines" (TC 75,77). Domingo Yaotl also had movable property he wanted sold, saying he had "a worn-out boat; it is to be sold and the proceeds will be used to help me be buried" (TC 52,53). Pablo Quechol paid for his burial in another way. "There is cacao with which I was going to get married, the two thousand beans that my mother and father left me. And when I die, one part will be used there [for the burial]" (TC 88,89). Pablo's parents had hoped to give him a good start in life, but instead gave him the means for a decent burial. Miguel Oçoma was in the minority, with cash on hand for his burial. "I have in keeping two pesos in money, and when I have died, let me be buried with it, and with what should be left, a mass is to be said for me" (TC 244,245).

Since death found people at home, the corpse had to be moved to the church for the funeral mass. Ana Tlaco had foreseen this problem. "For two tomines, the church attendants will come to take my body; [the money] will be given to them" (TC 190,191). Apparently this was the standard fee, for Joaquín de Luna also set aside "two tomines so that the church attendants will come to take me and accompany my earthly body to the church of our Lord when I am buried" (TC 154,155).

When Angelina Mocel's husband Juan Velázquez made his final testament, he wanted the proper accoutrements for his burial. "There are some green trousers [*zaragüelles*] of mine; it hasn't been long since I bought them. And they are to be exchanged for white cloth, and when I die, my earthly body will be wrapped in it" (TC 206,207). At death, he wanted native cloth rather than his fancy European pants. He still had native clothing, "an embroidered cloak of mine which I wore," but rather than using that as his shroud he said, "it is to be sold to buy candles for my burial when I have died" (TC 206,207). Juan Velázquez was not alone in lacking a shroud when he died. Juana Tiacapan of Aticpac noted in her testament that "the cloak with which my late daughter was enshrouded when she died belonged to Martín Tlacochcalcatl Xochicuetzin," and she wanted the debt to him repaid (TC 68,69).

Juan Velázquez's use of a plain white cloak [*tilmatli*] for a shroud rather than his more elaborate cloak may have been a postconquest change in native practice. The Franciscan Motolinia said "when the lords died, they were clothed and buried in [their cloaks and mantles], some in many and others in few, each one in keeping with his station in life" (1951:196). Other burial practices might have changed too, for Motolinia goes on to say "They also buried with the lords the jewels and precious stones which they possessed," something not found in late sixteenth-century Culhuacan. But he noted that there was regional diversity, "in other places the lords left these possessions to their children" (1951:196). Though no one in Culhuacan had valuables buried with them, Juan Rafael Tlacochcalcatl had "five precious stones [that] I give to my wife Mariana" (TC 144,145). Mariana, for her part, ordered them sold for a mass. When she died one was gone, and she somewhat gratuitously denigrates the ones remaining saying, they were "four white stones, just little ones" (TC 128ff). And as mentioned earlier, there was doña Ana de Coronado whose emerald was pawned for her burial.

Angelina Mocel did not specify where she wanted to be buried, but other people had definite requests. In the will of her great uncle, Antonio de San Francisco Tlemachica, there was the formula phrase "and my body I give to the earth because from earth it came," but he ordered that his body "is to be buried at our church of San Juan Evangelista" (TC 96,97), the main church of Culhuacan. The desire for burial in the church was not unusual.[12] Joaquín de Luna, a resident of Mexico City who died in Culhuacan, perhaps surprisingly did not want his final resting place in the Spanish capital. He set aside a peso in money saying "I make it an offering, so that when I have died I will be buried at the church of San Juan Evangelista" (TC 154,155). The noblewoman doña Luisa Juana, left no doubts about exactly where she wanted her body to rest. "When I die I will be buried inside the church before [the image of] the noblewoman Saint Mary."[13] In Europe until the eighteenth century, burial in the church was a practice of the wealthy. To request a final resting place close to a saint was to gain "the benefits of indulgences and chances of grace." Closer proximity increased the benefits (LeRoy Ladurie, 1979b:278–79).

A European introduction to the New World was the use of wax candles, which became an integral part of church services. Angelina Mocel ordered that "a metate is to be sold in order to buy candles for the burial of my body when I have died" (TC 182,183). As we have seen, her husband, Juan Velázquez, also wanted candles for his burial, asking that his cloak be sold (TC 206,207).

Candles were lighted on special religious festivals, especially the feast of the dead. María Tiacapan of the ward of Tianquizçolco wanted to be remembered after her death, saying "I put my husband Mateo Opan in charge of seeing to it that on the day of the dead [*miccailhuitl*] he remember me before God and bring candles [to the church] each year. Let him not forget me" (TC 194,195). Ana Tlaco wanted the same, giving some land to her younger brother, Miguel Itztic, hoping that in return "perhaps he will favor me with some candles on the feast of the dead" (TC 190,191).

In the prehispanic period, the dead were remembered on special days, particularly on the anniversary of the person's death. According to Motolinia

> ... they had other days in memory of their dead, when they mourned for them ... And this was the manner of these days: they buried and mourned the dead man, and then twenty days later they mourned him again and offered food and roses on his tomb, and after eighty days they did the same thing again, and repeated it every eighty days. After a year they mourned the dead and made offerings every year on the anniversary of his death. This they did

for four years, and then they stopped entirely and never thought of the dead man again to pray for his soul (Motolinia, 1950:53–54).

In the colonial period, the Christian Day of the Dead, November 2, became a major religious festival in Mexico,[14] likely because it coincided with a similar prehispanic custom. Whether in late sixteenth-century Culhuacan the two women who wanted to be remembered on the day of the dead meant the Christian feast or the traditional anniversary is not known. Only two Christian holidays are seen in the wills, the Day of the Holy Cross (May 3)[15] and the feast of Saint Catherine (November 21) (TC 278,279).

Feasting marked all kinds of occasions and death was no exception.[16] Motolinia reports that part of the mourning for the dead involved "eating and getting drunk" (Motolinia, 1950:53). In colonial Culhuacan, the testator Miguel García, who at times acted as a notary (TC 86ff), made provision for his own wake. "The four hens will be eaten here when I have died" (TC 104,105). Doubtless mainly close family participated, but Miguel Oçoma set aside "a pot of shelled maize [which] will be eaten by those who will bury me, and they will taste the beans in the little pot when I die" (TC 244,245).

Angelina Mocel's estate, like most people's, contained houses, land, and movable goods, which were listed and disposed of separately. Angelina's house "that my late father Pablo Huitznahuatl gave me" was listed first and was to be sold for her burial. Houses were often the first item declared. Angelina also had land, each parcel being separately listed and bequeathed. She worried that her son would not last to inherit it, saying "I give [land] in Tetla in the place named Texalpan to my child Nicolás, if he lives. And if he does not [live], then it too is to be sold in order for masses to be said for us" (TC 182,183). Nicolás was very much on her mind, and she tried to care for him by another bequest. "The chest my late husband and I bought belongs to my child Nicolás; it is to be sold, and with it he will be given milk" (TC 182,183).

Angelina had a few final bequests to make before she was finished. She listed some cloth and some yarn that was going to be woven into cloth. And then there was a matter she had not gotten to before she died. There was "a cloak which was my late husband's. If I had lived, I was going to help my husband with it and request some masses. And now I say it is to be sold and is to belong to my husband. Perhaps someone will want to buy it" (TC 182,183). Her husband Juan Velázquez had died in mid-February of 1581, wanting it sold for candles for his burial. Now it was the beginning of May. Someone else would have to see to Juan's cloak. One wonders if he got his candles.

Pious bequests were a feature of testaments. Burial on sacred ground, perhaps in front of the saint, provision for candles for the funeral mass and later, on the feast of the dead, were expressions of the importance of religion. The number of masses the people ordered also could be a measure of their piety. Although rarely expressed in colloquial language, people were concerned with providing salvation for themselves through masses. Standardly the dying would request at least one mass for themselves, and often one for their departed mate if they were widowed. María Teicuh of Tezcacoac ordered that her entire estate go for masses for her and her late husband, though she had surviving children (TC 240ff), but she was unusual.

The money for masses came from the sale of land and houses and movable goods. The amount of money realized from these sales would determine how many masses could be said. The noblewoman doña María Juárez had a clever scheme for perpetual masses. She had declared that "my field in Tlalachco is not to be sold, but is just to be rented out each year, and with the money that is acquired there, masses are to be said for us" (TC 250,251). This system of rental is similar to the Spanish institution of *capellanía* in which a wealthy person would set aside monies for the support of a priest who would say masses for the capellanía's founder. In Culhuacan, whether this was a borrowed Spanish concept, a new innovation, or something with local precedent is not known.[17] Donations to religious institutions had been a prehispanic custom, but this was a gift for the general support of religion. Doña María's gift was for the salvation of her soul, a Christian notion.

Sometimes the dying provided generalized bequests for charity, to the poor and the sick. In sixteenth-century Catholic belief, the poor were the image of Christ on earth. Making provision for the poor on earth helped the spiritual accounts of those immediately on the way to the afterlife (LeRoy Ladurie, 1979b:281). In Culhuacan, sometimes sale of land would provide money for charity. Luis Tlauhpotonqui ordered that some of his "patrimonial land is to be sold, and with the proceeds in money, alms are to be given to the sick" (TC 139ff). Juana Tiacapan of Aticpac gave some land to the ward heads, saying "Perhaps they will give to some poor person" (TC 68,69). Sale of movable goods also went to charity. Pablo Quechol, a trader, ordered some baskets and mortars [*molcajetes*] to be sold, "and the proceeds are to be given to the sick" (TC 88,89).

In Culhuacan there was a church-run hospital where the sick could be taken care of. By 1583 the Archbishop of Mexico wrote that "in all the Indian villages with the rank of head town, there are hospitals run with the labor, money and alms of the Indians themselves" (Ricard, 1966:155). The physicians in Culhuacan's hospital were Spaniards[18] who seemingly were paid. Diego Sánchez, who was fatally knifed, ordered that the assailant "pay [what it costs] here in the church hospital where I am being treated. And he is to pay the physicians and give them what they should ask" (TC 220,221).

Other bequests also indicated piety. Angelina Mocel's great-uncle Antonio Tlemachica assigned some land "to the city, and perhaps the city elders, those in charge of Culhuacan, will raise a cross there" (TC 98,99). Ana Tiacapan of Tepanecapan went so far as to have two of her houses torn down "and the stone... brought here, and with it a house [chapel] will be built for the image of our Lord" (TC 94,95). And Simón Moxixicoa echoed her bequest, giving to his ward's patron saint "the stones for corners of houses... to our dear father San Francisco, with which to make his house [chapel]" (TC 158,159).

The most direct statement of piety was that of Tomás de Aquino. After ordering church burial for his body, recorded in classic notarial phrases, he spoke directly and from the heart. "I have made an offering: I went to give it to our dear and honored father, prior fray Juan Núñez, in person, and I said to him, 'My dear father, here is my voluntary offering of six pesos that I make for no special reason; neither did I steal it, but I say that during all the time that I have lived, our Lord gave me all that I needed; let me likewise thus return it to him'" (TC 64,65). His idea of reciprocity is clear. God had provided good fortune on earth and the way to repay it was through his earthly servant, the Augustinian prior. The sum of six pesos was quite a substantial gift, especially since it seems to have been in cash.

Possession of religious objects can also indicate piety. Foremost among these objects were religious books. Christian texts helped spread and reinforce belief. Miguel Oçoma gave to his child a "minor [book of] hours and two [books of] doctrine" (TC 245,247). He was not the only one with Christian texts. The notary Miguel García ordered that "a book of hours, a breviary... and three [breviaries?] in Nahuatl, and a confessional manual are to be sold. The church attendants are to buy them" (TC 104,105). In the same breath, he bequeathed some of his other religious objects: "three rosaries, after they are cleaned, will be sold" for masses. The "image of the savior on the cross" was to be sold for debts (TC 104,105). Angelina Mocel's great-uncle, Antonio Tlemachica, had a crucifix, declaring that it "is entirely my property. I say that it is not to be taken anywhere but just stay at my home" (TC 97ff). Juana Martina also had a cross, but its destination was other than her own house. "It is to be kept in the home [i.e. chapel] of our mother Santa María Magdalena," the patron saint of her ward of Cihuatecpan. In money, the cross was not worth much; Juana Martina asked the ward heads for just one tomín for it (TC 256,257).

The notary finished the text of Angelina's bequests and began the closing formulas. "Done before the witnesses: the executors Agustín Vázquez; Miguel Josef; Diego Elías, alguacil; Baltasar Téllez, topile; Bárbara Tlaco; María Salomé" (TC 182,183). The executors [*albaceas*] were Indian officials of the municipal government who had much to do with estate administration.[19] The three listed, Vázquez, Josef, and Elías, were executors for many estates. Although not identified as such, the other three witnesses (*testigos*) were Angelina's relatives—her uncle, her mother, and her sister-in-law.

It is not surprising that colonial Nahuatl testaments were witnessed. Two traditions converged, the prehispanic custom of performing important acts before witnesses and the European practice of witnessing wills, mandated by Molina's instructions to notaries. The *Siete partidas* had defined two types of wills, both requiring witnesses.

> The one... is called in Latin *testamentum nuncupatiuum,* which is to say that which is made publicly before seven witnesses..., in which he who makes it shows by word or by writing... those whom he establishes as his heirs and how he bequeaths or disposes of his other things. The other type is, as is said in Latin, *testamentum in scriptis,* which is to say that it is made in writing in no other way (Markov, 1983:442).

The statutes describing the *testamentum in scriptis* define in great detail who is a proper witness and how the will is to be validated.[20]

By the late sixteenth century, witnesses were identified by the Spanish loanword *testigos,* and individual witnesses named. In the early colonial period, groups of Indians whose individual members were not named acted as witnesses to wills (Lockhart, 1981:12). In Culhuacan, the executors were almost mandatory witnesses to wills, and they acted in an official capacity. How other witnesses were chosen is usually not defined. They could be relatives of the testator, recipients of bequests, the testators' creditors or debtors, owners of fields bordering on the testators', and an array of others whose connections to the testator often cannot be determined. The will of doña Luisa Juana was done "before the witnesses who were especially named and she herself found, Juan Itzpancalqui and Juan Tlacochcalcatl. And those there who cared for the invalid also heard it."[21] It sounds as if just two of her witnesses were chosen, and the rest just happened to be caring for her when the will was drawn up. There is a good possibility that the Indians did not have the same notion of witnessing a statement that Spaniards had.

The act of witnessing a testament necessitated a witness's being present at the scene and hearing the proceedings, but not observing them by sight. Felipe Andrés's blindness was no handicap to his witnessing Simón Moxixicoa's will (TC 158,159).

Angelina Mocel's son Nicolás received many bequests from his mother, but he was not a witness to her will, probably because he was just a little child, perhaps even a baby. She had tried to ensure that he would have milk, something only unweaned children drank. In Culhuacan, one identifiable minor child witnessed a will[22] and seemingly there are instances elsewhere (Lockhart, 1981:12). The *Siete Partidas* called for no witnesses "less than fourteen years of age" (Markov, 1983:442).

The Laws of Toro (1505) reduced the number of required witnesses from seven to five, and in some instances to three (Markov, 1983:441). In the New World, most Spaniards' documents standardly had three male witnesses and a notary to be valid (Lockhart, 1981:12). Angelina's six witnesses were fewer than the average number of eight for a Culhuacan testament. In the colonial period, the deathbed scene where written testaments were dictated was practically a public forum. The notary and the executors, who were town officials, church officials, relatives and associates, were witnesses and gathered "at the head [of the bed]"[23] (TC 268,269) of the dying. Ana Mocel had a real crowd, with eighteen people, not counting the town officials and Maldonado, the notary (TC 210,211). It was not just women who had great numbers of witnesses; Domingo Yaotl had fifteen (TC 48ff). If the written testament were lost, the larger number of witnesses would make it easier to recall what the dying person had ordered and more difficult to change the bequests underhandedly after the death.

Men and women testators both named men as witnesses more frequently, in a ratio of three to two. Although the *Siete partidas* excluded women from acting as witnesses (Markov, 1983:442), they were a standard feature of Nahuatl wills. Sometimes women were in the majority. Lucía Teicuh had seven women and only three men witness her will (TC 126,127). Two women, María Tiacapan of Cihuatecpan (TC 22,23) and the mother of Agustín Vázquez (TC 18,19), only had men witness their wills, as did five men.[24] Though it might seem that the woman's role as witness was less important than the man's, two men had just women as witnesses. Miguel Cerón had two women as witnesses, and Juan Rafael Tlacochcalcatl had three (TC 62,63; TC 146,147). Both men had their wives as witnesses, and interestingly, Miguel's other witness was Juan's wife, Mariana. Likely there was some kind of link by kinship.

Relatives acted as witnesses, even when they did not receive a bequest. Often men had their wives act as witnesses, but women seldom had their husbands do the same. Having close family members as witnesses may have been a device to insure that the estate was not subsequently challenged by them. Joaquín Matlalacan willed his entire estate to his young son, but his wife and his mother acted as witnesses to the will. The two women were, in effect, disinherited, but by acting as witnesses to the will, they may have been acknowledging and acquiescing to that (TC 236ff).

Some witnesses might have been included for legal reasons, to ensure they met their obligations to the one dying. One woman who owed money to Luis Tlauhpotonqui witnessed his will, perhaps affirming her responsibility for the debt (TC 134ff). A witness for Ana Tiacapan of Tepanecapan was Mateo Juárez Tecpanecatl, official in charge of masons [*tetzotzoncatopille*]. Ana said she "gave four tomines of my money to the masons who were to build me some walls." The work was not completed yet. At the point of her death, Ana was no longer interested in construction work. "I say let my money be brought back, and it will be spent when I die" (TC 94,95). Mateo Juárez was first among the witnesses named, perhaps thus affirming his obligation to pay the money.

Other witnesses to wills knew about previous transactions of testators. Melchor de Santiago Ecatl had been granted some land by the *tecpan* (noble house) of his ward. Witness to Melchor's testament was "Pedro de San Nicolás, [who] knows about this; he measured the land" (TC 118,119). Pedro's acting as witness would bolster Melchor's claims to the land. This kind of witness is typical in Nahuatl wills. Often witnesses appear to include a number of people who could vouch for the testators' right to bequeath property, as well as affirm that the testators made the wills. If someone bequeathed property before witnesses who raised no objections, this might be presented as proof that the testator had the legal right to bequeath that property in the first place. The fact that property rights were asserted through wills helps account for the numerous Nahuatl testaments in lawsuits before Spanish courts.

At times people with neighboring fields acted as witnesses. For example, one witness for Ana Juana's will was Martín Tlacochcalcatl Xochicuetzin ("flower skirt"), who had a field next to hers (TC 82,83). Since she was bequeathing the field, his acting as witness may have been a way to keep land titles and boundaries in order. Usually when neighbors were witnesses, the testators were women and the neighbors were men.[25]

Sometimes testators addressed those at the deathbed. Doña Luisa Juana spoke to her kin saying, "May you hear me, you who are here with me. In your presence I give my orders to my father, Juan de San Miguel and to the noble lady, my mother doña Elena Constantina."[26] Ana Tiacapan of Tezcacoac addressed her witnesses directly, "O my children, this is all I have declared and what you who are present and will be named here have heard" (TC 58,59). The final statement of Miguel Oçoma gives the sense that his words were written just as he spoke them. "Draw close, my lords, you Miguel Iuhcatlatzin and you, Miguel Coatequitzin, I instruct you, if I die tomorrow or the next day, to speak promptly on behalf of my soul." After giving some instructions, he again directly addressed one of his witnesses, entrusting him with a weighty task. "And you, Miguel Coatequitzin, I beseech you: my child Juan is poor and will perish; I give him to you; he is to live with you" (TC 244,245). More unusual is an exchange between Ana Tiacapan of Tepanecapan and her daughter María Xoco. Ana bequeathed a number of things to the girl, including a boat. "But then the daughter said, 'It cannot be that I should take the boat; with all my heart I give it to my father, because he gathers the hay tribute with it. He is to go about taking it'" (TC 94,95). Although much of the the text of wills is formula, as we have seen, the statements above convey a real sense of immediacy and intimacy.

When Angelina Mocel's husband Juan Velázquez asked her to sell his cloak to buy candles, he followed native practice of entrusting final tasks to someone other than the official executors. Instructions for third parties to dispose of property or take care of special arrangements are often found in Nahuatl testaments. Usually they were kin who were to care for minor children or to sell property for masses. These were informal instructions and exhortations not backed by any administrative hierarchy. Vicente Xochiamatl ("flower paper") entrusted a fellow stonemason to collect some money for land a Spaniard bought from him and give it to his son. Said Vicente, "Let him give a little something to the child. I make Fabián Jiménez, stonemason, responsible for it" (TC 112ff).

The elders of Culhuacan's residential wards were occasionally the third parties in charge of specific duties. Sometimes it was just to watch out for the testators' interests. The notary Miguel García listed movable goods he had that he wanted sold, saying "let everything I have mentioned, with which the various [debts] are to be paid back, be sold quickly. The ward heads will speak for me, along with my nephew" (TC 104,105). Vicente Xochiamatl, who had had his fellow mason look out for one transaction involving his son, had the ward heads take care of another. He gave some magueys to his son, but had worries about it. "Let those who cultivate there not fool [my son] [about the magueys]; let the ward heads speak for me" (TC 112,113).

Written testaments in Nahuatl are found from the midsixteenth century on, but the oral tradition was still strong. For example, the notary Miguel García stated that "eight pesos and four tomines have been paid publicly [toward buying my horse]" (TC 104,105). Reliance on the living testimony and support of witnesses to affirm that the transactions had taken place (or were about to) is rooted in oral tradition. Although Joaquín Matlalacan proved ownership by reference to a document, saying "I have the bill of payment (*carta de pago*) to verify that it is my purchased house" (TC 236,237), it was much more common to name someone who had witnessed a given event.

The oral tradition was strong, but there is evidence that people had the expectation that testaments would be preserved and could be used for future reference. Luis Tlauhpotonqui mentioned his father's will in the text of his own, and concluded saying "whatever I have forgotten is to be investigated again in the testament of my late father. One can see there if I have forgotten something and it was not written" (TC 140,141). After Simón Moxixicoa died, his wife wanted a division of the estate. Joined by her relatives she said, " 'Let us hear the testament that the deceased ordered.' And then the testament was searched for and was read and the relatives heard it" (TC 160,161).

Generally in Culhuacan the original wills were kept in a central repository under control of the town government, and sometimes copies were made. The will of Cristina Tiacapan was written by Baltasar Amaro and copied by Miguel Jacobo de Maldonado. Maldonado said the will was a good copy, "not one letter nor anything else was omitted; rather, the copy was made perfectly like [the original]."[27] He also made a copy of Andrés de San Miguel's will, using some of the same language concerning the trueness of the copy. According to Maldonado, "the wife [of the testator], María Ana, whose home is Santiago, will keep the original" (TC 212ff).

Miguel Jacobo de Maldonado finished Angelina Mocel's statement, dated it, and signed his name. For the moment, his job for her was at an end. He had written the statement in his clear notarial hand[28] in sharp black ink on European paper. Perhaps he read back the text to Angelina, following the instructions for notaries. It was now up to him to file the document with the proper authorities.

The Augustinian friars in Culhuacan had done their work well. Whether or not there had been a prehispanic testamentary tradition, by the late sixteenth century making a will was one of the standard pious acts before death. Not only did these statements bequeath property to living heirs, but they became the instruments for giving property and money to the church. European ideas concerning proper burial and provisions for insuring the health of the soul after death via masses were well entrenched. Culhuacan may have seemed a very provincial town, but it was participating in very European traditions only three generations after the Spanish conquest. Of course piety in any age is hard to judge. But if we use the same standards of assessing pious behavior of the people of Culhuacan as we do for Europeans, we conclude that the Indians had fully absorbed the *outward* expressions of religious belief.

In form and in content, Nahuatl wills conformed to European patterns. They diverged from those patterns in the way estates were administered. This topic will be taken up in the next chapter.

4 / TOWN GOVERNMENT

"Here in the city of Culhuacan"

In late May 1582, a little over a year after Angelina Mocel's death, her estate was still not completely settled. Estate administration was a function of town government, so the notary Miguel Jacobo de Maldonado returned to the page on which Angelina's testament was recorded. He began writing the opening phrases about the settlement, "We, the executors, Agustín Vázquez and Miguel Josef, and Miguel Jacobo, notary, declare...." Angelina's sisters-in-law, María Salomé and Petronila, had sold some of her goods to pay for masses. It was the duty of the notary and the executors to deal with the money for the estate. María Salomé and Petronila had said that "We will go and make an offering." And now the notary and the executors were called upon. "To verify it, (we declare) we saw the money, one peso four tomines, which was presented before us and was brought to the church, and which we gave to our beloved father the prior, fray Juan Zimbrón" (TC 183ff). The highest ranking Indian religious official, the fiscal Gabriel Maldonado, acted as witness to the statement. Delivering money to the friars so that they would say masses for the deceased was the usual government involvement in estates.

The officials who participated in the administration of Angelina's estate were part of the civil and religious hierarchies that regulated many aspects of Indian life. Although the Spanish conquest ended Indian political hegemony, nonetheless there continued to be considerable native autonomy over local affairs.

Culhuacan's civil government had been affected by the general Spanish colonial policy of reshaping native hierarchies to suit the viceroyalty's needs. Though the process continued to evolve somewhat over the whole colonial era, by the late sixteenth century most of the basic changes had been made. The structure of civil rule differed from its prehispanic precursor, yet its basic functions did not, for it was still concerned with questions of taxation, maintaining order, and defending the town's interests. Likewise native religious hierarchies of the colonial period were affected by Spanish priorities, but their basic concerns, spiritual affairs and sacred rituals, were continuations from the prehispanic period. Despite the fact that the ultimate authorities of both hierarchies were Spanish, the civil and religious structures in Indian towns were central institutions in native life. The structure and function of native hierarchies creatively adapted to colonial rule.

In the prehispanic era, the Valley of Mexico was divided into political units called *altepetl,* often translated as "town" or "city," which were essentially city-states. The meaning of the term is "water" (*atl*) and "hill" (*tepetl*), which "may indicate the two elements necessary for a place to be habitable" (Reyes, 1975:6). Altepetl were generally subdivided into residential wards usually called *tlaxilacalli* or at times *calpulli,* some of which were at a distance from the main settlement. Culhuacan consisted of the main settlement at the base of the Cerro de la Estrella and the outlying settlement of Tetla up on the mountain itself. The dynastic ruler of an altepetl was a *tlatoani* (pl. *tlatoque*), meaning "he who speaks." Sometimes an altepetl had several tlatoque, sharing power in complicated ways, though Spaniards considered a one-tlatoani altepetl the norm. Culhuacan's single tlatoani line was distinguished, and its ties to the Toltecs long gave the town prestige.

In the immediate postconquest period, Indian altepetl became the basis for organizing the first system of Spanish rule, the encomienda. As we have discussed, encomiendas were private grants of Indians' labor to the Spanish conquerors, in exchange for which the grantholder, the *encomendero,* provided his Indians with personnel for Christian religious instruction and owed the Spanish community military obligations. In practice the encomienda was mainly a funnel for Indians' goods and services to privileged Spaniards. The Oñate family claimed residence in Mexico City (González de Cosío, 1952:156), and the encomendero in 1580, Cristóbal's son Hernando, is never mentioned by any of the Culhuacan citizens who died about 1580.[1]

The encomienda was a private system of administration, but the Spanish crown worked quickly to assert its control over its domains. A viceroy and high court (*audiencia*) were established, and at the level of local administration, the area was divided into *corregimientos,* civil jurisdictions. The *corregidor,* the official in charge, carried out edicts from higher levels (such as the king's request for composing the Relaciones geográficas), and acted as a judge for petty crimes and local squabbles (Gibson, 1964:91). Indians had recourse to the high court in Mexico City and for some matters appealed directly to the king in Spain (see e.g., Anderson et al., 1976:177). However, for most matters, the corregidor was the primary contact Indians had with Spanish administrators.

Both the corregidor and the encomendero received income from the Indians in their respective jurisdictions, the encomendero as a private grant, the corregidor as his official salary. In some towns the encomendero and the corregidor were the same person, who thereby gained access to two separate incomes from the same Indians (Gibson, 1964:83). However, this was not the case in Culhuacan. In 1580, as we previously noted, the encomendero was from the Oñate family, while the corregidor was Gonzalo Gallegos.

Culhuacan was part of the corregimiento of Mexicatzinco, which included Ixtapalapa as well. The corregidor was assisted by a *teniente* or lieutenant, an *alguacil* or constable, a notary (*escribano*), and an interpreter (*interprete*). In the Culhuacan wills, the only clear reference to any one of these Spanish officials is to Diego de Paz, the teniente and official interpreter of the corregimiento who bought a piece of land from an estate (Gallegos, 1927:171; TC 38,39).[2] The Indians' last thoughts were not of the Spanish administrators, most of whom they would have seen only occasionally.

After the conquest, Spaniards applied many of their own concepts of urban organization to the Indian towns of Central Mexico (Gibson, 1964:32).[3] In Spain cities which were capitals of districts were called *cabezas,* "head towns." In New Spain, Indian altepetl were designated *cabeceras* (a variant form of the term cabeza), and their outlying settlements were dubbed *sujetos,* "subject towns." Culhuacan, as an altepetl, became a cabecera in the colonial period.[4] Subdivisions within Indian towns were termed *barrios,* "wards," if they were connected to the main settlement, and *estancias* if they were at some distance (Gibson, 1964:33). Culhuacan's outlying settlement of Tetla was called a barrio in the Libro de bautismos of Culhuacan (1588) (Gorbea Trueba, n.d.) and a sujeto in the Relación geográfica map (Monterrosa Prado, 1970). The status of Tetla is unclear.

The Spanish system of ranking communities by size and prestige was imposed on Indian towns. The largest and most important towns were ranked *ciudades,* followed by *villas* and *pueblos.* Mexico-Tenochtitlan, capital of the Aztec empire and subsequently the Spanish capital, was naturally a ciudad. Although the designations largely had no practical impact, towns which were called by the lesser names of villa and pueblo were lobbying to upgrade their status within a generation after the conquest (Gibson, 1964:32). In the populous municipality of Xochimilco, near Culhuacan and also part of the chinampa zone, Nahuatl documents from the 1570s carefully note that they were written *Y nican la noble ciudad xuchimilco,* "here in the noble city of Xochimilco."[5] The Spanish phrase for "the noble city" was taken over into Nahuatl. Other times the phrase was "altepetl ciudad," using both Nahuatl and Spanish terms in apposition.[6] Tlaxcalan documents have the Spanish phrase *la leal ciudad,* "the loyal city," recalling the city's role as an ally of Cortés in the conquest. Culhuacan documents of the late sixteenth century begin, *Y nican in altepetl Culhuacan,* "here in the city of Culhuacan," using only the word altepetl to denote the political unit, never any of the Spanish ranking terms. This was doubtless because in 1580, with a population of only about 3,600, Culhuacan's rank was as a pueblo. So quick to adopt other European ways, the heirs of the Toltecs chose to ignore their lowly Spanish designation.

Another change Spaniards made in altepetl was in their names. Each of the Indian municipalities and their individual wards acquired a saint's name. Culhuacan became San Juan Evangelista Culhuacan and each of the wards was given a patron saint. In one Culhuacan ward the designation in Spanish was translated to Nahuatl: Tres Reyes ("three kings") was standardly called Eitlatocan. When Angelina Mocel made her will, like most testators, she identified herself as a resident of a particular Culhuacan ward. Hers was Santa María Magdalena Tezcacoac. The ward of her father, Pablo Huitznahuatl, was called Santa María Magdalena Tezcacoac Cihuatecpan, a clue that wards had dual names, and likely dual structures. Some Culhuacan wards were known only by their patron saint's names, perhaps indicating that they were newly created subdivisions.

Towns often changed physically because of Spanish urban priorities. Practically all Spanish cities in the New World had a checkerboard pattern. A central plaza had the most important buildings, as well as the residences of the wealthy, around it. Many Indian towns in Mexico came to have this pattern also. In Culhuacan, the main church of San Juan Evangelista was situated across from the paper mill [*molino de papel*] on one side, and on the other, the water reservoir [*estanque*], along the main road to Coyoacan. Most of the streets shown on the Relación geográfica map were at right angles, with canals traversing the town in several places. [See Figure 1].

The reshaping of native institutions involved the creation of a Spanish-style city council or *cabildo*. New offices were created, the officeholders being elected by the elite native men. The high offices of the cabildo had titles which were loanwords from Spanish, indicating new creations. At the lower levels of administration, such as tax collection and land surveying, Nahuatl titles prevailed, probably as colonial continuations of traditional offices.

The highest official in the town was the *juez-gobernador,* "judge-governor." In the midsixteenth century, the tlatoani usually held the office, but significantly, the offices of tlatoani and juez-gobernador became separate. The office of tlatoani was hereditary, while that of juez-gobernador was elective or appointive, and the office holder thus was more malleable to Spanish demands. Although the Culhuacan evidence is fragmentary, it seems clear that the offices of tlatoani and juez-gobernador were separate by the 1580s, and likely well before that.[7] One of the perquisites of the office of tlatoani had been eroded by 1580. Land to support the office holder [*tlatocatlalli*] was held by someone who was not a ruler (TC 60ff).[8]

The two principal offices of the cabildo were those of *alcalde* and *regidor*. In Indian towns the number of people serving in these offices at one time often varied, but there were often two alcaldes and four regidores at a given time. The office of alcalde was prestigious, for not only did the official sit on the cabildo, but the office also carried judicial powers (Gibson, 1964:167). In Tlaxcala it was a suitable office as preparation for the governorship or as an honored post for the ex-governor. (Gibson, 1952:111). Regidores were the town councillors. In addition to alcaldes and regidores, there were other officials with Spanish titles, including the *escribano* or notary, the *alguacil* or constable, and the *alcaide* or jailor. *Diputados* or

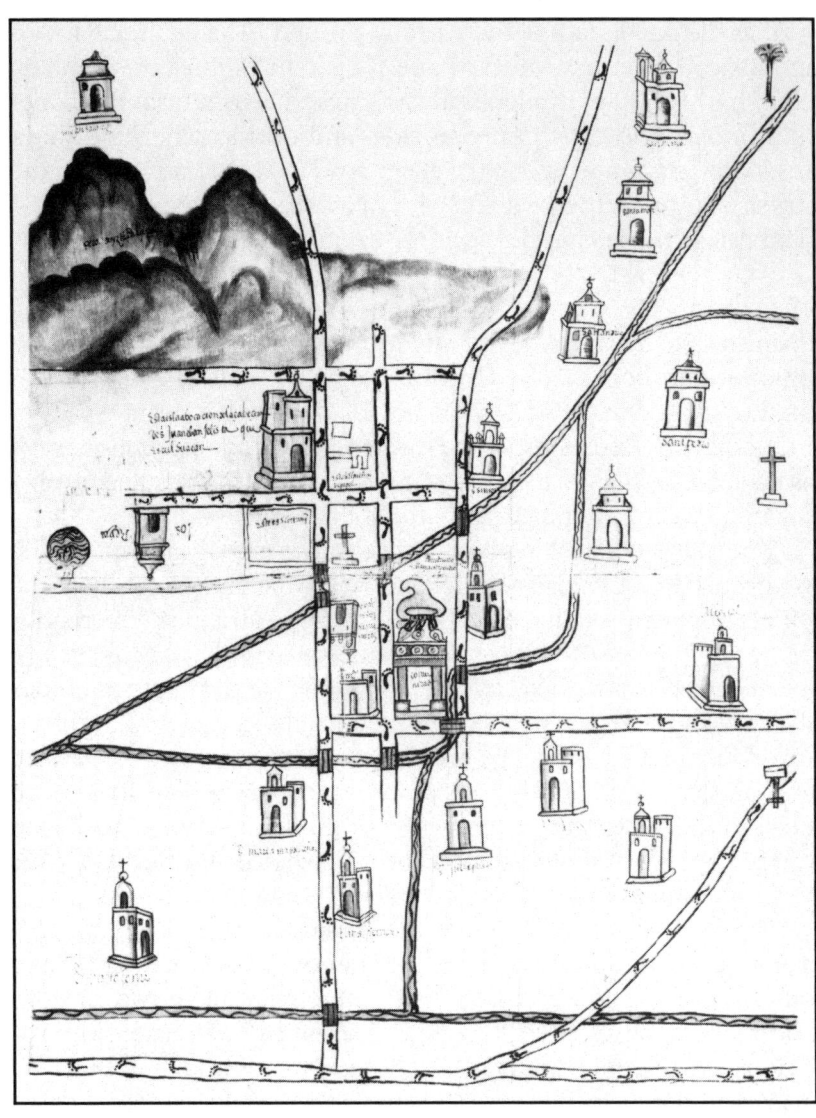

Fig. 1 Relación Geográfica map of Culhuacan, 1580. (Courtesy of the Benson Latin American Collection, The General Libraries, University of Texas).

deputies were low-level town officials whose functions were not clearly delineated; perhaps they simply acted as assistants to high cabildo officials.

At the lower levels of town government were functionaries having Nahuatl titles, especially tax collectors, the *tequiticatepixqui* and *tequitopile* (TC 242,243; 254,255; 268,269), and the official in charge of public works, the *cohuatequitopile* (TC 170,171). Officials dealing with land included the *tlaltopile,* who seems to have been generally in charge of land, and the *tlalpouhqui* or surveyor. These offices with Nahuatl titles were likely continuations of prehispanic offices which the Spaniards ignored or decided did not need transformation to some Spanish equivalent.

The men who held public office came from the upper stratum of society. In Tlaxcala "no one enters into public office who is not noble" (Torquemada, 1975:II,347). The different offices were rotated among the noblemen. In Culhuacan, for instance, Juan de San Miguel, Angelina Mocel's relative by marriage, held the offices of alcalde and *alguacil mayor* [chief constable]. Miguel Jacobo de Maldonado, who wrote a subtantial number of the Culhuacan wills, also served in more than one office during his lifetime. At some point someone scribbled some personal notes about him at the end of the book of testaments. "Miguel Jacobo was made notary for the year 1602 and alcalde for 1603, and notary for 1604 and 1605" (TC 280,281).

The town government was in charge of the municipality's official dealings with the outside world. We get but a glimpse of this function in the sources for Culhuacan. In 1580 the juez-gobernador, alcaldes, and regidores helped the corregidor and the prior to draw up the Relación geográfica of Culhuacan. The Relaciones geográficas, as we have noted, were questionnaires of royal government requesting information about New Spain. A man who served as alcalde in 1585, Pedro de San Agustín, was called upon to make the map for the Relación "by the order of the corregidor Gonzalo Gallegos" (Monterrosa Prado, 1970:13). Little else is known about the Culhuacan cabildo's dealings with the outside world.

More generally, town government regulated local life, levying taxes and demanding labor for public works, as well as keeping order and peace. The Culhuacan documents highlight the role of the government in overseeing transmission of property through inheritance and resolving disputes involving estates.

Taxation and public works, as we have mentioned, were concerns of lower level officials with Nahuatl titles. This reflected the reality that methods of taxation were entirely in Indian hands, though the amounts demanded were not. The encomendero and corregidor had to be paid, but no Culhuacan Indians mentioned in their wills specific taxes or labor obligations to these Spaniards. Generally Spaniards were only interested in total revenues and numbers of workers and did not care how the levies were raised. The town government levied public works duties [*cohuatequitl*] which in other towns consisted of construction projects, clearing ditches, labor on lands to support officials (Lockhart et al., n.d.). In Culhuacan there was a tribute of fodder [*cohuaçacatl*], one of the the products abundant in Culhuacan which they sold in Mexico City markets. Tribute in goods, *tlacallaquilli,* was occasionally mentioned by testators. Often these were levies for a certain amount of cloth.

An important function of government was to maintain public order, and the newly created office of *alguacil* or constable, was primarily concerned with it. The job was not without hazards, as doña Luisa Juana's father discovered. Miguel Huelihuitl spent some time in jail "because he broke the head of Juan de San Miguel when he was *alguacil mayor*" (TC 136,137).[9] The town had a prison [*teilpiloyan*], run by an Indian official, the alcaide. This was yet another office with a Spanish name, although the word for jail was Nahuatl.

Incarceration in the town jail was punishment for various offenses. When the town government rendered an official decision, there were often admonitions that "whoever says anything [counter to it] will have justice done him and will be put in jail" (TC 160,161). Sometimes the penalties were even sterner. The juez-gobernador ordered, concerning an agreement between Juan de San Miguel and his sister-in-law doña Luisa Isabel, that "in the name of his majesty that the penalty for anyone who wishes to break or dispute this agreement [will suffer]: imprisonment in jail for ten days and will receive 100 lashes in the plaza, and will be banished for six months, and will pay ten pesos that will belong to the chamber of your majesty."[10]

Unfortunately, we have no idea how often these penalties were imposed in practice. The ideas of fault, punishment, and compensation were clearly articulated, however. In the prehispanic period, the Aztecs had a highly structured legal system with written laws and a hierarchy of judges. Penalties were specific and legalistically applied. High status could not ameliorate the punishment, although the penalties were often applied according to the status of the perpetrator (Offner, 1983).[11]

In the only known case of fatal assault in Culhuacan, the victim, Diego Sánchez, said "the person who attacked me was banished . . . and now I say, if the black man by whose hand I was wounded by a knife should appear, he is to pay [what it costs] here in the church hospital" (TC 220,221). The assailant was described by the Nahuatl word for black, *tliltic,* not the Spanish word *negro*. Since he is not identified by name, he was likely an outsider. If the culprit were merely officially banished, the punishment was light. Friction in Indian communities between natives and intruding blacks and mulattoes was a standard occurrence in the colonial period and was one of the reasons prompting colonial legislation restricting non-Indians from living in Indian towns (Gibson, 1964:147; Mörner, 1967:45ff).

As we have seen in the previous chapter, town government, through its notaries, kept records relevant to the town, such as testaments. The notaries were the officials in charge of writing legal documents, such as minutes of cabildo meetings, petitions, bills of sale, testaments, and censuses. From the documents the notaries wrote, we get some clues to the difficulties involved in their profession. They dealt well with the problem of Spanish loanwords. Spanish has a larger inventory of sounds than Nahuatl, and there are more letters in the Latin alphabet than notaries had need of. Thus, recording words which were perhaps only imperfectly perceived presented a challenge to notaries. Nahuatl has no voiced/voiceless distinction such as between p/b, t/d, and k/g. There is also no l/r distinction. And distinct vowel sounds in Spanish, such as u/o, were merged in Nahuatl. Thus a Spanish word like *público* could be rendered by a Nahuatl-speaker as *bopligo,* substitutions of letters for sounds not distinct in Nahuatl. The methods which Culhuacan notaries used to cope with loanwords are consistent with those found among other notaries for the same period (Karttunen and Lockhart, 1976).[12]

Another problem with which Culhuacan notaries grappled was timekeeping in the Spanish system. In the early colonial period, there was a shift from the prehispanic calendar to the Christian calendar. Both calendars were intimately tied to their respective religious systems, and a change imposed by Spaniards was the Christian calendar. Dates in Nahuatl documents, such as testaments, are by the Christian calendar. There were set phrases for years, and a somewhat mixed system for the rest of the date. For example, the phrase *omochiuh yc xxi mani metztli de Julios mil y quientos y ochenta Anos* "Done the 21st of the month of July of the year 1580" (TC 48,49), contains Roman numerals for twenty-one, the phrase in Spanish *de Julios* [sic, for *Julio*] *mil y quientos y ochenta Anos* for "of the month of July of the year 1580" while the word for month, *metztli,* is Nahuatl. Some notaries also used the Spanish word for month, *mes.*

There is evidence that Culhuacan notaries quickly adopted the change from the Julian to the Gregorian calendar in the mid-1580s. To bring the Christian calendar into better alignment with the solar year, Pope Gregory XIII decreed that the day following 4 October 1582 would be called October 15, thus dropping ten days. Spain was was one of the countries which adopted the calendar immediately. Culhuacan notaries did not have word of the change four months later, in February of 1583, but by June of 1585, we know that the Gregorian calendar was in use by Culhuacan notaries.[13] Fairly quick adoption of the calendar would have been expected since the cycle of Christian feast days would have been affected by the change.

The Indian town government was typically involved in the final legal acts of its citizens. The notary recorded the statements of the dying, and town officials acted as witnesses and executors to wills. As discussed previously, a will was a religious document, a final declaration of faith, but it was also a civil instrument, passing on property to designated heirs. Much of the property that people had to bequeath was real estate, over which the town government had jurisdiction. Most heirs were citizens of the town over whom the cabildo likewise had jurisdiction. If there was a dispute over inheritance, the first hearing of the complaint would come before town officials. More often than not, however, estates were not disputed, and town officials simply delivered money to the church from the sale of people's property.

The executors of estates were town officials, who were called by the Spanish loanword *albaceas* (sing., *albacea*). In Spanish practice, executors were named by the testator, but in Culhuacan, the executors were regular officials of the government. As with other offices, the people named as executors changed in rotation. In September 1580 the former executors had left some duties undone. "We, Miguel García, Martín de Santiago, and Antón Jacobo, executors [say that] the other group of former executors Alonso Jiménez and Miguel Santiago left behind the goods of the dead . . . we collected it in order that they be aided with masses . . . for the property owners who died" (TC 72,73). Gabriel Maldonado, who was known as the chief executor [*albacea mayor*], went on to hold the office of fiscal, the highest Indian religious official. In the career of another man, Miguel Josef, stretches were devoted to being an executor of estates, serving 1581–82 and 1585–86 (with service as regidor in 1583).

Executors were officials of the town government, but being an executor seems to have been a role rather than an office. For example, although Miguel Josef was identified in texts of wills as an albacea and identified as such in other contexts, he had the Spanish title diputado.[14] Sometimes those identified as albaceas in the text signed their names using the title alguacil. All these were Spanish titles of some type, indicating a postconquest introduction. Sometimes however, the Nahuatl title *topile* "official," (literally: "one who carries a staff [of office]") was used. In the will of Ana Tiacapan of Tepanecapan, Martín de Santiago and Antonio Jacobo declared, "we the executors [albaceas] who went to hear the declaration here place our names and signatures to verify the declaration and the orders of the invalid," then each signed with the title "topile" (TC 94,95). Just as it is likely that some kind of prehispanic tradition underlay the Indians' enthusiastic adoption of testaments, likely the role of executor had prehispanic precedents. The alternate use of Spanish and Nahuatl titles for the same officials suggests this.

The notary was in charge of the preservation of the testaments he wrote, filing them together in a book. When there was some updating on the sale of a testator's estate, or the record of a disputed inheritance, the information was added to the appropriate will. For that reason, the delivery of money for Angelina Mocel's masses was certified immediately following her will. The town's friars also had access to the book, noting when masses were said (though none was noted for Angelina).

At times the notary not only kept the records of the deceased, but also became involved in estate administration. Notaries had a trusted position in estate administration since they oversaw the preservation of testaments. This situation presented an opportunity for fraud and mishandling of funds. (Similar problems are found among Spanish notaries in charge of testaments [Artiles, 1969:501–3; Parry, 1953; Gibson, 1952:78].) In June 1585 Culhuacan officials dealt with such a problem. As we have seen, "the book [of wills] was taken from Miguel Jacobo because he hid many testaments that the deceased ordered" (TC 222,223). The book was given to another notary, Juan Bautista, who "was ordered to take care of all the testaments." As with most important acts, this one was public. "The book was given to him before the lords executors, Miguel Josef and Francisco Vázquez" (TC 222,223). The proceedings were recorded by another notary, Pedro de San Pablo.[15] Precisely how Miguel Jacobo's suppression of testaments benefited him is not known, but testaments were often entered in evidence as proof of ownership of property. Disgruntled heirs might have bribed him to misplace the wills so that they could usurp the property. Or perhaps the notary himself was the usurper, collecting various monies meant for delivery to the friars. At any rate, municipal officials took steps to improve the preservation of the wills. Miguel Jacobo's lapse of ethics did not prevent him from going on to hold the office of notary again and also the office of alcalde (TC 280,281). It is unclear whether he was notary in 1585 when the governor and the alcaldes acted. The town's only known sanction against him was to deprive him of the book. The breach in ethics was dealt with locally because Indian governmental officials considered disciplinary action against their fellow office-holders as their jurisdiction.[16]

Indian notaries' involvement in estate divison may have been influenced by Spanish practice. In the early sixteenth century, the Spanish Crown set up the *escribanía de bienes de difuntos,* the notariate of the goods of the deceased. It acted as custodian for the estates of Spaniards who died in the New World and was the only newly created notariate for the Indies. Abuses by the tribunal and complaints by heirs marked the history of this body, and it ceased to exist in 1584 (Artiles, 1969:501–3). During the period when the bulk of the Culhuacan wills were drawn up, however, there existed a Spanish notariate exclusively concerned with estate administration, and this may have influenced procedures in Indian towns.

Notaries were involved in estate division, but the will of one notary and executor, Miguel García, shows other aspects of a notary's role. Listed in his will are a number of transactions for which he was responsible. They included keeping valuable property, "some hammered gold," belonging to Culhuacan ward officials; acting as an agent for the payment of various people's debts; and accepting money from testators for the purchase of goods for the church. When García was in charge of money matters, he seems to have kept the money for his own use, ordering the payments only at his death. Significantly, however, he did enumerate his obligations in his will, and was attempting to act in good faith, if not promptly (TC 100ff).[17]

As we have seen in the case of Angelina Mocel, native civil and religious officials delivered money to the friars from the sale of goods from the estate. Usually these were petty transactions and merited simple certification of payment with only a lump sum mentioned. However, the auction of movable goods from the estate of the nobleman, don Juan Téllez, was a more complicated matter. The Spanish prior, fray Juan Núñez, became directly involved in the sale, and the record of it became part of the town archives. Normally the prior would not have taken part in such a sale, but likely don Juan's own funds and those of the church got entwined when he served as fiscal. It seems he had made quite a mess of things, borrowing money which upon his death had to be repaid. After everything was sold, the prior addressed the noblewoman, doña Juana de San Gabriel, who was doubtless don Juan's relative, saying "My lady, guard the proceeds from these goods and collect all the remaining goods; let it all be sold. And when it is collected, whoever gave loans to [don Juan] will be satisfied by being given the money, for there are many who are requesting money. Where are we going to get it? They will not have enough even if 20 pesos are collected with which they are to be compensated" (TC 42,43,45). Fray Juan Núñez took it upon himself to repay the creditors.

The highest levels of town government were involved in the divison of the estate of doña Luisa Juana, Angelina Mocel's relative. This was an unusual division in many ways. Rather than the notary drawing up the will, the official in charge of the choir [corotopile], wrote the statement;[18] the executors from the town government were not witnesses to the testament, nor did they play any role in the administration of her large estate. Doña Luisa Juana had appointed the prior, fray Juan Núñez, as her executor. Her personal appointment of him is closer to Spanish practice than to native. When he failed to divide the estate, however, the heirs and town government became involved. The size of the estate and the importance of the heirs doubtless contributed to an ultimate division before the cabildo.

The juez-gobernador himself, don Juan Marcos de Velasco, and the alcaldes supervised the division of doña Luisa Juana's property. It was complicated because she had inherited land from her grandmother and her mother, but essentially their estates remained undivided. Doña Luisa Juana and her aunt (her mother's sister), doña Luisa Isabel, continued joint possession. Now that doña Luisa Juana was dead, her father inherited her portion, and he wanted the lands divided from those of his sister-in-law. One of the steps in the division was to establish his daughter's rights to the property, and her testament was used as evidence. In June 1580, two months after her death, her will was brought to the juez-gobernador. When don Juan "saw it and understood it, he said that he ruled the testament valid, and no one is to violate it."[19] By November 1580 Juan de San Miguel, doña Luisa Juana's father, and her aunt doña Luisa Isabel had come to an agreement about the division of the lands, and "came to show their written agreement and accord" to the juez-gobernador and other town officials. Seemingly the same day that their statement was presented, the juez-gobernador gave them possession of the fields "when the alguacil mayor has gone to put stakes to show the lands which belong to each as his property."[20] The juez-gobernador also set penalties for violating or disputing the agreement.[21]

In April 1581, eleven months after his daughter's death, Juan de San Miguel addressed the juez-gobernador, saying that he "wishe[d] to take possession of all the fields that belong to him and that he inherited so that no one at some time should take them or dispute them in the future."[22] The juez-gobernador "gave orders for a writ to be made that possession be given to Juan de San Miguel."[23] The alcalde carried out the orders for actually dividing the estate. Addressing the alcalde concerning the writ of possession, the juez-gobernador said "if someone says something counter to it and disputes the possession, let him be brought before me so that I will hear his declaration. And I will do him justice."[24] The alcalde was merely the agent for carrying out the juez-gobernador's authority.

The alcalde Lorenzo de Francisco personally oversaw the division of the lands. Going to each of the places which the writ specified, "the lord alcalde took Juan de San Miguel by the hand, and to give him possession he went taking him from one place to another on [the land]."[25] Juan de San Miguel "dug in the corners [of the field] with a wooden digging stick to show that he took possession of all his land." To complete the act of possession, "the lord alcalde said 'in peace and safety I give you possession of all your inherited fields.'"[26] There was no trouble with taking possession for "no one there disputed it or impeded it."[27] All of the proceedings were witnessed by a number of town officials and other noblemen, including don Juan Ramírez, who had been tlatoani, don Juan García, Agustín Jiménez, the alguacil mayor, and two relevant officials specifically dealing with land, Pedro de San Bernardino, official in charge of the land [*tlaltopile*] and Juan Bautista Quenitoloc, land measurer or surveyor [*tlalpouhqui*].[28]

A week or so earlier, also in April 1581, the town government had considered another matter concerning doña Luisa Juana's estate, that of selling her house to Spaniards. "When the young woman died, she made her testament concerning her inherited house and enclosure; all of it is to be sold, and with the proceeds in money masses would be said for . . . her."[29] These were not such unusual requests; but there was a problem. "No citizen here in Culhuacan has appeared who wants to buy the house and enclosure, because they are worth a lot of money."[30] Thus in April 1581 Juan de San Miguel asked the town government to "give him their license and legal power so that some Spaniard can buy the house and enclosure."[31] In order to live in Indian towns and buy property, there was a requirement to obtain a license and permission from the native government. The colonial government had enacted measures to control the number of non-Indians in native towns in an attempt to control Spaniards' rapaciousness.[32] In the case of doña Luisa's house, the town council considered the matter and decided in favor, for two weeks later Juan de San Miguel was before them with the Spaniards. In the cabildo's presence he declared "that I truly take and receive 40 pesos in money from the hand of Señor Diego de San Román and from his wife, Elvira Núñez, with which they are paying for the house and enclosure."[33] The new homeowners were the sister and the brother-in-law of Culhuacan's prior, fray Juan Núñez,[34] whom the town council deemed Spaniards worthy of a license for residence.

The cash sale was to pay for masses for the souls of doña Luisa Juana and her mother, doña María Motecuhçoma. The town council saw to that Juan de San Miguel received the money "and immediately he divided [it]. Thirty [pesos] he gave to our dear father, fray Juan Núñez, in order that he say masses for the said deceased. And the ten pesos remaining, Juan de San Miguel took to spend on himself,"[35] since he had already paid ten pesos toward masses for his late wife and daughter. Everyone got something from the sale. Diego de San Román got a house; his brother-in-law fray Juan Núñez got 30 pesos; Juan de San Miguel got back the cash he had advanced; and doña Luisa Juana and her mother presumably got their masses.

Ecclesiastics were direct beneficiaries of estate division, and sometimes actively participated in them, but the cabildo had no jurisdiction over the number of masses that were actually said. Often the friars did certify at the bottom of wills that a certain number of masses were celebrated, but it is my impression that fewer were said than the testators had ordered. It is clear that if no cash were forthcoming from an estate, there would be no masses, despite the wishes of the dying. For instance, Juan de San Miguel had petitioned to sell the house and enclosure to get money for masses for his deceased wife and daughter, because "masses have not yet been said to help their souls."[36] Masses were on a fee-for-service basis.

The division of doña Luisa Juana's estate was undisputed, and the cabildo acted as the legal authority to divide it. However, not all divisions were so amicable, and officials of the town council sometimes had to arbitrate. When Simón Moxixicoa made his will, he wanted his wife María Justina to bring up his children at their marital residence, "and not go away to another place" (TC 156,157). She was a witness to the will, perhaps by so doing giving the impression she would accede to his wishes. However, four months later, "before the lords alcaldes Lorenzo de San Francisco and Juan Téllez and the fiscal Gabriel Maldonado appeared the widow of Simón Moxixicoa" (TC 158ff) to dispute the estate. She had brought along her relatives to back her up. Simón's testament was found and read. Her relatives "complained about [María's] unshelled maize; they disputed greatly over it and were very discontented about it" (TC 160,161). The family wanted her goods, especially the corn, separated from her late husband's.

Some form of settlement had to be made, and it was up to the alcaldes to exercise their judicial power. They addressed the widow María Justina saying, "Abandon the house and take the firewood and your unshelled maize and all your woman's [weaving] things. No one is to quarrel, but you are to take your property in peace" (TC 160,161). The alguacil mayor was to oversee the actual division, probably because penalties were involved. "Whoever says anything [counter to it] will be put in jail" (TC 160,161). The division was accomplished; María Justina took her property and left; but the officials gave to a third party, the "precious green stones of the little children of Simón Moxixicoa, to keep [for them]" (TC 160,161). This seems to imply that the children did not go with their mother.[37]

The cases of doña Luisa Juana and María Justina show that at the local level the cabildo could both oversee undisputed estate divisions and render judgment in disputed cases. Very likely these functions were a continuation of prehispanic practices, even though the structure of the town government had been altered by Spanish colonial policy. In the prehispanic period, evidence was heard and assessed, judgment rendered, and penalties mandated. What changed in the colonial period was the Indians' access to another level of redress: the Spanish courts. Far from being reluctant about utilizing this method of justice, Indians actively sought it out when they were not satisfied at the local level.

A Culhuacan lawsuit of the 1590s is typical of the genre, for the case involved a dispute between heirs. One Miguel Huitznahuatocatl had died, according to his daughter Marta Petronila, "without making a testament."[38] The problem was that Miguel had married a second time, and his second wife, Cristina Tiacapan, had possession of his property. When she died, she excluded her stepdaughter Marta Petronila from the estate by simply not mentioning her in the will. Apparently not receiving satisfaction in Culhuacan, Marta Petronila took the matter to court in Mexico City, arguing that she was the legitimate daughter of her father, and that by rights she, rather than her stepmother's heirs, should receive the property. As evidence she presented a pictorial genealogy and a houseplan, both to show her direct link to her father and to the particular property.[39] [See Figures 2 and 3]. The suit was heard by the Spanish court with Spanish lawyers [*procuradores*] presenting their respective clients' cases. Witnesses were called and interrogated through interpreters.

Often in these cases, the final decision was based on Spanish principles of inheritance (Borah, 1983:46); therefore Indians framed their suits in terms completely comprehensible to the Spanish judges. Marta Petronila's case was strong, for she was the legitimate daughter of the original owner of the property, Miguel Huitznahuato-

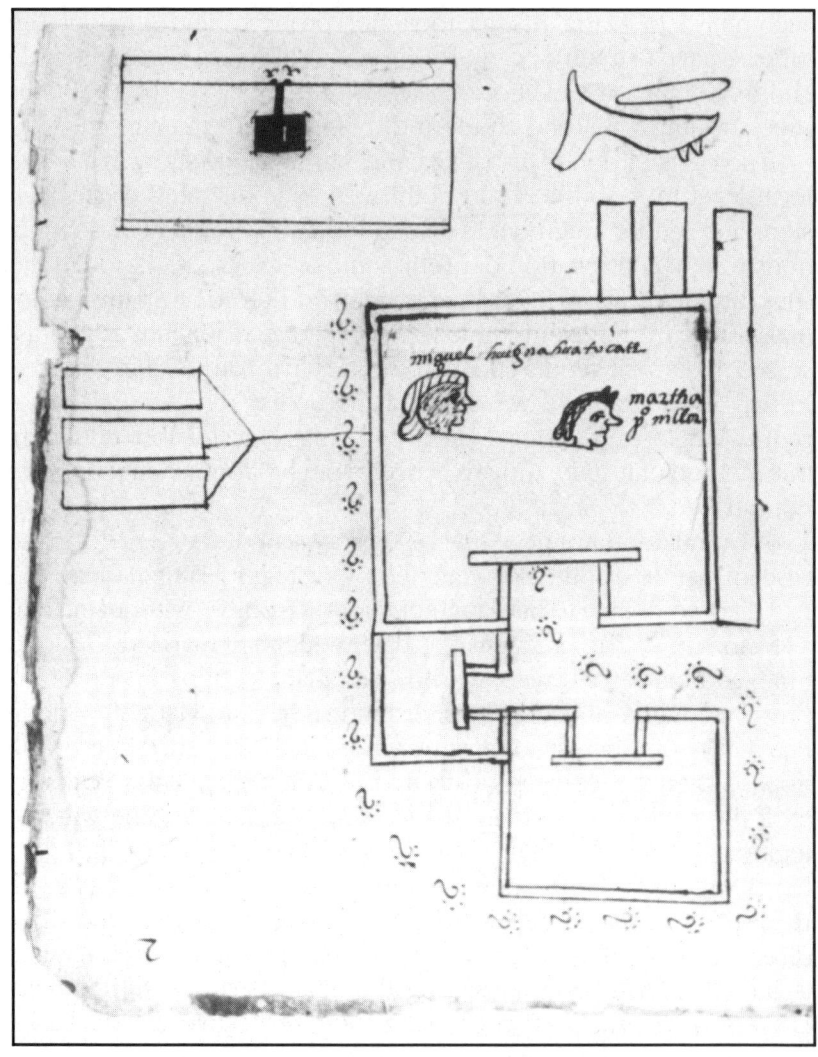

Fig. 2 A Culhuacan house plan. (Courtesy of the Bibliothèque Nationale of Paris).

catl. And in the end she won.[40] Although Spanish law provided for a wife receiving a specified portion of her husband's estate, it also provided for the children. Second wives (and their heirs) were often in a vulnerable position, however, as this case suggests.

A disproportionate number of Indian women argued their cases before Spanish courts (Kellogg, 1984). Perhaps this was because their testaments were open to challenge. Or perhaps Indian custom made fewer provisions for women as heirs, but Spanish law gave them access to a new means of acquiring property. Women appeared in courts both as plaintiffs and defendants; however, plaintiffs of either sex had better chances to win their suits before the courts (Kellogg, 1984).

The cabildo dealt with problems of town finance, justice, estate division, and policies toward the outside world, and the Mexico City courts dealt with problems that could not be dealt with locally, but there was another level of administration, that of the residential wards. They were the lowest level of organized rule and administration. In Culhuacan wards were consistently called *tlaxilacalli,* while elsewhere they were sometimes called *calpulli,* and in Amecameca there existed units called *calpoltlaxilacalli,* an amalgamation of the two terms.[41] Ward organization and the criteria for a person's affiliation with a given ward remain the subject of debate. Some scholars assert that kinship was the primary organizing principle of wards, while others contend that residence was the overriding criterion for membership. The report of the Spanish judge, Alonso de Zorita, for the Puebla-Tlaxcala area is the principal Spanish source on the calpulli. According to this report, officials of the ward [*calpulleque*] regulated landholding by its members (Zorita, 1963b: 105ff). In Culhuacan the wards regulated aspects of residence, land transactions and petty money matters, and protected the rights of their residents regarding inheritance. The ward elders, called *tlaxilacalleque,* were in charge of these matters. There is some possibility that the term tlaxilacalleque simply refers to the people of the ward and not especially to ward elders.[42]

The people of Culhuacan were under the jurisdiction of their wards. When on the verge of death, they stated their residence by their ward affiliation.[43] Angelina Mocel's aunt, María Tiacapan, was rare in not stating where she lived (TC 174,175). Angelina's husband, Juan Velázquez, declared his affiliation to be Santa Ana Tlacuilocan

Xallah (TC 204,205) while hers was Santa María Magdalena Tezcacoac (TC 180,181). Where they lived, however, is unknown.

Residence was something quite different from ward affiliation. A person could be living in a given ward without having a legal connection to it. For example, Ana Tlaco "whose home is Yecapixtla," a town in the Cuernavaca area quite some distance from Culhuacan, was "living in the [Culhuacan] ward of San Francisco Tlacatecpan" at the time of her death. Apparently she was originally from Culhuacan, and her brothers remained there. She seems to have been only visiting one of them when she died, for her declared residence, Yecapixtla, was that of her husband (TC 188,189). Another woman was also away from her ward of residence when she died. Juana Tiacapan stated that "where I lie sick [is] in the ward of Santa Ana Iyauhtenco," a subdivision of Culhuacan's outlying settlement of Santiago Tetla.[44] She claimed residence in Santa María Asunción Aticpac, in Culhuacan proper. When she died, she gave her husband, Lázaro de San Pablo, a houselot in Iyauhtenco. She attempted to shore up his chances of residence, by asking permission for him. "I have addressed the people of Iyauhtenco, and I said to them, 'My husband will remain here among you'" (TC 66,67). These two reports suggest that a wife became affiliated with her husband's ward, but this does not seem always to have been the case, as noted previously with Angelina Mocel and her husband, Juan Velázquez.

Movement of people from one town to another was quite common, and the formalities of establishing residence were important.[45] Where a person was affiliated was relevant to the tribute obligations, residence rights, and possibly also landholding.

The ward elders included women, one of the few instances of women serving in an official capacity.[46] Some women are identified as having noble status, but few performed official duties. A woman named Juana Tiacapan was a *tlaxilacalleh* for the ward of Coatlan (TC 130,131; 133,135). On the same day, she acted as a witness for the testaments of two women: Mariana, the widow of another testator, Juan Rafael Tlacochcalcatl, and María Tiacapan. Culhuacan women also served as *cihuatepixque,* officials in charge of women. The Dominican friar Diego Durán said that "in order to gather the women, there were old Indian women, appointed by all the wards, who were called cihuatepixque, which is to say 'keeper of women,' or guardians" (Durán, 1967:I,189).

The ward elders were called upon to regulate certain property transfers by testators. Vicente Xochiamatl gave some magueys to his son, and wanted the ward heads to look out for the boy's interests. "Let those who cultivate there not fool him [about the magueys]. Let the ward heads speak for me" (TC 112,113). When Ana Tiacapan of Santa Cruz bequeathed to her son some land that she had purchased, she said "I [am] notify[ing] the ward heads," about it, doubtless to protect his interests. In another case, doña María Juárez notified the ward of some of her land dealings. "I have divided [the chinampas]; 10 of them I alienated, as all the ward heads of Santa Ana Cal[tenco] know" (TC 248,249).

On occasion, the ward heads were recipients of bequests of land. Juana Tiacapan of Aticpac, who as we mentioned earlier, was trying to secure residence rights for her husband from the ward heads of Iyauhtenco, left to those officials some land she had received as a girl. She suggested that "maybe they will give [the land] to some poor person" (TC 68,69). Perhaps this donation was to sweeten her other proposition of allowing her husband to reside there. Diego Sánchez gave a similar donation of land saying "I leave it in the hands of the ward heads. Perhaps they will give it to someone" (TC 218,219). The account by the Spanish judge, Alonso de Zorita, says that ward heads redistributed land to those in need (Zorita, 1963b:108). These Culhuacan donations of land are interesting in light of that report. However, the Culhuacan donations may have been an innovation brought about by Christian ideals of charity.

The ward heads also funded small transactions by ward residents. María Icnocihuatl of Cihuatecpan was twice widowed and at her death had outstanding debts to them. She began her testament by saying, "here is what worries me and what my late husband Martín Huitzilcoatl and I have done wrong: we borrowed four tomines in money belonging to the ward heads and they have not yet been paid back." This was not all. "My late second husband named Francisco Quauhtli and I borrowed a peso belonging to the ward heads so that we could leave jail when we were both imprisoned" (TC 78,79). Unfortunately she does not state *why* she was in jail, but the ward heads lent bail money to her and her husband. Money dealings of this nature were apparently standard and denials of such involvement were seemingly formula. When Pedro Cano Acatl declared that "I have no money at all of the ward heads; no one is to accuse me of anything," Miguel Jacobo de Maldonado used the notarial catch-all phrase *et cetera,* to cut off the statement (TC 198,199). On the other

56 / CHAPTER 4

Table 3 Wards of Culhuacan c. 1580

TC[1]	LBC[2]	RG[3]
—	Otomites	—
—	S. Agustín Tecpaneca-Mexica	—
S. Andrés Amaxac[4]	San Andrés	San Andrés
S. Bartolomé Xallatenco	San Bartolomé Xallatenco	San Bartolomé
S. Fran[co] Atenpa	S. Fran[co] Tlacatecpan-Atenpan	—
S. Juan Bautista Ollopan	S. Juan Bautista Ollop [sic]	S. Juan Bautista
S. Lorenzo[5] (Tetzonco?)	San Lorenzo	San Lorenzo
San Miguel[5]	San Miguel	San Miguel
San Pedro Çacaapan	San Pedro Çacaapan	San Pedro
Santa Ana Aticpac	—	—
Santa Ana Caltenco	—	—
Santa Ana Tepanecapan	Sta. Ana Tepanecapan-Tzapotla	—
Santa Ana Tlacuillocan-Xallan	—	—
Sta. Ana Tzapotla	Sta. Ana Tepanecapan-Tzapotla	—
—	—	Santa Ana[6]
—	—	Santa Cruz[6]
—	Santa Cruz Apilco	—
Santa Cruz Tlallachco	—	—
—	—	Santa María[6]
—	—	Santa María[6]
Sta. Ma. Asunción Amantla	—	—
Sta. Ma. Asunción Amantla-Tianquiçolco	—	—
Sta. Ma. Asunción Aticpac	La Asunción Aticpac	—
Sta. Ma. Asunción Atotolco	—	—
Sta. Ma. Asunción Tianquiçolco	—	—
Sta. Ma. Asunción Tzaqualco	—	—

Table 3 (Continued)

TC[1]	LBC[2]	RG[3]
Sta. Ma. Magdalena Cihuatecpan	Sta. Ma. Magdalena Cihuatecpan	Sta. María Magdalena
Sta. Ma. Magdalena Cihuatecpan Tezcacoac	Sta. Ma. Magdalena Cihuatecpan	
Sta. Ma. Nativitas Tomatla	—	—
—	La Natividad de Nra. Sra.	—
Santiago Tetla[7]	Santiago Tetla	Santiago
Santísimo Atlacapan	—	—
Transfiguración Tlacatecco	Transfiguración	Transfiguración
Eitlatocan [Tres Reyes] Coatlan	Los Tres Reyes	Los Reyes
—	—	church, no name
—	—	church, no name

   1. TC = Testaments of Culhuacan, (1572–1606). Listings in this column are as they are found in the individual testaments. Some wards have dual names, but if a testator gives only one, it is recorded as a separate entry.
   2. LBC = Libro de bautismos de Culhuacan (1588) has a listing of wards on the first page (Gorbea Trueba, n.d.).
   3. RG = Map of the Relación geográfica de Culhuacan (1580) shows churches with names of most appended. [See Plate 1].
   4. In the TC, one will links the saint's name with the Nahuatl toponym, others merely list Amaxac (TC 68,69).
   5. In the TC, no one claimed this as a residence.
   6. RG names which cannot be linked to LTC or LBC data.
   7. Tetla also had subdivisions of its own.

hand, denials were not always formula. Miguel Huantli declared that "I have not borrowed anything at all, nor do I owe anything to anyone, and I have no money of the ward, nor anyone's goods" (TC 202,203). The ward heads were witnesses to his will, seemingly backing up his statement. His worry may have stemmed from the term he served as topile, when he was likely administering official funds. As we have seen, official positions allowed funds to be appropriated for personal use.

Tribute and finance were concerns of town government. In Culhuacan at least some tribute collection was the domain of the ward heads. Miguel Huantli, just discussed, asked the ward heads to take some of his maize. "Let them take it because it is our tribute as subjects" (TC 202,203). Whether this was a local levy or tribute destined for elsewhere is not known. Interestingly, the parcels of land donated to the ward heads for redistribution (discussed earlier) seem to have been especially liable for taxation, and this perhaps was a motivation for the donations.

When the Aztec confederation was defeated by the Spaniards in 1521, cabecera towns like Culhuacan no longer rendered tribute to a native superstructure. Levies supported the local Spanish officials, the encomendero and the corregidor, as well as local town projects. The corregidor and his teniente were additions to the political system, but the core of Culhuacan's political structure was the juez-gobernador, the cabildo, and the wards. The noblemen who ruled the town evolved into a group of professional office holders. They rotated their duties, serving in various civil and religious offices. Spaniards ultimately held power over Indian towns; nonetheless, there was considerable native autonomy. Natives had redress in the Spanish courts, but to a large extent local affairs were dealt with locally. The new structure of native rule had deep roots in prehispanic practices, yet it could respond to new pressures from the Spanish world. The Spaniards had dismantled the Aztec confederation, leaving largely intact the native altepetl, the political units which could continue orderly rule.

5 / FAMILY AND INHERITANCE

"Let all my relatives forgive me"

When Angelina Mocel lay on her deathbed, she thought of those close to her, her family living and dead. The family was the most fundamental level of social organization. Of course the quality and intensity of social relations between family members varied, but the ties of blood and affection that bound people together were affirmed through donation and bequest. How much property people had to give and to whom they bestowed it are revealing of social structure and the dynamics of personal relations. Since the information on the family comes from comments having to do with bequests, and since inheritance patterns are important for understanding family structure, family and inheritance are discussed in the same chapter. Outlined here are the Aztec kinship system and the ideals of kin behavior. More important for understanding the social system, examples of actual social behavior between kin are provided, and bequest patterns are examined to determine the strength of kin relationships. Finally, the effects of Spanish law and family patterns on colonial native society are considered.

In any kin network, a person has many relationships. Angelina Mocel was the daughter of Pablo Huitznahuatl,[1] the elder sister of Mónica and Elena, the wife of Juan Velázquez, the mother of Nicolás, the aunt of Juan Bautista, the sister-in-law of María Salomé and Petronila, the niece of María Tiacapan and Baltasar Téllez, and the grandniece of Antonio Tlemachica. Angelina benefited materially from some of these relations and was the benefactress in others. The webs of kith and kin were the fabric of society.

Marriage created new families and linked old ones. In Christian doctrine, marriage is a sacrament, an institution not to be entered into lightly. The prehispanic Aztecs also had great respect for marriage. It was marked by a ceremony which included tying the cloaks of the man and woman together, literally tying the knot. Prehispanic marriage clearly meant sexual fidelity for the woman, because, by definition, adultery involved a married woman.[2]

Partners brought their own property into marriage, and in case of divorce they both took what they originally had (Durán, 1967: I,57). According to Durán, "when they were not getting along well [they] asked for divorce.... each one being set free.... giving the women license to marry someone else, and he someone else" (Durán, 1967:I,57). In colonial Culhuacan only marriages terminated by death are known, though in a number of cases we know partners had not been getting along well.

The Nahuatl terminology for spouses sometimes gives clues to the strength of the relationship. The term for husband and wife is the same, *namictli*.[3] Sometimes the term *oquichtli*, "man," and *cihuatl*, "woman," were used in the narrowed sense of husband and wife, perhaps indicating consensual union rather than church marriage. One widowed woman insisted on her true status as a legal spouse. "I will rest satisfied as the legitimate wife I was" (TC 22,23). The phrase she used, *teoyotica nitenamic onicatca*, is literally translated "by means of divinity I was the spouse of someone," which indicates she was married in the Christian church.[4] People often called their partners, "my honorable spouse" (*nonamictzin*), using the honorific *-tzin*. The absence of the honorific sometimes meant trouble in the marriage. One Culhuacan woman, Ana Juana, referred to two husbands to whom she had been happily married (in succession, presumably) as "my honorable husbands" (*nonamictzintzinhuan*). She said of them "with them we carried out the duties of life on earth" (TC 82,83). Her current husband, Gabriel Itzmalli, whom she denounced as a "great scoundrel," she just called "my spouse" (without the honorific) and gave him no bequest. On the other hand, absence of the honorific did not always mean that the spouse was denied an inheritance. Juan Tezca left practically his entire estate to his wife, but consistently referred to her without the honorific (TC 30ff).

A concern of the Christian church was to stamp out native

practices it viewed as incestuous or immoral, such as multiple wives. Polygyny was practiced in the prehispanic period and was suppressed in the colonial, although it continued in some places and has an underground existence in modern times (Carrasco, 1972, 1974; Nutini, 1965). In the Culhuacan wills, there is evidence that people did have more than one spouse, but seemingly in serial monogamy. New unions were prompted only by the death of a partner.

Marriage was a major rite of passage in colonial Aztec society, generally a marker of adult status. For women this meant that they were identified as their partner's wife rather than as their father's daughter. Men were identified in terms of their wives only in lists of witnesses. For example, Angelina's aunt María had as witness to her will "Baltasar Téllez, topile, spouse of the one about to die" (TC 178,179). On occasion, some women even after marriage continued to be identified by their links to important males other than their husbands. María, Angelina Mocel's aunt, though twice married was called the "maiden/daughter of Tlemachica" [*tlemachica ychpoch*] (TC 174,175). Similarly, Angelina herself was called "the maiden/daughter of Pablo Huitznahuatl," though she had been married and had borne a child (TC 180,181). Women continued to be identified with their spouses (or occasionally their fathers or uncles) even when the men were dead. On the other hand, men who dictated testaments never primarily identified themselves as husbands or fathers of particular women.

Both men and women sometimes calculated time by when they were married. Juana Tiacapan of Aticpac identified some of her chinampas as those "that were given to me when I was still unmarried" (TC 68,69). Juan de San Pedro distinguished one of his houses from another by saying "I was still a young man when I built [it], not yet married." He had another which he said "my wife and I built after [we were married]" (TC 172,173). This type of notation might have been to establish outright ownership of property acquired before marriage.

People never said why they chose a particular person for their partner. Ward endogamy was not the rule.[5] On a number of occasions, such as in the case of Angelina Mocel and her husband Juan Velázquez, partners were from different wards. In the case of Ana Tlaco, she was originally from Culhuacan while her husband was from the distant town of Yecapixtla (TC 188ff). Nobles tended to marry each other, as seen in the case of don Pedro de Suero and both his first and second wives (TC 224ff).

Trust and cooperation often marked marriages. Women were full partners, and in the view of one Spaniard, sometimes the dominant ones. Gonzalo Gómez de Cervantes, who had served as *alcalde mayor* in various Indian towns, observed interactions between husbands and wives in court.

> When some Indian has some lawsuit, despite his being a very important Indian, able and skilled, he will not appear before the court without bringing his wife, and they inform and say that which by reason of the lawsuit it is necessary to say, and the husbands are very timid and quiet; and if the court asks something that it wishes to know, the husband responds: "here is my wife who knows it"; and in such manner, it has happened to me upon asking to one Indian and to many, "what is your name?" and before the husband responds, the wife says it; and thus in all the other things, in this manner the people [men] have submitted to the will of the woman.[6]

This forthrightness seems not to have been the ideal behavior of wives, for Alonso de Zorita reports that mothers exhorted their daughters to be obedient and modest. "Do not be disrespectful to [your husband]; listen to him and obey him, and do cheerfully what you are told" (Zorita, 1963b:150).

Marriage was a partnership which included joint dealings in financial matters. Husbands and wives were usually aware of each others' debts and expected their partners to repay them. On occasion, debts contracted by just one partner would be paid by the other if given the resources to do so. Angelina Mocel's aunt, María Tiacapan, had been married twice. "In Tzapotla where I was married the first time," she said, her first husband and she had debts. María wanted some stone sold, and the debt repaid. In addition, "with part of the money that remains, masses are to be said for . . . both of us, [me] and my late first husband . . . My present husband will speak for us" (TC 178,179). Thus María depended on her current husband, Baltasar Téllez, to attend to her financial affairs from a previous marriage and provided him the goods to accomplish this. Baltasar received the bulk of her estate after the debts were paid.

Angelina's aunt was not the only one to contract a debt jointly with her husband. As discussed previously, when María Icnocihuatl died, she worried about the unpaid debts she and her two late husbands had contracted with the ward heads. She took responsibility only for those debts because they had been contracted jointly. However, her second husband had contracted one with his first wife, and María made sure that *she* would not be held responsible. "I didn't know about something bad that my late husband named Francisco Quauhtli ["eagle"] did: he left a peso and four tomines unpaid. And now I say, let someone go and inform my stepchild named Gaspar. Let him pay the peso and four tomines. Let him aid his father and his mother, since they were the ones who borrowed it." The tale had a happy ending. Her stepson Gaspar "immediately replied, 'Very well, let me pay it for my father and my mother if our lord God give me life, for I am sick too.'" At this, "his stepmother was very reassured" (TC 78,79).

This situation was handled amicably, but others were probably not. The thrice-married Ana Juana enumerated her current husband's faults. Prominent on the list was her statement that "I don't know how many debts he has" (TC 82,83). Likely this was to prevent claims on her estate from his creditors. According to her, there were "debts of my husband that I have paid, as he very well knows: one peso which belongs to don Francisco Flores, alcalde, and four tomines that belong to his younger sister named Juana Xoco, and four tomines that belong to someone whose home is San Mateo" (TC 84,85). If a debt was contracted by one partner without informing the other, there was no feeling of joint responsibility.

As we have seen previously, a characteristic of Nahuatl wills was to put third parties in charge of carrying out particular transactions. People often chose their marital partners to play a role in estate division. The request of Angelina's aunt María Tiacapan that her husband pay off her debts is typical. In another case, Ana Tiacapan of Tepanecapan ordered one of her houses torn down so that a religious monument could be built. "My husband Pablo and my daughter María Xoco know about this, they will do it and carry it out" (TC 94,95). Her husband received nothing from her estate, but she trusted him with the responsibility. Men also had confidence in their wives' acting as their agents. As we have noted previously, María Ana, wife of the testator Andrés de San Miguel, kept the original of his will, and she was to deal with some of his bequests (TC 212,213).

Marital partners brought their own property into a marriage. After being wed, men and women could continue to acquire property either separately or together. Angelina Mocel and her husband bought a Spanish chest [*caja*] together (TC 182,183). More major purchases of other couples included horses. María Tiacapan of Tianquizçolco and her husband owned horses. One, she said, "my husband earned... entirely by himself. But the second we earned together; it cost us trouble to acquire it" (TC 192ff). Houses were also bought or built jointly. Miguel Hernández lay dying in a house that used to belong to Gabriel Acol. "We bought it, and there is a judgment about how [the purchase] is valid, because the both of us, my wife and I, bought it" (TC 274,275).

Bequeathing property to a partner was common, and it may have been an index of the affection felt. Angelina Mocel's father, Pablo Huitznahuatl, left his wife, Bárbara Tlaco, a house in which to raise their children. He cared about her reaction to his death, for he left some property to someone of unknown relation "so that sometime he will take pity and come to see my children, let them come to console my wife when I have died" (TC 168,169).[7] At the close of his testament in which he had given only a residence to his wife, he tried to make sure his will would be carried out. "No one is to violate my statement, because my wife Bárbara Tlaco and I have spoken concerning this and come to agreement" (TC 168,171). Bárbara Tlaco had inherited property from her uncle Antonio Tlemachica (TC 96ff). Since she was provided for, Pablo Huitznahuatl probably felt free to bequeath his land as he wished, though clearly in consultation with his wife. Another example of care for a spouse was Angelina's aunt María Tiacapan, who willed most of her estate to her husband.

Feelings of affection could survive the death of a marital partner. Widowed men provided masses for their late wives about half the time, while widowed women remembered their partners somewhat more frequently.[8] Women seem to have provided more masses all around, almost invariably setting aside money for themselves, while men were not so consistent. One woman, María Teicuh of Tezcacoac, ordered that her entire estate be sold for masses for herself and her late husband, despite her having surviving children (TC 240ff).[9]

Some marriages were not good matches. Ana Juana's third marriage was an unhappy union. As we have seen, Ana had recalled happily her two previous husbands but denounced her third husband, Gabriel Itzmalli, for a variety of reasons. He was a "great scoundrel.... He never gave me anything whatever, not money nor telling me 'poor you,' as did the three who died, two of whom were my husbands.... But look, this one, if he went to fetch fruit or if he went to fetch maize he would sell it himself without showing me how much he had bought. But as to the maize he gave to me, he just measured it out. For this reason I say that I am afraid [that he will do something bad].... And my husband asked me for a peso and said 'I am going to get fruit with it,' and he just collected it and didn't buy the fruit" (TC 82ff). Unsympathetic, stingy, and a spendthrift with his wife's money, Gabriel Itzmalli does not seem to have been the ideal husband. Ana was particularly worried that he would try to usurp her son's inheritance.

Ana's complaints about her husband were not ideal behavior for wives. According to Zorita, women exhorted their daughters that "if [your husband] supports himself by your industry, do not on that account scorn him, or be peevish or ungracious.... Tell him meekly what you think should be done. Do not say offensive words to him in front of strangers or even to him alone; for you will harm yourself thereby, and yours will be the fault" (Zorita, 1963b:150). Perhaps Ana held her tongue during the course of her marriage, but she was certainly willing to complain about her husband on her deathbed.

Marriage insured the continuation of the social system, producing the children who would become the legitimate heirs to property. Since in both the prehispanic Aztec legal codes and Christian doctrine partners were to be sexually faithful to each other (though male infidelity seems to have been tolerated in practice), both systems tried to insure that a husband was the father of his wife's children, that his children were his legitimate heirs. Nahuatl has terms distinguishing legitimate from illegitimate children. A legitimate child was one "born within the household.... The spiritually acceptable child," whereas an illegitimate child was a "secret child, the bastard [*calpan pilli*]... the child of a slave" (Sahagún, X:2).

Legitimate children were favored over illegitimate offspring when property divisions were made. A member of the Motecuhçoma family, don Diego de Motecuhçoma, had two illegitimate children who seemingly did not directly share in his estate. Heirs to the estate gave the illegitimate children some land "just for the sake of our lord God [for charity]."[10] Legitimacy was an issue in legal arguments before Spanish courts. One of the points that Marta Petronila made when she was litigating in the Spanish courts, trying to establish her right to her father's property, was that she was his legitimate daughter.[11]

The Aztec kinship system and kin terminology reflected the importance of both mother's and father's families. When asked to describe Aztec kinship relations, the native informants of fray Bernardino de Sahagún told of the "human cordage,"[12] the *tlacamecayotl* (Sahagún, X:1–9). Both verbally and visually, kin were conceived of as being roped together. In pictorial genealogies kin relations are shown by thick cords linking one person with another, perhaps a visual reminder of the umbilical cord.[13] [See Figure 3]. The verbal description of the tlacamecayotl is told from the point of view of a single individual (Sahagún, X:1–9), listing both the direct lineal relations (parents, grandparents, and children), but also collaterals (aunts and uncles, brothers), and relations created by marriage (in-laws and stepkin). The emphasis is seemingly on lineal relations, and includes kin who could act as surrogate parents (Calnek, 1974b:198). However, the tlacamecayotl may simply be a personal kindred, allowing an individual to emphasize certain relations for his or her advantage (Offner, 1983:200). Evidence from lawsuits suggests that both men and women invoked links to male kin more frequently than to female (Kellogg, 1984:37), but the bilateral kinship system allowed the flexibily to stress certain links when it was advantageous.

One interesting aspect of Aztec kinship terms which can cause confusion is that kin terms can be used for more distant relations of the same generation.[14] For example, terms for brother and sister could be used for cousins.[15] In addition, in order to show respect, terms for younger and older are reversed. For example, Angelina Mocel's sisters-in-law, María Salomé and Petronila, called Angelina "our younger sister" [*ticuiuhtzin*], though the two of them were probably younger than she (TC 184,185).[16] Thus when someone is referred to by a given kin term, we cannot be absolutely sure that the true relationship is being described.

Sahagún begins by emphasizing the male role, although other passages stress the equivalent importance of fathers and mothers (Sahagún, VI:175,216). The tlacamecayotl says that "One's father [is] the source of lineage ... diligent, solicitous, compassionate, sympathetic; a careful administrator [of his household]. He rears, he

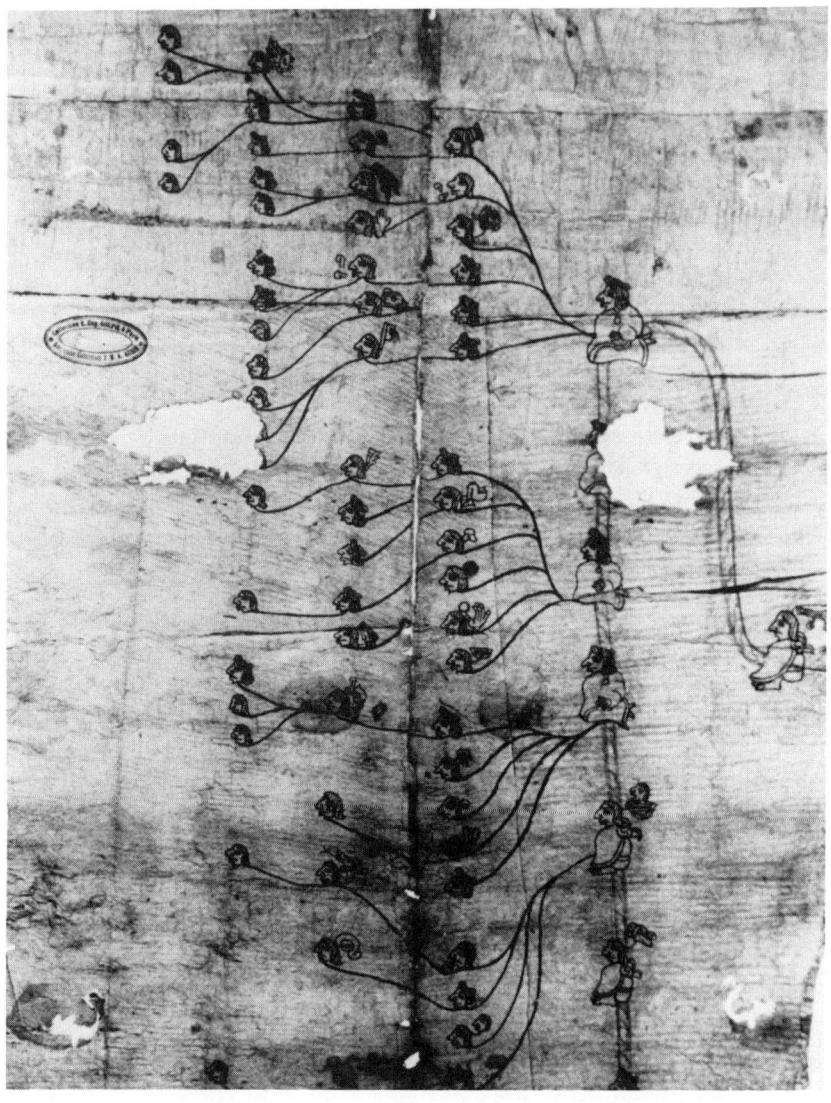

Fig. 3 A Culhuacan genealogy. (Courtesy of the Bibliothèque Nationale of Paris).

teaches people" (Sahagún, X:1). In Culhuacan the importance of fathers is emphasized when daughters were identified with them even after marriage. As noted previously, the notary Miguel Jacobo de Maldonado still identified Angelina Mocel as "the maiden of Pablo Huitznahuatl" (TC 180,180). This was despite Pablo's being dead and Angelina's having been married and become a mother. Pablo had raised and provided for her, but probably more importantly, he was a more prominent man in Culhuacan than Angelina's husband, Juan Velázquez.

When Pablo died, he made Angelina one of his heirs, giving her a house and some land. Angelina called him "my honorable father" (*notatzin*). Her father called her *nochpoch,* "my maiden" (a term which also denotes daughters). Calling her a maiden may have been out of respect for, according to Sahagún, a maiden [*ichpochtli*] is virtuous, "modest, pure, pleasing of appearance, honest... [she is] one's daughter" (X:12). Pablo called his other two daughters, both little girls, *nopilhuan,* "my children."

The tlacamecayotl also affirms the important bonds between mothers and their children, though not the mother's role in the lineage.[17] The ideal mother is "sincere, vigilant, agile, an energetic worker—diligent, watchful, solicitous, full of anxiety. She teaches people; she is attentive to them. She caresses, she serves others; she is apprehensive for their welfare; she is careful, thrifty—constantly at work" (Sahagún, X:2). Angelina Mocel was typical of other mothers who died leaving little children, for she tried to make sure her son was well taken care of. From the proceeds of the sale of a chest, Nicolás "will be given milk" (TC 182,183). As we have seen, he was not to live long, nor did his mother or father expect him to. Angelina gave him land "if he lives" (TC 182,183). Because his father, Juan Velázquez, was not very hopeful about the boy's survival either, the bequests indicated his doubt. He gave Nicolás one parcel of land which was given "if our lord God gives him life" and another one "if he lives" (TC 204,205). In addition, Juan gave him a small house, saying "it is to belong to my child if he lives. My wife will be there, but if the child dies, then it is to be sold and [the proceeds] are to belong to him" [i.e., for masses] (TC 206,207). Angelina sold this house while the boy was still alive and she felt she had to justify it. "I did not spend this money for any idle purpose; it was spent on my child whom my husband left behind" (TC 182,183). Infant mortality was a recognized phenomenon, even in normal times without pestilence. Sahagún's informants describe the "bad infant" as "without resistance to sickness, full of sickness.... It... becomes very sick, dies" (Sahagún, X:13).

Good children were a delight and are described in terms easily recognizable to us. "The good child [is] happy, laughing, joyful, rejoicing... it laughs, it jumps about (Sahagún, X:13). However, the Aztecs also had standard metaphors for children which are not universal descriptions. The testator Marcos Hernández Acolnahuacatl compares his grandchildren to birds. He gave some land to them, "to all four, as if they were little birds, because they left the egg..." (TC 278,279). The phrasing of this metaphor echoes part of a speech by fathers to their sons recorded by Alonso de Zorita. "You have emerged like a chick from its shell, and as the chick prepares for flight so you prepare yourself for labor" (Zorita, 1963b:141).

Parents usually entrusted their surviving partner to care for their minor children. Often the survivor was given custodial care of the children's inheritance. Pablo Huitznahuatl gave land to "my little children Mónica and Elena, if they grow [until they are adults], for it is their property. Their mother Bárbara Tlaco is to guard it for them" (TC 166,167). To his grown daughter Angelina, he gave some property with no strings attached. Similarly Gerónimo Teuhcihuatl bequeathed his houses to "my wife named María Tlaco and to my child just born if it grows up; they will be there" (TC 184,185). Another of Gerónimo's offspring received land in his own right, with no period of guardianship.

Adult offspring at times took off on their own. Doña María Juárez's daughter was sick at home, but her son "Juan Juárez has always been looking about and has not come to settle down anywhere" (TC 248,249).

Parents took special care of children in various ways. Ana Tiacapan of Tepanecapan gave her daughter a house, which she assumed would be torn down and rebuilt. "If [my daughter] marries somewhere, she should build herself a house there with the wood" (TC 94,95). Pablo Quechol's parents had also looked to the time when he would be married. "There is cacao with which I was going to get married, two thousand beans that my mother and father left me" (TC 88,89). As we have seen, the beans ended up paying for Pablo's burial.

One way to promote stability in the family was for those who were widowed with small children to remarry, recreating a nuclear family. Remarriage could be harmonious for all. The net of the tlacamecayotl includes stepkin, recognizing the importance of these relationships. The stepfather is one "who adopts children; one who provides support, who works steadily, who accepts his stepchildren as his own" (Sahagún, X:9). Stepmothers were also to care for their stepchildren, although they are not similarly urged to treat them as their own. "The good stepmother [is] one who is gracious, who loves, who is merciful [to her stepchildren]" (Sahagún, X:9).

Harmony prevailed in some stepkin relations. Tomás de Aquino declared that "my wife's children took care of me [greatly] every time I was sick, and they showed me much affection [treated me very well]" (TC 66,67). Stepchildren also remembered their stepparents fondly. Doña Luisa Juana's stepmother, doña Elena Constantina, won her stepdaughter's affection. Although Nahuatl has a term for stepmother, *chahuanantli,* doña Luisa Juana used the term for mother, *nantli,* for doña Elena Constantina. Addressing her father and his wife from her deathbed, doña Luisa Juana said "May you hear me, you who are here with me as in your presence, I give my orders to my father, Juan de San Miguel, and to the noble lady, my mother, doña Elena Constantina."[18] Likewise Juan Bautista's stepmother Magdalena acted well toward him, and he left her some land when he died. He divided a large parcel giving a portion to her, ordering the rest sold for masses for his mother and father. It seems that Juan's stepmother had outlived his father, carrying on her duties as surrogate mother.

The tlacamecayotl also outlines the undesirable behavior of stepparents. "The bad stepfather [is] one who desires, wishes, yearns for the death [of his stepchildren]" and the "bad stepmother [is] sad, hateful, rancorous, impatient. She looks at one with anger; she foretells the worst for one" (Sahagún, X:9). It is clear that bad stepparents were not apocryphal. In the case of the much-married Ana Juana, she was not getting along with her current husband, Gabriel Itzmalli, when she lay dying. Because of that, she tried to ensure that her son Juan Francisco, not her husband, received her property. She worried about his treatment of her son after her death. "Let him never bother my son, nor let him not accuse [my son] of anything..." (TC 82,83). To forestall difficulties, Ana Juana took the step of asking someone to look out for her son's interests, to prevent Gabriel from usurping the inheritance. As we have seen in the case of

Marta Petronila, who sued in the Spanish courts to receive a share of her father's estate, stepparents did usurp stepchildren's property.[19]

On the other hand, women often performed the role of stepmother well, although they tended not to leave their stepchildren any of their own property. María Tiacapan of Cihuatecpan was typical in leaving her stepdaughters only the property coming from their father's estate. "I leave all the fields and chinampas to them; all of it will belong to them, because it is their father's property . . . they will not make objections" (TC 22,23).

Grandparents also could be surrogate parents, but it was not an expected role.[20] When the widower Vicente Xochiamatl died, he put his mother-in-law in charge of raising her grandchildren. "My mother-in-law . . . is to care for [the children] here" (TC 114,115). In another case, María Tiacapan of Coatlan was orphaned in childhood and abandoned by her uncles. Her grandmother took over raising her. "My grandmother truly has performed meritoriously; she came to give us pieces of bread to eat. . . . She has acquired merit in the whole time since we were left orphaned" (TC 132,133). This grandmother went beyond the ideal behavior of "the good grandmother [who is] a reprimander, a leader of an exemplary life, a counselor" (Sahagún, X:5).

A new element in colonial Aztec family relations was the Spanish introduction of fictive kin relationship, *compadrazgo*. Godparents could also act as surrogate parents. Ties were established between godchildren and godparents and between the parents and godparents. The relationship between the adults was viewed as a "co-parenthood," and in this relationship, people addressed each other by Spanish terms *compadre* (co-father) or *comadre* (co-mother).[21] As early as the sixteenth century many Aztecs embraced compadrazgo (Gibson, 1964:152; Ravicz, 1967). Its quick and widespread adoption was likely related to the disruption of family life due to epidemic-related death and the need to stabilize family life (Gibson, 1964:152). In Culhuacan, a number of people indicated they had godchildren or had ties to compadres.[22] Ana Juana, who had tried to protect her son's inheritance against her third husband, called upon her compadre, don Francisco Flores, to act as a guardian for his godson. "I beseech lord Francisco Flores, alcalde, to speak for [my son] and come to take him, because [my son] is his godchild. Let him not abandon [my son]" (TC 82,83). Since she could not trust her husband to act as a good father, she called upon her compadre to do so.

In general men seem to have taken their duties as godparents more seriously than women, and men gave bequests to their godchildren more frequently.[23] Vicente Xochiamatl, who seemingly had just one child of his own, made provisions for his son and his godson, calling both "my children" (TC 114,115).

A more traditional way of caring for minor children was for uncles and aunts to take on the duties of parents. "One's uncle [is] the provider for those who are orphaned, the entrusted one, the tutor, the manager, the provider of support; the one who takes charge, who directs . . . a caretaker, a guardian" (Sahagún, X:3). The Nahuatl terms for father, *tatli,* and uncle, *tlatli* are very close, echoing the social reality of uncles playing the role of surrogate parent.[24] In Nahuatl as in English, "uncle" can denote the brother of either the mother or father, or the husband of a parent's sister. In the prehispanic era, the levirate was practiced, with a man marrying his brother's widow. This may indicate a father's brother was more important than a mother's brother in preserving family arrangements. However, there is evidence from colonial Mexico City that the mother's brother could also play the role of surrogate parent (Calnek, 1974b:197). The levirate was suppressed in the colonial era because the Spaniards viewed the arrangement as incestuous.

A niece or nephew is "an orphan—parentless—who serves in another's house; a servant; one who lives with others" (Sahagún, X:4). While the ideal behavior of aunts and uncles was to treat their orphaned nieces and nephews like their own daughters and sons, the tlacamecayotl description suggests that they were second-class relatives in a household. In Culhuacan nieces and nephews sometimes did suffer at the hands of their uncles. For example, María Tiacapan of Coatlan and her sisters were left orphaned, and her uncles did not fulfill their obligations as surrogate parents. "During all the time we have lived on earth we have been the dependents of others, and those uncles[25] of mine, my relatives never said 'Our nieces are afflicted [poor], they just live in the corners of other people['s houses], next to their walls they spread out their humble [beds?]; they are poor and perhaps they have nothing to eat.' Nor do my uncles even now say 'Our niece is sick, let's go see her.' They show me no affection [charity]" (TC 132,133). Her tirade was likely designed to put off her uncles from receiving any of her estate. This was not the first case of conflict in María's family. "My late grandfather Tomás Cacama[26] . . . and my late mother disputed with my late uncle Lucas" (TC 132,133). The disagreement was serious enough to be taken to the Spanish courts in Mexico City. All the parties to that dispute were dead, but María stated her right to the property the courts awarded, perhaps to forestall claims from her uncle Lucas's heirs.

Not all uncles were walking examples of the "bad uncle" who is "a dissipator, an alienator of people; he squanders, dissipates, wastes his possessions; he hates, despises, detests one" (Sahagún, X:3). Tomás Motolinia left his nephew some land so that he could "establish himself as an adult man with the tribute" (TC 162,165). Another generous uncle was Antonio Tlemachica, Angelina Mocel's great-uncle. He provided well for two nieces, Bárbara Tlaco, Angelina's mother, and María Tiacapan, Angelina's aunt. María soon followed her uncle to the grave. Identifying María in her will, the notary Miguel Jacobo de Maldonado called María the "maiden of Tlemachica" [*tlemachica ychpoch*], perhaps because Antonio had raised her. Antonio was seemingly a more prominent man than María's husband Baltasar Téllez.[27] Antonio consistently calls her his honored niece [*nomachtzin*]. For her part, María always referred to him as "my honored lord" [*notecuiyotzin*].[28] She never mentions her parents. Though Antonio had provided well for her, María left her late uncle no masses.

Aunts also could be providers for their nieces and nephews. "One's good aunt [is] merciful, of good memory, kind; an intercessor, solicitous, of noble birth, loving. She admires others, cares for them, is solicitous of others" (Sahagún, X:4). In Culhuacan aunts provided for nieces and nephews even when they had children of their own. Angelina Mocel had already sold one house to benefit her son Nicolás, and she ordered a house that her father had given her sold to pay for masses for herself, but she had yet another. "To my nephew Juan Bautista [I give the house] with all the chinampas which accompany it" (TC 180,181). In the absence of their own children as heirs, aunts chose their nieces and nephews. María Tiacapan of Cihuatecpan had stepdaughters to whom she left property coming from their father's estate, but she left her own property to her nephews. She mentioned three, and divided up her land among them. One was beholden to her already, for she had given her nephew Melchor Tleçannen "all the chinampas [of the house] which he is already working" (TC 20,21). She trusted another nephew, Gaspar Cuetli, to provide a mass for her. Another aunt lent her niece money. María Inés was the aunt of doña Elena Constantina, doña Luisa Juana's stepmother. Though María Inés had a modest estate, she was connected to one of the wealthiest families in Culhuacan. At her death, she wanted her wealthy niece to repay her peso.

Nieces and nephews never provided for the souls of their deceased aunts and uncles, but those still living did occasionally receive bequests. Juan Bautista, whose parents were dead and who had remembered his stepmother with a bequest, also left property to his uncle, don Francisco Flores. "With all my heart I declare that I am giving [land] to my uncle, don Francisco Flores, alcalde. No one is to take it from him" (TC 36,37). The orphaned Juan Bautista was probably a young man, since he mentioned no wife or children and bequeathed his property to older relatives. Another man in similar circumstances also left property to an uncle. Luis Tlauhpotonqui ordered some land sold "in order to help my uncle Toribio Tecmilotzin" (TC 138,141). One other person who remembered the older generation was not an unmarried young man.[29] Juan de San Pedro, who was a widower with children, gave the bulk of his estate to them, but also gave something to his aunt. "I say that my late father left me a house facing Xochimilco; I give it to my aunt, Ana Xoco; the reason why I give it to her is that she took much care of me and served me in my illness. For this reason I say that I make it her property; no one is to ever claim it from her" (TC 172,173). This kind of prohibition echoes the one Juan Bautista issued when he gave land to his uncle. Such exhortations are typical of Nahuatl testaments, but might have been used only when there are unusual heirs or extraordinary circumstances.

Another person who could play the role of surrogate parent was the older brother. In the prehispanic period, extensions of the term for older brother were used to designate high priests, principal judges, and lords. In ideal kin behavior, the older brother is "a bearer of all the burdens [of his father's household]; one who counsels [his younger brothers], who prepares them for the work of men" (Sahagún, X:9). In Culhuacan, Diego Sánchez played that role for his brothers and sisters, "I was as their father and ruled them" (TC 214,215). This role was one that the Franciscan Motolinia had observed in Cuernavaca. Fathers "left their houses and lands to their children, and the eldest, if he was a grown man, possessed it, and took care of his brothers and sisters, as the father had done during his lifetime" (Motolinia, 1971:134–135). This emphasis on lateral ties to brothers and sisters does *not* appear to be typical in late sixteenth-century Culhuacan. Whether the Cuernavaca region and Culhuacan had similar patterns in the prehispanic era is unknown. Diego Sánchez was widowed and had remarried, with neither marriage producing children who survived to receive a bequest. He devoted his attention to some of his younger brothers and sisters, who were seemingly living with him. Another brother and sister lived elsewhere and were barred from inheriting from him.

There are more Nahuatl kinship terms for siblings than for any other category of relations. Separate terms denote both older and younger brothers and sisters. As we have noted, terms for brothers and sisters were also sometimes used to denote kin of the same generation, such as cousins.[30]

The relationship between siblings may have been important in the prehispanic era, but the tie was not especially emphasized with bequests of property among the people of Culhuacan. Less than a third of the men mentioned siblings, while a little less than half of the women did. While men mentioned sisters as frequently as brothers, women mainly mentioned sisters. We have a fair amount of information about the social relations between siblings because they sometimes received minor bequests.[31]

Trust and consideration were part of brother-sister relationships. This tie might have been especially strong when the brother was not married. The widower Miguel Huantli was seemingly survived only by his older sister Ana Tiacapan, whom he put in charge of settling much of his estate. He left to her "the amaranth sown [on someone else's chinampa]; she is to take it. No one is to claim it from her" (TC 200,201). In order to pay for the funeral arrangements, he had two old boats, "perhaps someone will want to buy them, and with [the money] I will be buried, or candles will be bought." But his sister did not have to take care of this. "Let my older sister not be bothered over this, for I've bothered her [too much] already" (TC 202,203). Another man also trusted his sister with postmortem transactions. Joaquín de Luna was a citizen of Mexico City, but was present in Culhuacan when he died. He was a trader, owning a pack animal. "When I have died, my younger sister Juana Tiacapan will take [my horse] and have it . . . she is to aid me with six masses, as if she bought it... she has the responsiblity of arranging the masses" (TC 154,155). Someone else was going to arrange for a cross for Joaquín, but he declared that "my younger sister Juana Tiacapan knows about this," probably to make sure the request was carried out. Both Miguel Huantli and Joaquín de Luna were without a wife when they died, and they depended on their sisters to look out for their interests. Perhaps brothers' reliance on sisters only occurred when a wife was absent.

Often because of parents' bequests to children, siblings ended up sharing ownership of houses. Tomás Motolinia was in such a situation and made no move to consolidate ownership. "As to our patrimonial house, which faces Xochimilco, where I lie sick, when my late mother died, she gave each one part. We just divide the house, my elder sister Ana Tiacapan and I ... it is to continue thus, since that which belongs to me I in turn assign to my children. They can decide, if they live, if they will sell it or not" (TC 162,163). Tomás does not seem to have been very concerned about what his sister thought about the sale of part of the joint housesite, for she was a potential buyer. This type of transaction was not unheard of. For example, Miguel Sánchez had a "purchased house which stands in Tianquiztenco. I gave [paid] three pesos to my older sister for it" (TC 38,39,40).

Brothers sometimes bequeathed land to their sisters. As we have seen previously, Ana Tlaco, resident of Yecapixtla, had received land from one younger brother, which she in turn bequeathed to another younger brother. She hoped that "perhaps he will favor me with some candles on the feast of the dead" (TC 190,191). The motivation for this bequest was likely shaped by the special circumstances of her residence. Since she was originally from Culhuacan and, more importantly, was there when she died, she wanted masses said in the church of San Juan Evangelista Culhuacan. Masses were usually said in the town of burial, not of residence. Her younger brother, Miguel Itztic, apparently remained in Culhuacan and would take care of the masses, while her husband, Juan Bueno, would remain in Yecapixtla. In another case, María Tiacapan of Tianquizçolco received land from her older brother. "What my elder brother Luis Tlauhpotonqui gave me in Ayahualolco I give to my younger sisters" (TC 192,193).[32] She, like Ana Tlaco, wanted candles on the feast of the dead, but she left this in her husband's hands, not her sisters'.

Women's brothers generally received only token bequests from them. Juana Tiacapan of Atempan surprisingly bequeathed the bulk of her estate to her brother-in-law[33] and gave just a minor bequest to her brother, Diego. She gave him movable property, saying "I have put much effort into [this]: I planted a field . . . the crop I give to my younger brother Diego, who is to reap it" (TC 148,149).

In Culhuacan, women's ties to their sisters seem to have been stronger than those to their brothers. Sisters were often present at women's deathbeds, acting as witnesses to the wills. The sister of Juana Tiacapan of Aticpac was married to a resident of Mexico City, but Marta Teuhccho and her husband Hernando García were at Juana's bedside when she died. However, neither of them was an heir. Juana's husband received almost her entire estate (TC 66ff).[34] Sometimes sisters received bequests. When Lucía Teicuh died, her brother-in-law and her older sister Ana Tiacapan were witnesses to her will. Her sister was given token bequests of a chest and a metate (TC 126,127).

Sisters did sometimes receive land and houses from each other. María Teicuh of Cihuatecpan inherited a house from her younger sister Francisca. When María died, she ordered the component parts of the house sold for masses for the two of them (TC 232,233). Another woman, Ana Tiacapan of Tepanecapan, received a house from her sister. Ana ordered that it "should be torn down and the stone be brought here, and with it a house [chapel] will be built for the image of our Lord" (TC 94,95). Since her sister acted as witness to the will, she seemingly had no objection. As we have seen in another case, the estate of María Tiacapan of Tianquizçolco included land she got from her older brother, Luis Tlauhpotonqui (TC 134ff). She declared, "I likewise give it in turn to my younger sisters.[35] They know about it, since it belongs to them" (TC 192,-193). In addition, "the patrimonial house, which our progenitors left us, is all to belong to my younger sisters" (TC 194,195). Most of the other parcels of land she left to her husband, Mateo Opan.

In Culhuacan, inheritance was the primary way that property passed from one person to another, from one generation to another.[36] People retained their property until death. Rarely did anyone indicate that property was given in the lifetime of the donor. There were some exceptions, however, the most notable being Diego Sánchez. As we have discussed, he acted as a father to his younger brothers and sisters, and gave most of his property to them at his death, but he seems to have made a settlement with a brother and sister who lived apart from him. He warned his witnesses, "if another younger brother of mine, Juan Tototl ["bird"] comes, and another female person [younger sister] named Magdalena, we have gone to great trouble over the two of them, both of us, my younger brother Gaspar Chichimecatl and I, for we paid a lot of money for them ... And I say that [the money] is to be considered their inheritance. They cannot claim anything more" (TC 216,217). Perhaps he felt a twinge of conscience, for he concluded his testament with the exhortation: "Let all my relatives forgive me" (TC 220,221). Another exception to postmortem donations was María Teicuh's exclusion from her estate of two men of unknown relation. "The two can make no further objections because they took their [property],[37] they cannot claim more" (TC 232,235).

Sometimes parents allowed their sons and daughters to work land that the parents owned, but the children owned just the crop. Retention of ownership by the older generation was a guarantee of their continued control over their resources and their potential heirs. In parts of early modern Europe, aging parents made donations to their offspring in exchange for retirement conditions defined by legal agreements. In these circumstances, testamentary bequest was much less frequent (Spufford, 1976). As we have seen, among the colonial Aztecs the testament became an important type of legal and religious document. In sixteenth-century Culhuacan there is little evidence that *inter vivos* donations were made.

In the case of Diego Sánchez, it is clear that residence played a role in determining who would share in his estate. Two siblings left the residence and received portions then. But how did residence generally affect bequest patterns? Unfortunately the Culhuacan wills shed virtually no light on residence patterns, although there are references to it on occasion. For sixteenth-century Aztecs, there were a variety of residence patterns, detailed in house-to-house censuses. Among the high nobility in some locations in the Cuernavaca region, there is evidence of complex household structures including household heads with multiple wives (Carrasco, 1972). There existed joint families among commoners in the Cuernavaca region, with father and married sons, or brothers and their wives being coresident (Carrasco, 1964, 1974). These joint families also occurred in early colonial Mexico City (Calnek, 1972, 1974b, 1976). However, the nuclear family was an important, possibly the preferred, family type, with the joint family only a stage in a cycle when children or younger siblings did not have enough resources to set up a separate household.[38]

Among the colonial Aztecs an estate could be divided to multiple heirs chosen by the testator. This type of system, partible inheritance, contrasts with systems having a predetermined heir or heirs (such as those with primogeniture), systems of impartible inheritance. Angelina Mocel and her family were typical in bequeathing their property as they chose. Certain patterns of choice of heirs emerge from all the bequests of Culhuacan testators. A bequest to the church for masses for the testator's soul was almost obligatory, but the range of other recipients was wide. Both men and women willed property to members of the opposite sex as well as to their own. Most heirs were family members and occasionally fictive kin, though a significant number of people left property to heirs whose relation to the testator is unknown.

Most testators, both men and women, had three types of property to bequeath: houses, land, and movable property. Men and women held the same types of property and in approximately the same amounts, but the bequest patterns of men and women testators differed somewhat. This is more evident in bequests of houses than of land or movable goods.

When Angelina Mocel began her list of bequests with a house, she followed a regular pattern found in virtually everyone's will. As noted before, Angelina ordered this house sold, "because I have no assets at all with which to be buried." In addition to paying for the burial, "whatever money should be left of the proceeds from the house will be spent on me, for masses to be said for me" (TC 180,181).

There were differences in the way Culhuacan men and women bequeathed their houses. As often as not, Culhuacan women ordered houses sold for masses. They seem to have felt free to dispose of their houses as they wished, not feeling constrained to bequeath residences to living heirs. For example, María Salomé declared, "I have a house in Coltonco which is divided ... it does not belong to my child, María Ana; it is to be sold for a mass for my first husband, now deceased" (TC 26,27). María Salomé had given practically all her land to her daughter, but not the house.[39] Unlike women testators, men generally bequeathed houses to close relatives, almost never ordering houses sold for masses. The few who did had no living wives or children. Pablo Quechol, for example, apparently was survived only by some nephews and/or nieces living in the town of Cuitlahuac (TC 86ff). His house went for masses, along with just about all the rest of his property. Miguel Huantli and Melchor de Santiago Ecatl both ordered their houses sold for masses for themselves and their late wives (TC 116,117; 200,201).

When Culhuacan women did bequeath their houses to heirs rather than having them sold for masses, they did not seem to have a preferred class of heirs.[40] At Lucía Teicuh's death, she left her house to her niece instead of her daughter. "I give [it] to my niece named Francisca Tiacapan, who is in Cuitlahuac, because it is her home;[41] let no one trick her" (TC 124,125). María Teicuh of Cihuatecpan tried to insure rights of residence in the tecpan for her children and granchildren (TC 232,233). However, a house she had received from her late younger sister was to be sold for masses for the two of them (TC 232,233). Among Culhuacan women, there was no special affirmation of lineal female ties to daughters and granddaughters.[42]

Women did sometimes leave houses to sisters but not to brothers, possibly an affirmation of lateral ties only to females.[43] As we have seen, María Tiacapan of Tianquizçolco bequeathed her house to her sisters rather than her son (TC 192ff). María Tiacapan of Coatlan left her younger sister "the house that belonged to my late father Baltasar Cipriano," as well as another house complex (TC 132,133). A third María Tiacapan (Angelina Mocel's aunt) left her sister Bárbara Tlaco a unit in her house compound (TC 176,177).

Women's sisters were not invariably recipients, however. Angelina Mocel gave her house to her nephew Juan Bautista, ignoring her younger sisters Elena and Mónica. True, their mother Bárbara Tlaco had received a house from her husband, Pablo Huitznahuatl, and from her sister, María Tiacapan, so Bárbara was not in great need of a residence for the girls.

In Culhuacan, husbands generally did not receive bequests of houses, but there was no uniform exclusion of them.[44] María Tiacapan, Angelina's aunt, left one house to her sister, sold two other structures, but also left one to her own husband, Baltasar Téllez. It might be significant that María had no children (TC 174ff).

Though María's bequest to her husband was exceptional, men often left houses to their surviving wives.[45] Since care of minor children was an important matter on their minds when they lay dying, men usually left houses to their wives so that they could raise the children there. Bequests of this type might have been aimed at limiting the wife's ability to bequeath property independently. When Miguel Cerón died, he had three houses. "I assign it to my wife; all of it will belong to her, named Juana Xoxopanxoco. There she is to be in charge of my children, since it is their property and their house. Let no one take it from them" (TC 60,61). As we have seen, Simón Moxixicoa unsuccessfully tried to keep his wife at their marital residence by bequeathing the house to her and his children (TC 156,157). However, ownership and residence rights were not sufficient to keep her there, and members of the cabildo separated out her property when she left.

Culhuacan men seldom left houses to siblings, with notable exception of Diego Sánchez, the guardian of his brothers and sisters. In order that his younger brother Gaspar carry on his duties, Diego assigned him "the house that our grandmother built, that faces west, (all that goes right up to the hearth where we warmed ourselves goes with it).[46] There he will take care of my [other] younger brothers" (TC 214,215). As discussed above, women on occasion left their sisters shares in houses or parts of dismantled houses.

Men but not women took their responsibilities as godparents seriously enough to provide residences for their godchildren. Tomás de Aquino lived with his wife, her children from a previous marriage, and also apparently with his godchild, "Gaspar, child of Marcos Morelos." Tomás initially said, "I have a two-story house facing toward Xochimilco; all of it together will belong to my wife and my godchild that I adopted [embraced]" (TC 64,65). But then, thinking about the condition of the house, Tomás said that "the wood is already old" and suggested an alternative. "My wife is to give some small thing to the boy with which he will be brought up, if he lives"[47] (TC 66,67). That Tomás had no children of his own might go a long way to explain the seriousness with which he discharged his obligations as godfather. Tomás acknowledged the kindness his stepchildren had shown him, however. Another man adopted an orphan and left a patrimonial house to him and his own grandson. "My grandchild is to take [the part of the house] toward Mexico City and Juan, the orphan, is to take [the part] toward Xochimilco." Perhaps because this was a slightly unusual bequest, García added, "The two of them are just to share it; let no one ever trick them" (TC 102,103).[48]

Overall, Culhuacan men assumed responsibility for providing a residence for wives and children, and less frequently for brothers and sisters, nieces and nephews, and those to whom they had acted as surrogate father, such as godchildren. Culhuacan women seem less concerned with providing their kin with houses, perhaps assuming that men would do so.

Most people had land to bequeath, and both men and women left it to a variety of heirs. Angelina Mocel and her family were typical in their disposal of land. Some went for masses, some to charity, but most of it went to a variety of heirs. Donations of land seem to have been spread more widely than those of houses. Bequeathing a house was often tied to complicated questions of rights of residence. Land did not carry the emotional overtones of where people would live or with whom.[49]

There were two civil categories of land, patrimonial land and purchased land,[50] which were generally not bequeathed to spouses, but seem to have been given to heirs of the same sex, often lineal descendants—children and grandchildren. Purchased land was almost invariably willed to children and grandchildren, if it was not sold for masses. If both sons and daughters survived, the daughters would share equally. However, both men and women viewed purchased land as particularly alienable. In the estate of María Tiacapan of Tianquizçolco, it was the only piece of land that we know she ordered sold (TC 192ff).[51]

Testators' practice of specifically disinheriting people with possible claims occurs more frequently in women's testaments than in men's. These women may have felt their estates were particularly vulnerable to claims they did not wish to honor. However, there may have been a more general pattern of women's estates being vulnerable. The women who disinherited likely heirs—such as their children—usually said why. María Teicuh of Tezcacoac, the widow of don Juan García, gave her entire estate to the church. She said, "the reason I assign everything to the church is that no one cared for me during my illness, neither my children nor my grandchildren, nor anyone, for if they had cared for me I would have given them something" (TC 240ff). To forestall their sharing in her estate, she declared that "my children already have what belongs to them" (TC 242,243), property from their late father's estate. María Tiacapan of Coatlan, whose uncles had treated her so miserably, enumerated their faults at length. She left property to her grandmother, an unusual choice of heir, but the old woman had raised her and her younger sisters (María's other heirs.) María's will concludes with the exhortation, "Let no one violate my statement" (TC 132,135). It sounds like formula, but this type of formula prohibition may have appeared when something about the testament was unusual. Digressions about relatives' bad behavior served both as explanations and justifications for disinheritance. This type of complaint about relatives to prevent claims on estates occurs in colonial Spanish women's testaments as well (Lavrin and Courturier, 1979:299).

Culhuacan men also occasionally explained why certain people were not heirs. One example is Diego Sánchez's brother and sister who received a share of the estate during his lifetime. Another example is Pablo Huitznahuatl's assurances that his wife and he had consulted about how his estate would be divided. However, some cases of disinheritance were not explained. For instance, Joaquín Matlalacan left some land to his younger brother Marcos, but the bulk of his estate went to his own son Sebastián. Joaquín's wife and also his mother acted as witnesses to the will, but neither was an heir. They were thus disinherited, but Joaquín gave no explanation as to why (TC 236ff). Wives may not have had automatic claims on their husbands' estates, although they usually did share in them.

In the late sixteenth century the people of Culhuacan primarily left their property, houses, land, and movable goods to their children and to their spouses, and to a lesser extent to grandchildren, nieces and nephews, and to brothers and sisters. They treated their estates as divisible, and they carefully chose their multiple heirs. Fully aware that some of their heirs would not survive, they named alternative recipients. Usually they did not prefer one sex over another, generally treating sons and daughters equally.

The effect of this system of partible inheritance was to redistribute property widely with each succeeding death. Landholding which consisted of scattered plots of various sizes was thus further fractionalized. Shared bequests of property, as to children receiving shares in a house, were fairly common and suggest that at some point the property might be divided, or shares retained but residence relinquished. Testamentary bequests put property in the hands of women, sometimes as heirs with full rights and sometimes as custodians for their children's property. Only occasionally did someone put the estate in the hands of a single heir. This is not evidence that partibility was not operating, but probably that there were very few possible heirs. There are cases of a sole surviving child or the spouse in a childless marriage receiving the bulk of an estate.

How close these bequest patterns were to those of the prehispanic era is not known. One clear change was the bequests of money to the church for masses, which necessitated the sale of large amounts of land. Some buyers were not members of the Indian community. No longer was inheritance a closed system of redistribution of resources to succeeding generations of Indians. One question is whether inheritance patterns were affected by the epidemic conditions. Land and houses, while still valuable, were in greater supply as the Indian population declined. Was it easier for women to inherit under these conditions? In one modern Nahua-speaking community, daughters inherit equally with sons when there is enough land (Taggart, 1983:44). Among sixteenth-century natives in Mexico City, women appear to have held less land and more movable goods than men, and they seem to have preferred emphasizing their ties to women. If these patterns genuinely existed, likely it was due to scarcity of resources in Mexico City where Indians were competing with each other and with Spaniards.[52]

To what extent were Indian patterns of inheritance affected by Spanish ideas of inheritance? This too is unclear. Spanish courts systematically made judgments about disputed Indian estates following Spanish principles of inheritance (Borah, 1983:54). In the only known case of a disputed Culhuacan will, a legitimate daughter of a first marriage succeeded in overturning the will of her father's second wife.[53] In most other Culhuacan wills, testators generally chose those that did, in fact, fit Spanish conceptions of proper heirs. However, this may have been a convergence of two independently developed systems. In native society, the possible weakening of the ties between siblings may have been the result of Spanish pressures, since Spanish inheritance stressed lineal ties from parents to children rather than lateral ones to brothers and sisters. Another possible way in which Spanish law might have affected native inheritance patterns was in the assertion of the rights of wives and daughters. In Spanish law, a widow was guaranteed a fixed proportion of her husband's estate, and daughters inherited equally with sons. In Culhuacan, women's control of property does *not* appear to have been a postconquest innovation, the Spanish legal system may have particularly benefited women who wanted to assert claims.[54]

One clear area where Spanish family patterns had an effect on native society was the introduction of ritual godparenthood. With the decline in Indian population and the disruption of traditional patterns of caring for minor children, Indians embraced compadrazgo. This was a means to extend family ties, providing stability when native society was under great stress. By including their godchildren as heirs, men seem to have taken their responsibilities as godparents more seriously than women did.

6 / WEALTH

"And my horse is always to be kept hired out"

Angelina Mocel was the owner of houses and land that she had received from her father Pablo Huitznahuatl. The land helped supply the food needs of her family. In addition, she used her skills as a weaver to produce textiles for her family's use or for sale in the market. In this chapter is a discussion of several sources of wealth, such as land, money-lending, and commerce. Wage labor is examined as some people's source of income. In addition, some forms of wealth, such as houses and movable goods, are surveyed.

Wealth is a relative term, but in a preindustrial society like Culhuacan's, the amount of land people owned is the best index of it. If someone held large amounts of land over and above what was needed for subsistence and tribute, surpluses of food could be produced to be traded or sold. In the prehispanic period, the crops from some tracts of land supported institutional needs. Tlatoque had land which supported their offices. Temples had lands to support their religious activities. Palaces [*tecpancalli*] also controlled land. In addition, there was private land located in conquered areas which was given to nobles in reward for their services. Long-distance merchants [*pochteca*] invested in land (Calnek, 1975). None of the heads of institutions or other elites worked the land themselves, for dependent labor and labor duty by free commoners produced the crops on these lands.[1] Free commoners are generally considered to have had usufruct rights to land held by the calpulli,[2] producing enough for subsistence and tribute, as well as surpluses for the market.

The people of Culhuacan held varying amounts of land, easily seen because in colonial Indian testaments, each parcel of land was listed separately. From these enumerations, a general estimate of someone's *individual* holdings can be made. Since we generally have the testament of just one member of a family, we do not know the total amount of land a person would have had access to through other relatives. However, knowing the holdings of an individual is an important step in establishing that there were significant differences in wealth in colonial Culhuacan.

Ideally the listings of land gave the length, width, soil type, and location of each parcel. Not all parcels have such complete descriptions, for often someone just listed a field in a given place, giving no measurements at all or giving the measurement of just one side. However, the number of parcels is known, and it is clear that some people owned many more than others. Simply counting the number of parcels people had gives at least an impression of their holdings, and the measurements of even one side of fields suggest their sizes. However, we can evaluate holdings a little more precisely because most people owned chinampas, extraordinarily productive land whose size is known. Seven chinampas could support the food needs of one person for a year.[3] When people owned chinampas and other types of land greatly in excess of what the subsistence needs of their families were, then they should be considered well-off.

The range of holdings among testators was substantial. At one extreme were some of the titled testators, such as Pablo Huitznahuatl tecuhtli ("lord"), who had large holdings. He owned fifty-two chinampas and six other parcels of land, one of them two hundred by twenty, another twenty by twenty (the units of measure are not specified but were likely *matl* [1.67 m]), and four other plots forty units long and an unspecified number wide (TC 164ff). His chinampa land alone would provide subsistence for over seven people. Another person who had even more impressive holdings was doña Luisa Juana. Seven plots of her land totalled 35,210 square matl (about five hectares). A third person with substantial holdings was don Pedro de Suero. He held seven and a half hectares of chinampa land (enough to support 150 people) plus one and a half hectares of other land (TC 224ff). With holdings of this size, likely none of the owners cultivated the land themselves, but none of them gave any indication of how the land was, in fact, worked.

In the middle range were people who had seemingly enough land to support their families, perhaps also producing small surpluses. Small landowners included people like Angelina Mocel, who owned fifteen chinampas and two plots of other land to help support herself and her husband Juan Velázquez and their child (TC 180ff). Juan owned five chinampas and one plot of other land (TC 204ff). Others testators' wills are found in isolation, so that we do not know what other land they might have had access to. These include the widower Domingo Yaotl (TC 48ff), who had just five small chinampas and three other parcels to support himself and his son, and the young woman María Tiacapan of Coatlan, who had seven chinampas and two other plots of land to support herself and perhaps also her sister and her grandmother (TC 130ff).

At the other extreme from the wealthy were those who owned little or no land. Two were Ana Tiacapan of Tepanecapan (TC 92ff) and Antonio Toca (TC 194ff) who had no land but owned several houses. Others like María Icnocihuatl (TC 76ff) and María Inés (TC 266ff) owned a house and one plot of land. None of these landless or nearly landless people mentions any other means of support.

For those who did not have much land, however, there are a number of possibilities for how they made a living. While they owned little or no land on their own, they might have been allowed to cultivate land owned by relatives. This is clearly the case with some offspring who predeceased their parents. The testators' parents permitted them to plant fields, and the testators owned the crop. For instance, Domingo Yaotl, mentioned above, owned land of his own, but also used some of his mother's land. He gave his son "what I have planted, the maize, the beans, and the magueys that are on the field of my mother. And the land is my mother's property and I have nothing to do with it" (TC 50,51). Juana Tiacapan of Atempan owned five chinampas and two other parcels, and also sowed other land. Of this she said it "is not my property nor my land, but that of my father. But I give the crop to my younger brother Diego, who is to reap it" (TC 148,149).

Landless people might have engaged in wage labor. In Mexico City, there were full-time artisans of various kinds. However, in sixteenth-century Culhuacan, there is only fragmentary evidence that people engaged in wage work. Weavers were hired for pay, at least on a short-term basis, and production of textiles was both for domestic consumption and for sale.[4] When Angelina's aunt María

Tiacapan died, she had finished "only a quarter [i.e., one length] of my yarn which was going to be a huipil to sell" (TC 178,179). Clearly at least some production was for the market. Though María owned land through her inheritance from her uncle Antonio Tlemachica, she pursued activities to bring in money. She assigned the yarn to her husband,[5] saying "perhaps some hired person can finish it for him" (TC 178,179). Evidently María assumed her husband would not do the job himself, and someone would have been hired for pay to do such work.

Some people supplemented work on their own land both with skilled wage work and work on others' land for pay. Vicente Xochiamatl said "I worked a field for someone for two pesos that I was paid." Apparently in order that his own heirs did not claim the crop, he ordered that the "owners come to take the maize [which is on the field]" (TC 114,115). It is unclear how widespread wage labor for agricultural work was; but it is interesting that it is known to exist just as population was in drastic decline. There was a labor shortage and widespread use of wage labor may well be a colonial innovation. Some artisans demanded payment, such as Vicente, a stonemason, who expected pay for his professional work. "I worked in the church of San Francisco Tequixquipan and they haven't paid me yet" (TC 114,115), he complained. Culhuacan had an abundance of stone. There were quite a few masons, enough to warrant an official in charge of them. Vicente had a moderate amount of land owning thirty-three chinampas, plus four plots of other land, and some magueys. The total of his holdings could support a household of about five people.

Some landless people in Culhuacan engaged in trade, for commerce and money-lending were also ways to make a living and accumulate wealth. In the prehispanic period, an elite group, the *pochteca,* were long-distance traders. Women pochteca do not seem to have gone on expeditions, but they did invest in these ventures (Sahagún, IX:14). The pochteca held a privileged position in society because their activities not only brought luxury goods from distant points, but were also spy missions for future Aztec conquests, and were therefore backed by the power of the state. With the Spanish conquest, the pochteca lost their privileged position as agents of the state. Colonial native traders remained important to the economy, however.

In addition to long-distance traders, a local market economy flourished both in the prehispanic and colonial periods, and continues today. An incredible variety of goods could be purchased from local traders. The Spaniards were amazed by the great market of Tlatelolco when they arrived at the seat of Aztec power (Díaz del Castillo, 1966:144). Many of the traders in local markets were women who sold capes, herbs for medicine, tobacco, raw foodstuffs, such as beans, maize, chilis, and chocolate, as well as prepared food, such as atole, a type of corn gruel, and tamales.[6]

Wills from several Culhuacan trading families give insight into native commercial patterns. Luis Tlauhpotonqui and his sister María Tiacapan are especially interesting. Both claimed residence in the ward of Tianquizçolco, a name which literally means "at the old market," indicating there may have been an enclave of traders residing together. When Luis died in February 1581, he left a will detailing his father's business transactions as much as his own. His father, Antonio de Santa María, was a money-lender and trader who had died with many debts owed to him. Luis enumerated his father's debtors and the amounts they owed in his own will, making what was likely a futile effort to have the money collected. In the prehispanic period, debts could be inherited (Torquemada, 1975:II,566); in the colonial era, it seems clear that credits were also. Credit was important, money was put to work, but there are no clues to interest rates or collateral.[7] Payment to Antonio was in cash and kind, and presumably he made a profit. The Aztecs had notions of fair value and good business practice. According to Sahagún's informants, the "bad merchant" is a "usurer, a profiteer, a thief," but a "good merchant" is one who "sets correct prices, who gives equal value" (Sahagún, X:43). Antonio loaned substantial amounts of cash to debtors in many places. Indians seemed not to keep money on hand, a pattern also found among European peasants who depended on money-lenders for cash (Sabean, 1976:101; Weber, 1976:37).[8]

While most transactions in Culhuacan involved amounts of a few tomines,[9] many of Antonio de Santa María's loans were in the tens of pesos. For instance, one loan was to "one called Elías, whose home is Quauhtlalpan, [who] still has not paid 20 pesos and a blanket together with it" (TC 136,137). It is notable that a Spanish blanket [*frezada*] was counted as part of the debt, reminiscent of the prehispanic use of native mantles as a medium of exchange. Another of Antonio's loans was to Miguel Huelilhuitl: "nine pesos are not yet paid." Part of the debt was retired, although not by a money payment for "he just worked at our home to pay it." The loan was bail money; "with this money, he got out of jail, because he broke the head of Juan de San Miguel when he was alguacil mayor" (TC 136,137). This was not the only loan for a specific purpose, for one of Antonio's debtors was don Miguel de Castañeda, who borrowed some money to engage in litigation (TC 136,137).

Antonio also lent money to other traders. To "a person named Hernando, whose home is Xomiltepec," Antonio lent twelve pesos because Hernando "was going to carry on commerce with it but was not able to do it" (TC 136,137). Making money in commerce was obviously not a sure thing. Even Luis Tlauhpotonqui himself could not match his father's success. While his father dealt in big loans, Luis operated on a modest scale. "What I myself have lent to others" was a loan of nine tomines to one man, and two pesos to another (TC 136ff).

The debtors of Antonio de Santa María (and then his son Luis) were far-flung and diverse. One was a woman named Juana Tiacapan, a resident of Mexico City. She was a good credit risk, however, for of her thirteen-peso debt she just "has yet to pay another peso and four tomines" (TC 136,137). The other debtors were men. Some were also from outside Culhuacan, although the exact locations of their homes is not known. Antonio lent money to people in Quauhtlalpan, Huapalcalco, and Xomiltepec.[10] Apparently the law could be invoked to get payment when it was not forthcoming. Luis noted that "the money that was paid in Ixtapalapa, [someone] paid by legal order" (TC 140,141). The term for legal order, *justiciatica*,[11] indicates that the Spanish legal system was involved. Luis had not retrieved the money at the time of his death. "Six pesos are [still being] kept at the jail," indicating that the legal system was still involved in the matter.[12] In Culhuacan, Luis had other means for collecting. One way was to call on witnesses who knew about the debt. Someone who was apparently a resident of the town, "still has not paid eight pesos. Juan de San Miguel knows of this from when he was alcalde." If this important witness were not enough, Luis went on to say "it is [also] in the testament that my father ordered" (TC 136,137). Although that will is not extant, the municipal government was in charge of keeping the wills of its citizens. Luis relied more directly on local officials to collect debts. "The topileque interceded in the matter of Lazaro Hualmoquetza, who still must pay twenty-(one?) pesos because he stole two horses" (TC 136,137).

Horses were an important means of transportion, and were a vital part of most traders' capital. In the prehispanic period, overland traders used bearers [*tlameme*], since there were no pack animals (Hassig, n.d.). Horses were brought by the Spaniards when they first arrived in 1519, and these animals were a factor in the conquest. In the early sixteenth century Spaniards restricted Indians from owning horses, in part due to military considerations, but by midcentury Indian nobles were petitioning to have the legal right of ownership. Most of the high nobles seem to have wanted the animals as a prestige item, so that they could ride (like any self-respecting Spaniard) rather than walk. By the fourth quarter of the century, horses (and mules) were part of traders' estates in Culhuacan. The Spanish colonial government in the midcentury had banned the use of men for bearing burdens, and allowing Indians to own horses was an absolute necessity so that commerce would not be disrupted (Borah, 1983:53).

Antonio de Santa María had a number of transactions involving horses. In the case of Lázaro Hualmoquetza who "stole two horses," son Luis used Culhuacan officials to get recompense. In another case, Antonio and his son Luis seem to have kept a running two-way account with don Alonso of Xomiltepec. Apparently don Alonso owed fifteen pesos to Antonio at one time, reduced it to ten by outright payment, then paid five and a half pesos toward a horse which subsequently died after Luis had taken it back. That amount was counted toward the original debt along with three pesos worth of honey that don Alonso gave Luis. This left one and a half pesos outstanding at Luis's death (TC 136,137).[13] It is not known whether don Alonso wanted the horse for bolstering his prestige or for trade; perhaps it was for both. None of Culhuacan's high nobles whose testaments are extant owned a horse, although others, non-nobles, did.

Some merchant families intermarried. Luis Tlauhpotonqui's sister María Tiacapan was wed to a trader named Mateo Opan. The couple had between them two horses; "my husband earned one of them entirely by himself. But the second we earned together; it cost us trouble to acquire it" (TC 192ff). María determined where the profits went from the jointly owned horse.[14] Mateo Opan and his brother-in-law Luis Tlauhpotonqui cooperated on some transactions and were perhaps partners for some enterprises. Luis, at any rate, had a job for Mateo to do regarding his estate. He had a tecomate in the form of a bird, quite an unusual item, that he had "given as a pawn," apparently to get cash. He wanted it back, and said "the bird tecomate is in the house of someone in Te[tla]. Let someone go to collect it from him. Perhaps my brother-in-law Mateo Opan can go; let him deliver the four tomines" to pay the man who had it (TC 138,139). The notion of pawning seems to have been a European introduction, since the Spanish loanword *prenda* is used. Another instance of pawning is a precious green stone that doña Ana de Coronado's relatives relinquished in order to bury her (TC 72ff).

Joaquín de Luna, who claimed residence in Mexico City, was also a trader. He owned no land in Culhuacan (or anywhere else); all his capital was tied up in horses.[15] He gave one horse to his "younger sister Juana Tiacapan [who] will take it and have it." In exchange he wanted her "to aid me with six masses, as if she bought [the animal]" (TC 154,155). The value of this horse might have been as low as six pesos, since a peso paid for one standard mass; however, he may have requested a lesser amount for the animal than it was worth, giving his sister a discount on the price. He had loaned another pack animal, for which he expected compensation. "In Cuitlatetelco someone named Martín Cano is keeping a horse of mine valued at eight pesos... it has been there for a year in the service of Martín Cano,[16] [who] is to pay for the horse's work" (TC 154,155).

The merchant community in Culhuacan was tightly knit. María Tiacapan, an investor herself, was the sister of one trader (Luis Tlauhtpotonqui), and wife of another (Mateo Opan). In addition, she acted as witness to the will of the trader, Joaquín de Luna (TC 154,155). Another witness for Joaquín was Juana Tiacapan, perhaps his sister though not identified as such, who was in debt to Luis Tlauhpotonqui.[17]

Another non-Culhuacan resident engaged in trade was Ana Tlaco. Married to Juan Bueno and resident in the town of Yecapixtla (in the Cuernavaca region), Ana was originally from Culhuacan and was there when she died. She, like María Tiacapan of Tianquizçolco, owned a pack animal which was used for trade. "They are taking [the mule] about in Yecapixtla" (TC 188,189). She paid a good sum of her own money for the animal, saying "when I bought it I gave 15 pesos for it" (TC 188,189). The mule constituted virtually all her wealth and she wanted it "brought here [to Culhuacan] and sold." Half of the money was to stay in Culhuacan for masses, the other "will go to Yecapixtla." At her death, then, she disposed of her capital, rather than directing the profits from it. Through inheritance from her brother she owned one field, her only land. She bequeathed yarn and other weaving materials to her daughter, as well as a skirt, but she was vague about her movable goods. "As to our other property [i.e., movables] that is in Yecapixtla, my husband Juan Bueno knows about it" (TC 190,191).[18]

That pack animals were valuable is known, but one man, Miguel Hernández, went so far as to go into a formal partnership [*compañía*] with someone else for a mule [*cavallo macho*]. The circumstances of this partnership were not felicitous. Miguel declared that his partner, "Agustín Yaochihualoc, whose home is San Francisco Tlaxoxiuhco, killed [a mule] of mine; it cost 16 pesos and he killed it." Miguel, however, assumed some responsibility for the loss, saying "when [Agustín] killed it, we made a partnership, because it was the fault of both of us." Because of the shared responsibility, Miguel forgave him eight pesos of the debt, directing that "he will promptly pay the eight pesos [remaining]" (TC 274,275). The fact that the two men called their arrangement a compañía, a formal partnership, reveals that Indians knew the terminology for a standard Spanish commercial venture. In the colonial period, Spaniards made agreements to invest in particular enterprises and share the profits according to the amount each partner contributed. Although in theory partners were only committed to each other for one venture, partners often reinvested together in others. The notion of investment was certainly not foreign to native traders, for in the prehispanic period, women pochteca invested in long distance expeditions.

The most interesting figure who engaged in commerce was Miguel García, executor and notary. Among his possessions was his horse (or mule) [*macho*], which he wanted "always to be kept hired out to someone" (TC 104,105). He seemingly had not completely paid for the animal, saying that "eight pesos and four tomines have been paid publicly [toward buying the mule]," but not that he owned it outright (TC 104,105). As a town official dealing with estate administration, Miguel García was in a position to collect money destined for payment of testators' debts and for masses. He seems to have delayed forwarding some of the cash. One example was the case of an old woman. "Magdalena made as an offering six pesos in money to buy wood for the church of the [ward of] Transfiguración. I kept it and borrowed it." He does not seem at all shy at admitting this, and ordered that "it is to be paid back" (TC 102,103). He was in a position of trust, which he honored. We have seen that not all officials were so trustworthy, for Miguel Jacobo de Maldonado took advantage of his position as notary to hide the book of wills, doubtless for some financial reason.

García functioned as a public official and engaged in trade, but some items in his estate show even more facets of his life. He owned Spanish carpentry tools. Did he let them sit idle, rent these out, loan them to relatives, or use them himself? As one of the few truly literate men in Culhuacan, it should not surprise us that García owned books. He had religious books including "a book of hours, a breviary . . . , three [breviaries?] in Nahuatl, and a confessional manual"[19] (TC 104,105). Books of hours were popular in Europe at the time, owned by literate and semiliterate people. They were "the only book to be found where books are not read" (Febvre, 1977:29). In Culhuacan, García was not the only one to own a book of hours and other religious books. The testament fragment of Miguel Oçoma lists "a minor book of hours and two [books of Christian] doctrine, all of which are my property" (TC 244,247). Likely the books of hours were similar to European ones of the same period which contained prayers, calendars, and almanacs (Febvre, 1977:29).

Those engaging in commerce, even part-time like Miguel García, were only modest landowners. Joaquín de Luna of Mexico City had no land at all, while Ana Tlaco, late of Yecapixtla, had just a small plot which she inherited. Both of them counted their pack animals as their only sizeable capital. Antonio de Santa María had just a couple of fields of inherited and patrimonial land, as well as some purchased land, worth twenty pesos, a large sum for Culhuacan. But even one large plot of land (which twenty pesos would buy) would not have catapulted Antonio into the category of large landowners.[20]

Although those engaged in commerce often owned horses and mules to transport their goods, canoes were still used. Culhuacan's location on the shores of Lake Xochimilco linked it to major population centers in the Valley of Mexico, including the capital of Mexico-

Tenochtitlan. One young man who seems to have been a trader, Pablo Quechol, had no horse but owned a boat [*acalli,* literally "water house"] (TC 88,89). Among the Culhuacan testators, more people owned boats than horses, and no one owned both. Boats could be quite valuable. Tomás Motolinia gives some notion of prices, saying he had "five pesos with which I was going to buy a boat" (TC 162,163). We can infer that some boats were worth almost half the price of a good horse (and equal to the price of some houses). The boat Pablo Quechol owned was old and of little value. "Let it be divided [into planks] and burned [for firewood]" (TC 88,91). Just as both men and women owned horses, both owned boats. Ana Tiacapan of Tepanecapan lent hers to her husband for the collecting zacate, but she willed it to her daughter (TC 94,95). Zacate grew in Culhuacan and the reed was used for animal fodder. It was rendered in tribute or sold in Mexico City markets (Gallegos, 1927:172). Gathering and transport to the capital was by canoe.[21] Indians used Spanish pack animals but Spaniards never took to boats. However, they did need the products delivered in them.

Among the movable goods of the testator Pablo Quechol were large caches of foodstuffs and big storage containers, which suggest that he was engaged in trading foodstuffs. The most valuable commodity was Pablo's two thousand cacao beans, which his parents gave him in order to get married. Cacao beans were used as a medium of exchange in the prehispanic period and continued to be used in the sixteenth century for some goods valued at less than a tomín. Some of the goods in don Juan Telléz's estate, such as a small reed basket (TC 42,43), were auctioned off for a few cacao beans, but payment of debts was generally figured in Spanish money.

Houses were part of most people's estates and were a type of wealth. "A house mattered less than land, but it did matter," Eugen Weber (1976:156) said of French peasants. This was also the case for the people of sixteenth-century Culhuacan. There were a number of different types of houses owned by the Culhuacan testators. Most houses were simply called *calli,* "house." Some calli may have been rooms in a house compound and others free-standing one-room houses. House compounds were several adjoining single-room structures, each with its own doorway which opened onto a patio. [See Figure 2]. Except for houses of the high nobility, Indian houses were fairly simple one-story structures of stone, adobe, or wood.

Inside they were sparsely furnished. The interior was often filled with smoke since the only opening for ventilation was the door or sometimes a window (Gibson, 1964:336). In Culhuacan, Indians tried to maximize natural light by building doors facing east, west, or south, but never north. Often the only way to distinguish one structure from another was by the description of the way the door faced.[22]

The value of houses varied. The house belonging to doña Luisa was worth forty pesos and was so expensive that no Indians could buy it. As we have seen, it was sold to the sister and the brother-in-law of the Augustinian prior, fray Juan Núñez, after the cabildo granted them a license. Most Culhuacan houses sold to Indians were much less expensive, varying in price from three to nine pesos.[23] House prices in Culhuacan were far below those for Mexico City in the same period. Two sixteenth-century litigations between Indians concerning property in Mexico City list house prices of several hundred pesos for one, and seventy for another.[24] An Indian town more comparable to Culhuacan than the Spanish capital was Xochimilco, where a few house prices matched those of the capital.[25] On the other hand, those expensive Xochimilco houses belonged to nobles.

Many people describe their houses in terms of size and age. Angelina Mocel's husband Juan Velázquez had a house which was "just small not large" (TC 206,207).[26] Many houses were described as small; few were described as being large. The house belonging to Juan Rafael Tlacochcalcatl gives us some idea of the size of a house. It was simply described as a calli without other qualifiers and was "five *matl* wide and three by the side" (about eight by five meters) (TC 142,143). Some people said their houses were new, and others had old ones. Descriptions of age and size were probably comparisons against some ideal house.

Attached to doña Luisa's house (and included in the purchase price) was a walled enclosure [*tepancalli*].[27] Enclosures were often attached to houses and surrounded the patio. The testator Ana Juana had an "[enclosure] standing beside the road that is not yet roofed" (TC 80,81). Angelina Mocel's aunt had an "[enclosure] that surrounds [the house]" which was "to be sold and [the proceeds] used for and spent on me [for masses]" (TC 176,177). The Relácion geográfica of Culhuacan says that houses were surrounded by *cetos de canas* (woven structures of reeds) (Gallegos, 1927:173). Less frequently, wooden fences or gratings [*quauhchayahuacayo*] were attached to houses (TC 194,195). As with most other possessions, Indians could (and did) bequeath or sell their walled enclosures and fences separately.

Surprisingly among the high nobility only doña Luisa Juana listed a house in her will. Doña María Juárez, don Pedro de Suero, and don Juan Téllez may have lived in their respective *tecpancalli,* palaces or community houses. The right to live in a tecpancalli depended on status. María Teicuh of Cihuatecpan, who was likely an elite but who had no noble titles,[28] owned houses, which she bequeathed, but attempted to insure her descendants' rights to live in the tecpancalli. "The house ... will be for the public because it is the tecpancalli, but despite its being public it is the home of all my children and grandchildren. . . . They will keep it swept and attend to the public there" (TC 232,233).

With a few exceptions, most Culhuacan houses only had one story. Even doña Luisa's house, which sold for forty pesos, was likely just one story, since she does not use any of the special terms for two-story structures. A description by Sahagún says that a two-story house had deep foundations and thick walls (Sahagún, XI:274), doubtless to support the extra weight. In Culhuacan, two-story houses [*calnepanolli*] were owned by relatively wealthy men, one of whom was a stonemason (TC 64,65; 112,113).[29] Another type of multistory building was the *tlapancalli,* a flat-roofed house or terrace, owned by Ana Tiacapan of Santa Cruz (TC 224,225).[30]

There were a number of different types of structures for storage. Some people had storage rooms or *tlecopatl*[31] attached to their houses. Maintaining them was not a high priority, for they are often described as old. One was downright decrepit, "a storage room that collapsed" (TC 216,217). Angelina Mocel's cousin, Bernardino Vázquez, described his as "where I sleep" (TC 264,265). Tlecopatl might also have been used as kitchens. Another type of storage area was a *tlatlatilcalli,* found in a complex of buildings owned by Ana Tiacapan of Amantlan (TC 58,59). Several people had granaries [*cuezcomatl*]. At his death, Miguel Oçoma had "a granary full of unshelled maize" (TC 244,245). Bins were made of wooden planks (TC 26,27; 102,103; 270,271).[32]

The estate of Ana Tiacapan of Amantlan contained a variety of buildings. She was the owner of a house which had some public functions, two other houses, a great hall [*oquichpan*],[33] a "woman's house" [*cihuacalli*],³⁴ and two storerooms (TC 56ff). In one of these structures Ana's late husband "Baltasar Nentequitl attended to the rulers and traders of Amantlan" (TC 56,57). Ana also owned "a great hall which . . . faces Xochimilco, where people used to warm themselves" (TC 58,59).

Another woman, also named Ana Tiacapan, a resident of Tepanecapan, owned a *temazcalli* (TC 94,95), a structure used for sweatbaths, the preferred method of maintaining personal hygiene (Gibson, 1964:339) and used extensively by women during pregnancy and after childbirth (Sahagún, VI:155). Temazcalli were built low and windowless, with a fire at one end (Sahagún, XI:275).³⁵ Temazcalli were shared among many people.

Ana was also one of the few who owned a hut, a more humble structure than a house built of adobe or stone. This type of structure was so common that the Nahuatl word *xacalli* passed into Mexican Spanish as *jacal*. Huts came in various shapes and were made of various building materials, including wood and reeds plastered with mud (Sahagún, XI:273). Ana's was made of wood, possibly with the typical straw roof described in the Relación geográfica (Gallegos, 1927:173).

The terminology for houses in Culhuacan is quite rich and complex, and includes an interesting usage for a well-known term, *telpochcalli,* "young man's house." In the prehispanic period, the term telpochcalli generally referred to schools for young commoner boys. After the conquest, these schools disappeared. In colonial Culhuacan, one man used the term telpochcalli not to describe a school but to refer to the house he had built as a young man. Juan de San Pedro gave this house to his children saying, "it is my 'young man's house,' because I was still a young man when I built the house, not yet married" (TC 172,173). It is unclear whether the meaning of the term telpochcalli changed in the colonial period or whether this meaning was always present and not emphasized.

A final type of structure found in Culhuacan was the "woman's house" or *cihuacalli*. Part of the estate that Angelina Mocel had received from her father was a "'woman's house' which faces east" (TC 180,181). What a "woman's house" *was* is unclear. The term may describe the function of the house, as a kitchen where women's work was done (Anderson et al., 1976:90–91) or a common room for family use (Lombrado de Ruiz, 1973:186). A "woman's house" might have been a civil category of property, connected in some way to dowry. The most obvious explanation is that it was a house owned by a woman. This was *not* the case, for a number of men owned them, including Pablo Huitznahuatl, who bequeathed his to Angelina Mocel. She ordered it sold to pay for her death expenses. This pattern was typical: men who owned cihuacalli willed them to women while the women ordered theirs sold for masses.[36]

Culhuacan houses were generally made of adobe and stone. Building materials for houses included stone, adobe, and wood, all valuable enough to be bequeathed separately. Wood columns, lintels, stone, foundation cement, wooden planks, and shingles were sold for masses or bequeathed to individual heirs. Stone was abundant in Culhuacan and is commonly listed in wills. Adobe could be made almost anywhere in the Valley of Mexico. The corregidor reported that in Culhuacan it was made "with lake mud called *tlalçacutle* which is to say paste of mud" (Gallegos, 1927:173). Wood shingles were used for roofing, and deteriorated rapidly if not taken care of.[37]

There were professional building trades, such as masonry and carpentry, (Sahagún, X:27–28). Culhuacan was an exporter of stone (Gallegos, 1927:172). The Culhuacan wills indicate the presence of stoneworkers. Vicente Xochiamatl was a stonemason who had not been paid for his work when he made his will. He called upon his fellow mason to speak for him about the money. "Let Fabián speak for me, because we both worked there" (TC 112,115). One woman hired professional builders for a construction project (TC 94,95). However, it is not entirely clear that when a woman was named as having built a house that she did not actually supply her labor. Although the Culhuacan wills do not indicate it, adobe bricks were made by women, one of the practices which "struck Spaniards as inappropriate or bizarre" (Gibson, 1964:152, 505).

Houses built by Indian workmen, were generally unchanged by European innovations. One exception was the door [*puerta*].[38] The Aztecs "never used doors in the time [before the conquest], because it was not necessary to protect anything with them, being secure, that without doors [their houses] used to be protected.... (Torquemada, 1975,II:381) . A device made of woven canes leaned against the entrance, and it was hung with objects for making noise as a kind of knocker (Torquemada, 1975,II:381). Doors were part of several Culhuacan estates, and were bequeathed separately.

The dismantling of houses was a common practice,[39] so common that when Ana Juana willed a house to her son Juan Francisco, she declared that "it is not to be torn down" (TC 82,85). Stones and wooden columns had lasting value. They could be sold easily or used to build other structures. The estate of Ana Tiacapan of Tepanecapan is extreme in the number of structures she owned and tore down, but hers was merely an exaggeration of prevalent patterns. She ordered two houses be "torn down and a [chapel]... be built for the image of our Lord" (TC 94,95). Ana's estate mainly consisted of buildings of various kinds. She had already destroyed one building. "I tore down a... little house and warmed myself with the wood" (TC 94,95). She inherited a portion of a sweathouse. "I and my sister... shared [it], the stone belongs to me" (TC 94,95). Perhaps she was going to have that torn down too. Ana willed to her daughter a house [calli] and a hut [xacalli], and she suggested that "if she marries somewhere, she should build herself a house there with the wood" (TC 94,95). She *expected* her daughter to tear them down. Ana was not entirely single-mindedly destroying buildings, however. When she died, she had hired builders. She had paid "four tomines of my money to the masons who were going to build me some walls" (TC 94,95). She wanted the money back and spent on expenses for her burial.

Movable goods constituted another type of wealth. The auction of goods from the estate of don Juan Téllez (TC 40ff) gives considerable insight into the types of native and Spanish movable goods in use in late sixteenth-century Culhuacan. Though furnishings in most colonial Aztec houses were sparse (Gibson, 1964:336), don Juan owned a variety of household goods, both native and European. The European items can be identified by their loanword names.[40] Most estates, including those of the other high nobles, do not have long lists of movable goods, probably because they constituted only a small portion of the total wealth.[41] As we have seen previously, don Juan's movable goods were being sold to pay debts. The kinds of these goods were typical of other estates, and his vary only in the number he had. Furniture, cooking and serving ware, containers for storage, tools, and clothing were auctioned. Because of that, their value is known.[42] Nothing was worth more than a peso, and some values were so low that they were figured in cacao beans.

Don Juan owned several types of native furniture, including five old petates (reed mats), which sold for half a tomín; two wooden seats, which also sold for half a tomín; and some other furniture for sitting of unknown value, four seats with backs, two benches, and four chairs. Most commoners slept on the ground or on petates (Gibson, 1964:336), but don Juan had a bed, which sold for six tomines. He owned some Spanish furniture, including "a chest with a hide spread out on it, with a lock," two other chests [*cajas*], "a big table made out of willow wood," and a ladder [*escalera*]. Chests were particularly popular and useful items in Culhuacan and appear in many estates, including Angelina Mocel's and her uncle Antonio Tlemachica's. Antonio gave his to his grandchildren, saying "they can put their clothing there" (TC 96,97). Juana Tiacapan of Atempan gave a small chest to her brother-in-law, so that "perhaps he will put his papers there" (TC 148,149). People often kept important legal documents at home, examples being bills of sale or receipts for payment, and occasionally testaments (TC 210ff).[43]

Don Juan also had a variety of native and Spanish goods for food storage and serving. He had "a tecomate in Michoacan style," four broken tecomates (one with a cracked rim), a jug, three jícaras, a small round basket with a handle, a reed basket, and a wooden basket tied with maguey cords. His Spanish goods of this type were a tin plate, a tin bowl,[44] a green glass bottle, and three red cups.[45] Tools also comprised part of don Juan's estate. He owned a native digging stick [*huitzoctli*], and Spanish tools, a pair of scissors [*tijeras*], a saw [*sierra*], and in addition, a broken Spanish sword [*espada*].

A final type of movable good in don Juan's estate was clothing and textiles. Don Juan had "striped cloth of various colors with rabbit fur." Weaving with rabbit fur produced luxury textiles, and the *tochomitl,* as this cloth was called, was owned by high nobles in the prehispanic period. While don Juan had clothing of native elites, he also had a pair of Spanish-style leather shoes and some boots[46] worth only a tomín.

Woven goods had considerable value. The trader Pablo Quechol had "a new skirt which cost four pesos" (TC 88,89), which he ordered sold for masses. Four pesos was the price of some Culhuacan houses. Of course, in this case, Pablo may have overestimated the price he could get. The executors certified the sale of his goods two months after he died, and the "skirt was sold for the price of two pesos," still quite a lot (TC 90,91). Value of cloth depended on the fineness of the weaving and its size.

There is evidence that Spanish woven goods were entering Culhuacan in the 1580s, for Spanish blankets [*frezadas*] occurred in several estates. Towards the end of the sixteenth century, when Indian populations were declining and populations of Spanish cities expanding, Spaniards began to direct the manufacture of coarse textiles for a mass market. Likely the Spanish blankets that Indians owned were made in New Spain, for such coarse cloth was not generally imported. On the other hand, blankets could be valuable. Pablo Quechol had a "new blanket for which was [paid] the price of three pesos" (TC 88,89). As with the skirt, Pablo's estimate of value for the blanket differed from what the executors could sell it for. The blanket sold for two pesos (TC 90,91). Nonetheless, two pesos was a substantial amount of money for Culhuacan. Compared to the half a tomín paid for the tochomitl in don Juan Téllez's estate (TC 40,41), the blanket was valuable indeed.

While native goods predominate in most estates, the number of items of European origin is impressive. Colonial Aztecs readily adopted some items, such as metal tools, because they were technologically superior to native tools of wood and stone. Don Juan's broken Spanish sword was mainly a status symbol.[47] Swords were one of the European goods restricted from Indian ownership in the early post-conquest period for military reasons. Restrictions were eased in the midsixteenth century, and weapons, such as swords and knives [*cuchillos*], which were also originally also restricted, soon found their way into Indian hands. Metal knives were valued for their superior durability.[48] Other people in Culhuacan owned Spanish tools, including the notary and executor, Miguel García, who had woodworking tools: a chisel [*escoplo*], a plane [*juntera*], as well as an axe [*hacha*] and a saw [*sierra*] (TC 104,105).

Land was the most important index of wealth in Culhuacan. Crops could be produced above the level needed for replacement of seeds and domestic consumption. Agricultural surpluses were rendered in tribute, but they were also sold in markets. Those people who controlled large amounts of land and labor could derive income from the surpluses produced. Those with little or no land could work land they did not own to raise food, or they could engage in wage labor to earn money to buy food, or both.

Commerce was also a way for the landless to make a living. In Culhuacan, traders generally owned a pack animal or boat for the transport of goods. The merchant community had ties to other communities in Central Mexico, with connections both to the Spanish capital of Mexico City and to the Indian town of Yecapixtla in the Cuernavaca region. The trading community was cohesive, with links of marriage and friendship binding it together.

Houses and movable goods were also forms of wealth. The value of most houses was quite low, indicating that in general the testators were not wealthy people. Inventories of movable goods were catalogues of sixteenth-century material culture. While goods of native origin predominate, the number and type of goods from the Spanish world are an indication of Indians' changing tastes and cultural aspirations, as well as developments in the Spanish colonial economy.

7 / GENDER AND STATUS

"Because she is a female, how is she going to work it?"

Angelina Mocel was a member of a prominent and wealthy Culhuacan family. She owned property in her own right and bequeathed it as she pleased. Her father, Pablo Huitznahuatl, was the principal source of her wealth, leaving her a house and parcels of land upon his death. In determining Angelina's and other people's status, we must take account of a number of factors. In this chapter the effects of gender, class, and wealth in shaping Culhuacan society are considered. The term gender is used to refer to those social consequences of a person's sex in determining roles in society. Class refers to the division of society into nobles and commoners. In addition, differences in personal wealth of individual nobles and commoners are examined. The interplay of gender, class, and wealth was complex. Although wealth and class were major factors in determining a person's status, gender was also an important determining factor of social roles.

Prehispanic society had been divided into two basic groups, elites and commoners, with gradations of status within each group. The nobility was mainly an hereditary group at the time of the conquest. The pochteca, a group with a privileged position though seemingly not part of the nobility, were long-distance merchants. Making up the bulk of the population were free commoners or *macehualtin*. In addition there were other commoners, including slaves, whose labor was restricted (Hicks, 1974).

By the late sixteenth century, much of the earlier complexity of social groupings had broken down, and a leveling process had set in. Within the Indian aristocracy, however, some distinctions were maintained and reinforced by Spanish colonial rule. Two factors were at work, one cultural, the other practical. Spaniards had respect for hereditary aristocracy, and Indian noblemen acted as intermediaries between the Indian masses and the Spanish colonial government (Gibson, 1964:153ff). Although the Culhuacan wills show no evidence of it, nobles in many sixteenth-century Indian towns were attempting to defend their rights and continue the divisions between themselves and commoners. Commoners in the sixteenth century took advantage of the general flux of society and of new economic opportunities to pass themselves off as nobles (Gibson, 1964:156). Nobles were exempt from tribute, and the men were eligible to be electors and hold office.

Within the colonial Indian elite there existed two groups, the tlatoque and the *pipiltin* or lesser nobility. High nobles in the early colonial era can be identified by their Spanish noble titles of *don* and *doña;* lesser nobles often continued to use traditional Nahuatl titles to mark their status. The collection of Culhuacan wills contains a large number of people who can be identified as nobles by their

Table 4 Titled Testators

Doña María Juárez
Doña Luisa Juana
Don Pedro de Suero
Don Juan Téllez

Pablo Huitznahuatl Tecuhtli
Juan Rafael Tlacochcalcatl
Miguel Sánchez Tlacatecuhtli
Miguel Chimaltecuhtli

Diego Sánchez, teopantlacatl
Juan de San Pedro, notary*
Diego Hernández, notary*
Miguel García, executor and notary
Miguel Cerón, alguacil
Miguel Huantli, topile

*Testator has the same name as a notary, but not clearly the same person.

titles, as well as people who were the kin of nobles. The latter did not have titles themselves but mentioned their titled relatives. For instance, the entire family of Angelina Mocel consisted of elites, but only her father, Pablo Huitznahuatl, had a title, that of *tecuhtli* or "lord."[1] (See Tables 4 and 5). In Culhuacan none of the titled people indicated privileges which might accompany their rank, although elsewhere the gradations of rank within the pipiltin were clear. In late sixteenth-century Tecali, for example, a hierarchy of elites can be established, with rich pipiltin measuring their wealth in land, labor, and numbers of pipiltin subordinate to them (Olivera, 1978:179).

Table 5 Testators with Titled Kin

Testator	*Title of Kin*	*Name of Kin*	*Relationship*
Angelina Mocel	tecuhtli	Pablo Huitznahuatl	daughter
María Tiacapan	"	" "	sister-in-law
Juan Velázquez	"	" "	son-in-law
Antonio Tlemachica	"	" "	"father-in-law"
Bernardino Vázquez	"	" "	nephew
Mariana	tlacochcalcatl	Juan Rafael	wife
Ana Mocel	topile	Antonio Xallacatl	mother-in-law
Mateo Juárez	regidor	Juan ———	brother
Juan Bautista	alcalde, don	Don Franco Flores	nephew
María Teicuh	" "	" " "	mother-in-law
Ana Juana	" "	" " "	comadre
María Inés	doña	Doña Elena Constantina	aunt
Doña Luisa Juana	alcalde	Juan de San Miguel	daughter
Doña María Juárez	don	Don Andrés Juárez	wife
Don Pedro de Suero	cihuapilli	Luisa Xoco	husband
Don Pedro de Suero	doña	Doña María Teicuh	husband
María Teicuh	don	Don Juan García	wife

Differences in class were often reinforced by differences in wealth. We have seen, for example, that many elites were also wealthy landowners. However, in the Culhuacan wills there are some elites who by virtue of their own property would *not* be considered wealthy. A case in point is Juan Velázquez, Angelina Mocel's husband, Pablo Huitznahuatl's son-in-law. Juan's Spanish surname suggests he is a member of the elite,[2] but his estate is very modest. He held just five chinampas and one other plot of land forty units of measure long, plus a small house (TC 204ff). If his will were found in isolation, we would believe he had been living on the margin of subsistence. However, we have the will of his wife Angelina Mocel, who owned eighteen chinampas plus a couple of plots of other land. Taken together, couple's holdings were above subsistence for a family the size of theirs.

There are other examples of elites with little wealth of their own. One was the aunt of doña Elena Constantina, María Inés (TC 266,267).[3] The assets of María's estate were a house and a plot of land, unspecified "goods," and a one peso debt owed her by doña Elena Constantina. María's niece was a member of one of the richest families in Culhuacan, but it seems to have had no effect on María's own wealth. Though her estate was small, María wanted her body buried "inside the church," an aspiration in European society usually fulfilled by the rich.[4] A final example of a poor relative of a known elite is Mateo Juárez, who actually described himself as poor.[5] He was the younger brother of a regidor. Mateo's estate confirms his poverty. He just had a small house, some trees that his parents left him, and some movable goods. He left his wife Inés "the old boat, since we don't have anything, she is to take that" (TC 76,77). Perhaps Mateo had access to greater resources through his brother, but on his own he had very little.

In some cases, the mention of a titled relative merely confirms that someone is both wealthy and a member of the elite. Antonio Tlemachica, Pablo Huitznahuatl's "father-in-law," had a substantial estate. His connection to the tecuhtli is icing on the cake, an unsurprising alliance between elite families.

Some elites seem to have been poor, and they said that was the case, such as Mateo Juárez, just mentioned; however, there were also commoners who declared their poverty and do not seem to have been that badly off.[6] One was Tomás Motolinia, whose very name proclaims his poverty. *Motolinia* means "poor" or "afflicted."[7] Tomás goes further, declaring that "I keep nothing for our lord God [i.e., having nothing] with which to make an offering at the church." In addition, he declared that "My daughter Bárbara Inés is poor" (TC 162,163). Confirming that his family is not noble is his bequest to a nephew to "establish himself as an adult man with the tribute" (TC 162,165). As noted previously, nobles were exempt from tribute. This self-declared poor person owned two houses, an unspecified number of chinampas and four other chinampas elsewhere. In addition, he had two good-sized plots of cultivated land, one of which was sown with magueyes. Tomás had bought two of the properties, one set of chinampas for six pesos and some other land, for three pesos. After his death, some of his property was sold for masses. Fray Juan Zimbrón acknowledged receipt of six pesos from the sale of Tomás's house, and five pesos "from the magueyes that were sold" (TC 164,165). The sales brought eleven pesos, and likely the purchased land held its value of another nine pesos. Thus, this self-declared poor man was worth at least twenty pesos. His protestations of poverty might have been some kind of formula statement, for this wording is echoed in other people's declarations.

The testator María Icnocihuatl ("widow") also declared that "I keep no property for God our lord... Let all my [close relatives] who see and hear my testament know this" (TC 78,79). Her estate could not satisfy any claims by kin, for it was quite small and thoroughly encumbered by debts. It consisted of the house that she and her first husband had built and the postage-stamp sized plot of land that it stood on. As we have noted previously, the two of them had contracted debts with the ward heads that the sale of property was to pay off. In addition, she had debts incurred with her second husband. After paying the debts she wanted that "with all that remains from the proceeds in money from the house, let them say masses for me" (TC 78,79).

Others had even more modest estates with no houses or land. At her death Ana Xoco just had "her maize, which was measured at six fanegas and a half,[8] and all her various things were sold, a huipil..., a small chest, a metate, and a hoe. All of her goods were sold and the money came to six pesos" (TC 262,263). The fiscal Agustín Vázquez sold the various movables, and all the money went to the church. In another case, Martín of the ward of San Andrés died, "and he had not left any testament." No property was enumerated except for "three pesos that belonged to him [which] had been discovered" and delivered to the church for masses (TC 28,29). A third case was that of Antonio Toca, whose estate, like Ana Xoco's, largely consisted of foodstuffs, "the unshelled maize, the amaranth, [and] the beans" (TC 194,195). His house had already been sold. And like Ana, he "left no children; all of them died and [he] made no testament; [he] just died" (TC 194,195).[9] All three people had small estates with no land, and they did not make wills. Officials drew up these posthumous statements, likely because money was given to the church. Perhaps if they had had heirs, the property would have passed to them rather than to the church.

In prehispanic society, a person's sex was a significant factor in determining the role he or she played. At birth Aztec babies were given tokens of their future occupations: a shield, a bow and arrows for boys, spindles, shuttles, and skeins of yarn for girls (Sahagún, VI:201). Division of work was by sex; work roles were gender roles. Females learned to grind corn, sweep, weave, and prepare food; their economic role was primarily concentrated in the domestic economy (Hellbom, 1967:235). Food preparation was women's main job, literally a daily grind of preparing corn for cooking. Boys learned to hunt, fish, farm and fight. Men practiced many skilled trades, including metal- and feather-work and construction. In essence, biology was destiny, an aspect of Aztec culture not disturbed by the Spanish conquest.

In colonial Culhuacan, there is evidence of division of work by gender. There were men who were stonemasons and tailors. Generally in Central Mexico, agricultural work seems to have been in the hands of men, although there is some evidence that women were involved in planting and harvesting, two periods of intense labor (Torquemada, 1975:II,481).[10] On occasion, there are remarks suggesting that Culhuacan women engaged in cultivation. Marcos Hernández gave "all the recent yield of ears of maize to my grandchildren and my daughter-in-law because it is the [result of] their work" (TC 278,279). Juana Tiacapan of Atempan commented on her own work. "Here is something I have put much effort into: I planted a field in Yahualiuhcan" (TC 148,149). However, men's role in agriculture is underscored by comments by two testators. Simón Moxixicoa gave some tools, "a hoe, an axe, and a metal-tipped digging stick," to his son "because he is male" (TC 158,159). In the other case, María Salomé gave a large amount of land to her daughter but wondered "because she is a female, how is she going to work it?" (TC 28,29).[11]

As we have seen, baby girls at birth received weaving equipment, practically a symbol of their femaleness. In the prehispanic period, cloth mantles that women wove on backstrap looms were rendered in tribute and were used as a medium of exchange. In the colonial period, cloth was replaced by Spanish money for transactions, but women continued to weave for domestic consumption and for the market.

In general, the types of movable goods that men and women had did not vary by sex;[12] however, in Culhuacan a number of females owned something called "women's equipment" [*cihuatlatquitl*].[13] This, in fact, consisted of goods used for weaving, such as spindles, shuttles, battens, and spinning bowls (Sahagún, VI:163). Juana Tiacapan of Atempan had an estate which consisted primarily of yarn and cloth at various stages of completion, as well as women's weaving equipment. In her lifetime she had asserted her economic independence. At death she ordered that her debt to her grandmother be paid "when my yarn is sold... Let no one ever say anything [against my statement] because in what I gave to others I have not touched my father's property." Further she declared that "nor with my women's equipment do I touch [my father's property]; during all the time I have lived on earth, I have acquired them by my own efforts" (TC 150,151). Other women, such as Lucía Teicuh, also had weaving equipment, which they ordered sold for masses (TC 126,127). In the disputed estate of Simón Moxixicoa, the cabildo officials ordered the widow María Justina to "abandon the house and take... all your women's equipment" (TC 160,161). In Angelina Mocel's family, her aunt María assigned all her woman's equipment to her husband Baltasar Téllez, "no one is to claim it from him" (TC 178,179).[14]

Women's estates also included yarn and half-finished weaving projects. Among Angelina Mocel's goods was "yarn, recently [spun into] lengths. It is to be for a huipil and is stretched on the canes [is on a loom]. The third length is not warped yet. And there are two hanks of black [yarn] and some rabbit fur cloth [*tochomitl*] that is worth one and a half tomines. And there is a little dark colored [yarn]... and cotton which is worth a tomín" (TC 182,183).[15] When her estate was being settled, her sisters-in-law took care of some of the weaving. "María Salomé and Petronila said, 'Let us make up the yarn [that was going to be a huipil] . . . and make the offering'" (TC 184,185). The executors received the offering in the form of money, so the women probably sold the huipil.[16]

In Culhuacan, women's kin often helped each other with weaving. In the case of Angelina Mocel, her sisters-in-law took care of the yarn for a huipil. Another woman, Juana Tiacapan of Atempan, had yarn "that belonged to my younger sister Antonia." At Juana's death she felt unhappy about not having woven it and bequeathed it to her brother-in-law, her late sister's husband, to have it finished. "Let him take it. He knows if perhaps he will hire someone [to finish weaving it]" so it could be sold for a mass for Antonia. But Juana had to explain why an outsider had to be hired. "The reason why I say this is so that God will not castigate me because I myself have not been able to do it" (TC 148,149). Clearly Juana had originally expected to do the job herself.

Clothing in the late sixteenth-century Culhuacan was a mixture of native and Spanish styles, but clothing styles varied by gender. According to the corregidor, men "go about now dressed in shirts and zaragüelles and long white cotton capes of the land [i.e. native cloth] . . . And in general all wear shoes and hats" (Gallegos, 1927: 172). None of the citizens of Culhuacan said a thing about owning hats. The corregidor is silent on what women wore. From the evidence in Culhuacan wills it seems that women tended to be more conservative in their dress than men.[17] There is no reference to any Culhuacan women owning Spanish-style clothing; they only mentioned owning skirts and huipils.

The adoption of Spanish clothing was evidence of changing tastes and cultural aspirations, and was likely also a marker of status. In the prehispanic period, clothing had been such a marker. Elaborate sumptuary laws attempted to control the wearing of many types of elite clothing by ineligible people. These laws were apparently unsuccessful, which is often the case (Anawalt, 1980). In the colonial period, Indian men's adoption of Spanish garb was likely an extension of the cultural pattern of clothing marking status. Angelina Mocel's husband, Juan Velázquez, for instance, had a pair of green Spanish pants [zaragüelles], which he wanted "exchanged for white cloth, and when I die, my earthly body will be wrapped in it"

(TC 206,207). The young trader Pablo Quechol had a Spanish jacket and a Spanish shirt [*camisa*] (TC 88,91).[18]

Among the Indian nobility gender was a significant determinant of a person's role. For example, women did not inherit offices,[19] although a woman's status affected the status of her children. Men's linkages with women were considerations for their qualifications for office, for the status of a man's mother in relation to his father— higher or lower—and her status as a legitimate wife or concubine affected a son's status as a potential ruler. In addition, a son's status was somewhat dependent on his birth-order among his mother's other children. The first son of the principal wife was often the first choice for a new ruler.[20]

There were rational reasons seen for not permitting women to hold high office, having nothing to do with their abilities. In Tlaxcala daughters did not inherit offices because through marriage "foreign blood, even though noble, would enter to disrupt the state" (Torquemada, 1975:II,348). In the numerous intermarriages of royalty from different altepetl, generally it was the women who moved, consolidating political alliances. Parental guidance given to daughters of rulers makes this explicit: "You know it is customary for a wife to follow her husband and live with him in his house" (Zorita, 1963b:147).

As we have seen in the discussion of the colonial town council, high offices were monopolized by noblemen, although at the ward level, some women served as ward heads [tlaxilacalleque] and cihuatepixque. One of the consequences of the general monopolization of office by men was that literacy in Nahuatl was a skill only of high status men. It was not a private vocation, but a public function; recordkeeping was in the hands of professional notaries, all of whom were male (Karttunen, 1982:414–15). A few Culhuacan cabildo officials could sign their own names or make a rubric, but no women could manage even that. Doña Luisa Isabel is the only woman whose name is signed to a Culhuacan document, but the signature is in the notary's hand.[21]

From previous discussion it is clear that being female was not a bar to ownership of property, which was usually given as inheritance or occasionally as dowry. Prehispanic elites "left to daughters very ample houses and land and other property [*haciendas*], in order that they live and sustain themselves and have ease" (Torquemada, 1975:II,348). Among native royalty, dowries are known to exist. In the prehispanic royal marriage between a noblewoman of Texcoco and the ruler of Teotihuacan, she brought to the union extensive lands, called "woman's land" [*cihuatlalli*], clearly dowry lands.[22] In colonial Culhuacan, "woman's land" occurs only in the estate of the noblewoman, doña María Juárez (TC 246ff). Dowries would be a way for a woman to share in an estate in the lifetime of the donor. Perhaps only the high nobility bestowed or held dowries.[23]

Dowry and inheritance, both ways of apportioning property, are known to have put wealth in the hands of elite women, but prehispanic property settlements for commoner women are poorly reported. In Motolinia's account (1971:134–35) of inheritance in the Cuernavaca area, where the elder brother took care of his brothers and sisters, it is not unequivocally clear that the sisters actually shared in the inheritance.[24] However, it is abundantly clear from colonial Aztec wills (from Culhuacan and elsewhere) that women both shared in estates and bequeathed property as they saw fit. In does not appear to be a colonial innovation, but the extent to which women shared in estates may have been determined by the decline of Indian populations and the relative abundance of resources. Women's right to inherit might have been only potential when resources were scarce.

The status of women in the colonial period was probably affected by the extent to which they owned property. As we have seen in the discussion of the family, women held property in their own right no matter what their marital status. Women brought property into marriage and continued to acquire it separately or together with their husbands. Culhuacan widows had a high rate of remarriage, perhaps because their estates were swelled by inheritances from their late husbands. For women, widowhood did not necessarily detract from their desirability as marriage partners, and may have in fact contributed to it.[25] When marriage was terminated by divorce, each partner took the portion brought into the marriage. I speculate that because Indian women had control over property, the way they viewed themselves and their actions toward others were affected. The Spanish alcalde's observation of Indian women's dominance of their men in courtroom situations[26] could well have been from an independence of spirit resulting from economic independence.

It is difficult to evaluate the effects of differences in gender found in language, particularly in Nahuatl where there are differences in language based on the gender of the speaker. For example, certain kin terms were used exclusively by women, such as *conetl,* "child," and *pilotl,* "niece, nephew." Certain constructions such as the vocative (e.g., "O my child!") had three forms, one used by men, one by women, and one by both. Language was clearly a way of reinforcing differences in gender. Crossing those linguistic lines was a violation of norms. "The [male] pervert [is] of feminine speech [*cioatlatole*], of feminine mode of address. [If a woman, she is] of masculine speech [*oquichtlatole*], of masculine mode of address" (Sahagún, X:37). In a highly unusual instance a Culhuacan man is recorded using a woman's word to refer to his godchild, employing the term *conetl* rather than *pilli* (TC 64).

An interesting and subtle cultural difference between men and women was in naming patterns. In colonial Aztec society, names were an important index of a person's status, as well as a marker of gender. Men's and women's given names as well as surnames give valuable clues about the culture, for there are substantial differences in the types of names men and women had. Women's names were stereotyped; men's were much more varied. It seems as if the naming of females was conservative and also not very important. In the colonial period, a sign that someone was baptized was a first name that was a Christian saint's name. Both males and females received these names, but among the Culhuacan women, the number of given names was small.[27] Three names—María, Juana, and Ana—were by far the most common given names for women. Among the women testators, only four, including Angelina Mocel, had given names other than these three common ones. In fact, Angelina Mocel and her female kin, Bárbara, Elena, Mónica, and doña Luisa Juana, are unusual in having such a diversity of given names.

In the sixteenth century, Indians adopted Spanish names but did not follow Spanish naming patterns. Spanish practice varied somewhat at this time, but there were clear distinctions between given names and surnames, and surnames were carried on from one generation to another. Indians, following prehispanic custom, chose names individually. Prehispanic Aztec babies[28] received several names, the first for the day of its birth, the second on presentation three months later; noblemen often received a third, designating their office (often inherited from their fathers) (Motolinia, 1950:60). Indian mothers and fathers in the prehispanic and colonial eras did not pass on their names to their children. In colonial Culhuacan there are clear examples of this. One is Andrés de San Miguel, whose son was named Mateo Juárez. Nor did don Pedro de Suero and his brother have the same surname; the brother was Josef de San Marcos. Doña María Juárez's son (and also her husband) had the name Juárez, but her daughter did not.

Use of patronymic family names might have caught on to some extent among the high nobility. The Culhuacan branch of the Motecuhçoma family carried their famous name through several generations. Angelina's relative by marriage, doña Luisa Juana, was the daughter of doña María Motecuhçoma and the granddaughter of doña Juana Motecuhçoma. Another member of that family was don Diego de Motecuhçoma, the grandson of the Aztec ruler at the time of the conquest, Motecuhçoma Xocoyotzin.

An innovation which Indian nobles took to readily was the use of Spanish noble titles of *don* and *doña*. In sixteenth-century Spanish society only nobles of the highest rank had these titles, and this was likewise the case in sixteenth-century Indian society. Angelina Mocel came from a prominent family, but she was not a doña, though she had relatives who were. Her cousin, doña Elena Constantina, married into the Motecuhçoma family.[29] Doña Elena's stepdaughter, doña Luisa Juana, and the girl's mother, aunt, and grandmother were all doñas. Another noblewoman, doña María Juárez, had the Spanish title, as did her daughter, doña Ana, but not her son, who was called simply Juan Juárez (TC 246ff).

Most people had surnames or second names which also varied by gender. Both men and women often had Nahuatl second names. Men's were often quite colorful or descriptive.[30] Angelina's great uncle Antonio had the surname *tlemachica* which means "what in the world for?" Other surnames were *quenitoloc,* "what was his name?"; *cocoliloc,* "one who is detested"; *acyehuatl* "who is he?"; *xochiamatl* "flower paper." *Yaotl,* "enemy, warrior," was a popular man's surname. One man had just the surname *macehual,* "commoner." Aztec calendrical names sometimes occurred as names for men. For example, one was *acatl,* "reed," and another was *quecholli,* a type of bird, which was the name of the fourteenth "month" of the Aztec calendar.

Men, such as Angelina Mocel's father, Pablo, used titles for names. He had a Nahuatl title of *huitznahuatl* as one of his names. "Huitznahuatl" was a title of one of the four supreme military commanders of the Tenochcan armies (Códice Mendoza, 1979: f.67r). Other men had titles for names. Juan Rafael's Nahuatl name, *tlacochcalcatl,* was also an Aztec military title. Miguel Sánchez *Tlacatecuhtli* (TC 38ff) had a title which meant "ruler of people"; and Miguel *Chimaltecuhtli* had an Aztec military title which meant "shield lord." One official, Francisco Cihuatecpanecatl, seems to have used his cabildo title *regidor mayor* as part of his name, merely extending prehispanic practice of using titles as appellations. *Cihuatecpanecatl* itself is a title, indicating the head of Cihuatecpan, a Culhuacan ward.

Women most frequently had a Nahuatl second name which indicated birth-order.[31] Angelina's aunt, María Tiacapan, had one of the most stereotypical names for a Culhuacan woman. (There are four testators with that name!) *Tiacapan* means "first-born." Other birth-order names were *tlaco,* "middle child," *xoco,* "youngest," and *teicuh,* "younger sister." *Mocel,* Angelina's second name, is also a type of birth-order name meaning "only."[32] In a number of cases we can see the successive birth-order names. Pablo Huitznahuatl's wife was named Bárbara Tlaco, and her older sister was María Tiacapan (TC 174ff). Diego Sánchez's sisters are classically named Juana Tiacapan, Agustina Tlaco, and María Xoco (TC 216,219).

What were these women actually called? Did *Xoco* become *Teicuh* with the birth of another sister? Did *Teicuh* or *Tlaco* become *Tiacapan* if the eldest died? Does Angelina Mocel's name mean that she was the only child of a first marriage and her sisters Elena and Mónica are from a second union? Since parents were not shy about giving two daughters the same first name—such as the two Magdalenas of María Teicuh of Cihuatecpan (TC 230,231)—were girls called by their Nahuatl names? There was specific symbolism connected with particular saints. In the case of María Teicuh with two daughters named Magdalena, the patron saint of María's ward was Magdalena. The choice of names was likely influenced by the desire to acquire some of the religious characteristics and power of a certain saint, or a wish to honor that saint.

Because *tiacapan,* and to a lesser degree *teicuh,* occur so frequently among the Culhuacan testators, I have differentiated these women by their ward affiliations, though in native practice, women were usually identified by their ties by blood or marriage to important men. The great duplication of women's names makes it nearly impossible to trace women through several testaments.

There is sometimes a similar problem in duplication of men's names. For instance, there were several men named Juan Bautista (John the Baptist). Angelina Mocel had a nephew and heir named that, but he was not the testator of that name (TC 34ff), who died a year before Angelina. However, it is impossible to tell if the notary having that name, who practiced at the end of the 1580s, was Angelina's nephew. Positively identifying men of the same name as single or multiple persons is difficult. For example, there was a notary by the name of Juan de San Pedro and a testator of the same name (TC 170ff), but is this one person or two? The will sheds no light, for his estate contains no goods, such as pens, inkpots, or a desk, associated with the notarial profession.[33] In the case of don Pedro de Suero, it is impossible to say if he was the same man as the one who served as tlatoani at some point (TC 224ff).[34]

At the end of the colonial period, two Spanish given names came to be *the* appellation for all Indians. In sixteenth-century Culhuacan, women with two Spanish given names were a significant proportion of the women who appear in the wills.[35] Among the women testators were María Salomé, Ana Juana, María Ana, Juana Martina, and María Inés. The use of two given names seems to have been a marker of slightly higher status among women, a step above use of a birth-order name. Several women with the title doña used double first names, such as Angelina's cousin, doña Elena Constantina, as well as the latter's stepdaughter, doña Luisa Juana, and the girl's aunt, doña Luisa Isabel. Men also had double Spanish first names, but that seems to be a less frequent pattern. One town official, Diego Elías, was consistently called by those two names and seems not to have had a Nahuatl name or a title used as a name.

For both women and men, a Spanish surname indicated high status. All the known Culhuacan tlatoque had Spanish surnames. In Angelina's family, several members had Spanish names, her own husband, Juan Velázquez, for example. Saints' names were popular for surnames.[36] Pablo Huitznahuatl's full name was Pablo de San Gabriel Huitznahuatl; his "father-in-law," Antonio, was Antonio de

San Francisco Tlemachica. In the cases of Pablo and Antonio, they seem to have been known primarily by their Nahuatl names. Some men who seem to have had double Spanish first names, like Andrés Miguel, may in fact, have had saints' names as surnames. Andrés de San Miguel was called in his will both by that name and simply Andrés Miguel (TC 210ff). The notary, Juan de San Pedro, even when signing his own name, on occasion left out the "de san" (TC 72). Incidentally, the sex of the saint did not have to correspond to that of the Indian namesake, for there was an Antonio de Santa María and a doña Juana de San Gabriel.

For women, Spanish surnames were used only by high nobles, usually those with the title doña. Just mentioned is doña Juana de San Gabriel; another was doña María Juárez. Doña María had her two younger sisters who were not doñas, and who had simple birth-order names: Magdalena Tiacapan ("first born") and Ana Teicuh ("younger sister"). Likely doña María also had a birth-order name she chose to ignore[37] when she married don Andrés Juárez. She may then have taken her husband's surname and the title doña to match his don. If she did assume the title for that reason, it was not necessarily standard practice. Plain María Teicuh of Tezcacoac was married to don Juan García. She had a stereotyped birth-order name and no noble title (TC 238ff). This was similar to don Pedro de Suero's first wife Luisa Xoco ("youngest"), who was identified as a noblewoman [*cihuapilli*], but who did not have the title doña. A few Culhuacan noblewomen had the title doña, but had birth-order names. Examples are doña Ana Tiacapantzin ("honorable first child") and doña María Teicuh ("younger sister"), who was don Pedro de Suero's second wife (TC 224ff).

A Spanish surname was an indication not only of high status, but also of upward mobility and success. Some of the Culhuacan noblemen used both Nahuatl and Spanish surnames. One was Pablo de San Gabriel Huitznahuatl. High nobles with the title don did not use Nahuatl surnames, sticking tightly to their Spanish names. The alcalde Juan de San Miguel, did not have the title don but is never known by a Nahuatl name. Sometimes the use of don was not consistent, such as with don Pedro de Suero, who is referred to in his testament without his title. His second wife is also referred to variously as doña María and María (TC 224ff).

The use of a Nahuatl surname in a generation after someone was known by a Spanish surname seems to have indicated downward social movement. The trader Antonio de Santa María, referred to consistently by that name, probably because of his success, had a considerably less successful son, Luis Tlauhpotonqui (TC 134ff). Perhaps had Luis proved himself, he would have assumed a Spanish surname also. In sixteenth-century Europe as well as Mexico, naming patterns were in flux, and men may have "changed names like shirts" (LeRoy Ladurie, 1979b:154). There is evidence from Tlaxcala that noblemen assumed different Spanish names as their status rose.[38]

An option open to Indian women but not to men was marriage to Spaniards. More Spanish men than women immigrated to the New World, an imbalance that prompted Spanish men to form unions with Indian women, although most of these unions were fleeting and the women were left with the resulting children. But some Spanish men legally married Indians. In Culhuacan at this period, few people are identified as Spaniards, for contact was face to face and there was no need to say that fray Juan Núñez or his sister Elvira were Spaniards. However, we do know one Spaniard in Culhuacan married an Indian woman. Pedro Ortiz,[39] busy buying land in Culhuacan, was married to an Indian noblewoman [*cihuapilli*] from Coyoacan (TC 196,197). It is likely that Ortiz was directly trading on his connections to Indian elites to further his acquisitions of land from Indians. The unnamed noblewoman was simply identified as Ortiz's wife, with no prejudice for or against her union with a Spaniard. The marriage may well have been advantageous for both.

Culhuacan society was shaped by many factors: differences between the nobility and commoners, between rich and poor, and between men and women. Class, wealth, and gender helped determine a person's status. That someone was female, for example, said nothing about her wealth or her class. However, being female had certain ramifications. Women would have used "women's speech," probably would have been called by stereotyped names, and would have been expected to follow the work patterns of their gender. They would have been excluded from high office in both the civil and religious hierarchies. They would have been illiterate. In Culhuacan, they tended to dress in traditional clothing rather than Spanish styles. But women were not pawns without property, mere vessels for producing children. They received wealth in the form of land and houses by inheritance and dowry and asserted their claims to property through the Spanish judicial system. Regarding wealth and status, it is clear that not all elites were wealthy. Substantial differences in individual wealth occurred within elite families. Wealth correlated highly with elite status, but in a number of cases, we have evidence that there were poor nobles and wealthy nonnobles.

8 / LAND

"And Spaniards are not to buy these chinampas"

When Angelina Mocel lay dying, she had the clarity of mind to enumerate her parcels of land. "And there are seven chinampas in Acatzintitlan by the field of the late Fabián, stone mason.... And there are two chinampas in Tlacatecco, and two more in a separate place... In addition there is some dry land in Ayauhtonco of 10 [units of measure]...." (TC 180ff). She bequeathed each parcel separately, some to her family, some destined to be sold for masses. Sale of land for masses was a change in land tenure from prehispanic patterns, one of the major changes during the colonial era. In late sixteenth-century Culhuacan, there is evidence of prehispanic patterns, of shifts in patterns, and of innovations in land tenure.[1]

Angelina was typical in identifying most of her parcels by a toponym or placename, describing the kind of land, such as dry land, and giving measurements of parcels. As with most landowners, Angelina held scattered plots of land with different agricultural potentials. Most of her land came through inheritance from her father. The general pattern of scattering was exacerbated by inheritance, because with partibility, people usually bequeathed land to several heirs. Each death brought about a redistribution of land, and people often inherited from several different kin. The effect of the scattering might have been advantageous for the owners, for they would have had access to several types of land with differing agricultural potentials. This effect was by default and not planned, for unless consolidated or supplemented through purchase of land, a person's holdings were the result of the luck of being named an heir.

People noted the names of the locations of their parcels. Angelina's were in Acatzintitlan, Tlacatecco, Ayauhtonco, and Santiago Tetla. There were many toponyms in Culhuacan, some of which can be pinpointed on a map, but often the placenames were merely descriptive of soil-type or terrain. Consistent and recurrent use of these identifications indicates that although toponyms might be descriptive, nonetheless there was agreement in Culhuacan as to what places they referred.

Sometimes a field's location is given in terms of another owner's field. Angelina's declaration of owning land "in Acatzintitlan by the field of the late Fabián, stone mason" (TC 180,181) is a typical entry. That Fabián was dead did not matter a bit. References to dead owners may have been a reflection of swift change in ownership due to epidemic conditions.[2] Angelina might not have known who the new owners of Fabián's land were. Or possibly not until the heirs reached maturity or prominence would the field be identified with them rather than with the deceased owner. Only occasionally were women, living or dead, named as the owners of adjacent fields. These women were almost always nobles, such as doña María Juárez (TC 144,145). Another reason dead owners might have been referred to was that many plots of land were ordered sold for masses, and the interval between someone's death and the sale of property may have left many plots without an owner. References to dead owners, such as Angelina's to Fabián, were likely attempts to keep order in a system undergoing rapid change. That there were so few references to women holding adjacent fields may indicate that widespread ownership of land by women was a recent phenomenon, perhaps another consequence of epidemic conditions.

Angelina's careful specification of parcel locations indicates that she, like other landowners in Culhuacan, knew the boundaries of her land. Boundaries of fields were sometimes marked by stones (TC 178,179). The importance of boundary markers in the prehispanic era is evident from a law decreeing death for anyone who moved them (Alva Ixtlilxochitl, 1977:I,385). Two actions by Juan de San Miguel, Angelina's relative by marriage, indicate the boundaries of his land were known and were then marked. When he took possession of the land he inherited from his daughter doña Luisa Juana he "dug in the four corners [of the field] to show that he took possession of his land."[3] In addition, the juez-gobernador ordered confirmation of the possession "when the alguacil mayor has gone to put stakes to show the land which belongs to each one as his property."[4]

As part of the land documentation for doña Luisa Juana's estate there were cadastrals, schematic plans of parcels like modern house plats, not in the form of a map, but showing the size, shape, and sometimes the soil type. [See Figure 4]. According to Zorita (1963b: 110), calpulli heads kept pictorial records of landholding, but we have no such Culhuacan documentation, just an isolated set for one estate.

Occasionally someone did not know the boundaries or precise location of a parcel. The testator Juan Bautista, for instance, declared that "there is a field of mine in Tlallachco [measuring] 40 [units]. I am not well acquainted with where the patrimonial lands are there. I declare that if they are found, let the noblemen [*pipiltin*] aid me when they appear" (TC 34ff). In the prehispanic era, wealthy landowners from Tenochtitlan who were awarded parcels in conquered areas often had no idea where their fields were since they never worked the land themselves (Calnek, 1975). Ownership and cultivation were separate affairs. However, with few exceptions, Culhuacan owners knew where their fields were either because they worked them or because they directly oversaw their cultivation.

Descriptions of property locations give insight into Indians' conception of space. Angelina Mocel's aunt, María Tiacapan, gave the following description of one parcel, "I declare that in Xilomanco I was given [a piece of land] . . . It is three *matl* wide toward Mexico City, and toward Coyoacan it is seven *matl* long" (TC 176,177). Rather than giving a cardinal direction, she gave a local point of reference. Most houses were identified by the directions they faced. To indicate south, for instance, Angelina Mocel said a house was "facing toward Xochimilco" (TC 182,183). Nahuatl has standard terms for east and west. East is *tonatiuh yquiçayanpa ytzticac*, "facing the sun's emerging place," and west, *tonatiuh ycalaquiyanpa ytzticac*, "facing the sun's entering place." Angelina's aunt, María Tiacapan, however, used an *ad hoc* way of saying west, "toward Coyoacan." Molina's 1571 *Vocabulario* gives no standard Nahuatl term for south, probably meaning that none existed. Nahuatl has a phrase which means "toward the north side," *mictlampa*, but its meaning is primarily metaphorical, indicating "hell." Avoidance of using that term for the cardinal direction may therefore have had some religious significance. In Culhuacan, Xochimil-

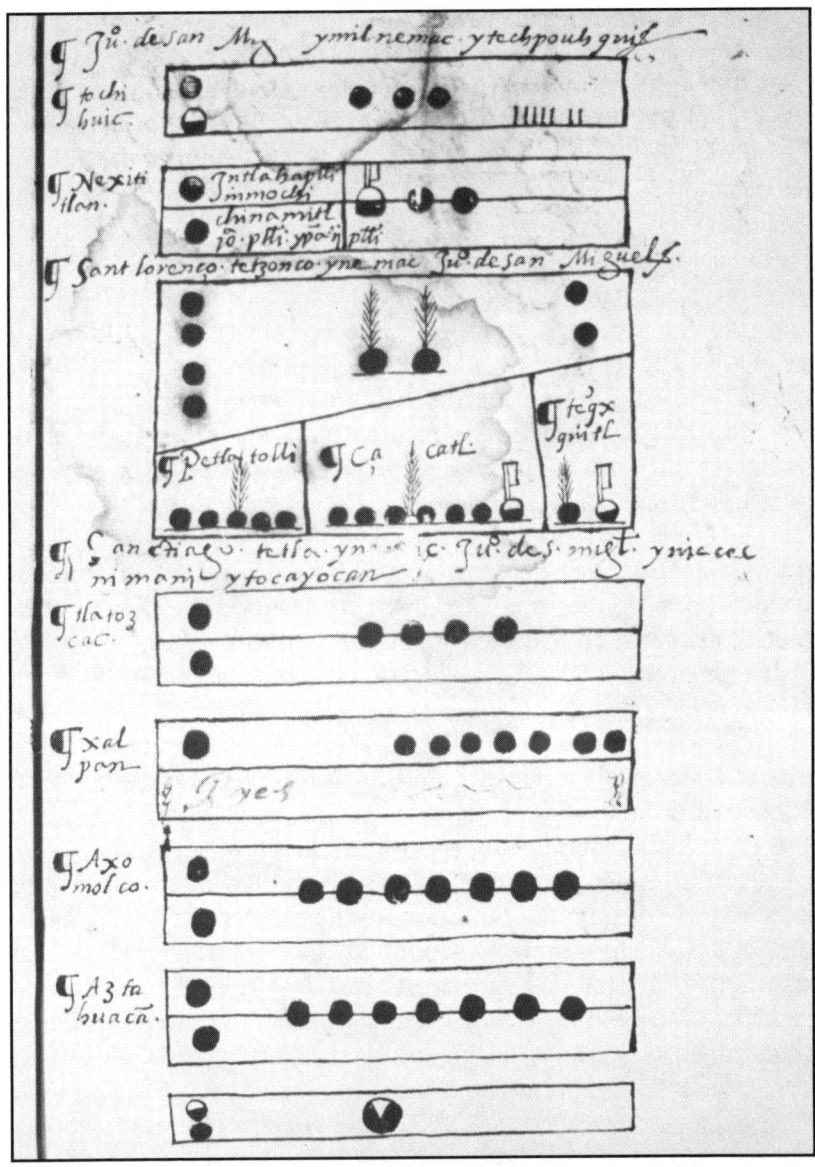

Fig. 4 Cadastral of Miguel de San Miguel's portion of doña Luisa Juana's estate. (Courtesy of the Archivo General de la Nación, México, and they reserve all rights to the reproduction of this illustration.)

co was the reference point for south; Mexico City was the reference point for north (although it was north-northwest). In Texcoco, the Spanish loanword *norte* was used as early as 1587 to fill the linguistic need for a term for north (López y Magaña, 1980:69,75).

Usually people knew the precise measurements of at least one side of their parcels. Frustratingly often, they gave the measurement for only one—making it impossible for us to calculate the area of a given parcel, though perhaps giving only one measurement meant that there was a standard width (or length?). All the terms for the linear units of measure for land were in Nahuatl, although the Spanish linear unit of the *vara* (one vara = 0.84 meters) was known and used to measure a fishing net (TC 172,175). Comparing native land measurements to each other and to European measures is difficult (Gibson, 1964:257–58; Cline, 1966:93–94). The *matl,* literally "hand/arm" in some places was equivalent to the Spanish *braza* (1.67 meters). The length suggests that the matl is a measure of a man's outstretched arms. In the colonial Spanish translation of Cristina Tiacapan's will, the translator gives *braza* as the unit of measure, though the Nahuatl will gives none, but the number of units in both documents is the same.[5]

Some people's fields were measured by the *quahuitl,* a term literally meaning "pole" or "rod" (TC 226ff; 264ff). In some places in Mexico, the quahuitl was larger than a matl but in others they seem to have been roughly equivalent. One owner of land measured in quahuitl was Angelina's cousin Bernardino Vázquez, who made his will in 1588. Another was the high noble don Pedro de Suero, whose will dates from 1572. There was not a shift in usage over time. No one described his or her land measurements in both units; the matl and the quahuitl are consistently used within a given testament.[6] Some people had other native linear units of measurement for their land. The *cenyollotli,* a term literally meaning "one heart," was a measure from the chest to the outstretched hand (Molina, 1970:sec.2,17).[7] María Tiacapan of Cihuatecpan stated that her houses had "land nine matl and a cenyollotli long, and four matl wide" (TC 20,21). A cenyollotli was smaller than a matl, perhaps exactly half.

Pablo Huitznahuatl described some of his land by a term for area. "And I declare that I assign to the city one *mecatl* [of land], 200 [units of measure] long and 20 wide" (TC 168,169). *Mecatl* literally means "cord." The measure was standard and passed into Mexican

Spanish as *mecate,* a unit 400 meters square (twenty by twenty) (Cabrera, 1974:90). Since Pablo's land is specifically two hundred by twenty, perhaps this was the standard measure in Culhuacan. This may be another example of variations of measurement in Central Mexico.[8]

Other Nahuatl units of measure such as the *cemmitl* ("one arrow"), a measure from one elbow to the fingertips of the other arm, and the *cemacolli* ("one shoulder"), a measure of shoulder to fingertips (Cline, 1966:93), were apparently not used in Culhuacan, more evidence of regional variation in units of measure.

There were glyphic representations for the native units of measure, a heart for a cenyollotli, a hand for a matl, an arrow for the cemmitl, a shoulder and arm for the cemacolli (Cline, 1966:93), for land documentation was one of the standard types of native pictorial records. In the only pictorial extant for Culhuacan, the cadastrals of doña Luisa Juana's lands, there were no units of measure given in glyphic form, though the written text gives the unit as the matl.[9]

The Culhuacan cadastrals have some unique iconographic features which differ significantly from standard native notations.[10] There were standard notations to show the numbers of the vigesimal (that is, base twenty) Aztec system. Vertical lines represent one unit of measure; twenty is shown by a black dot. For the next large unit of measure, twenty by twenty or four hundred, the standard sign was the *tzontli.* (See Table 6.) The Culhuacan cadastrals have some iconographic features which differ from these notations. Usually the vertical lines, signifying a single unit of measure up to twenty, were grouped by fives with a vertical bar across the top (making them look like combs). The Culhuacan cadastrals have the single strokes grouped together by fives, but the horizontal bar is lacking (Harvey and Williams, 1980:409). A more significant departure from standard notation is that single strokes are used only for numbers less than ten. Instead, modifications of the dot, usually meaning twenty, were used. Three-quarters of a dot meant fifteen, confirmed in the written text. Ten was indicated by half a dot.

Multiplication by twenty is usually shown by a combination of flags [*pantli*] with other signs. The Culhuacan cadastral shows the partial dots in combination with flags. A flag and full dot combination is rare since dots usually mean twenty, as do flags. The com-

Table 6 Numerical Iconography

Standard Signs		Culhuacan Signs
ı	1	ı
⁄ɪɪ\	5	ıııı ı
⁄ɪɪ\ ⁄ɪɪ\	10	◐
⁄ɪɪ\ ⁄ɪɪ\ ⁄ɪɪ\	15	◑
●	20	●
● ● ● ● ● ● ● ● ● ●	200	⚑ pantli ◐ (20 × 10)
● ● ● ● ● ● ● ● ● ● ● ● ● ● ●	300	⚑ ◑ (20 × 15)
🌿	400 (20 × 20) tzontli	🌿

bination of the two yields four hundred, which can be shown more succinctly by the tzontli sign. However, the half dot for ten and three-quarters of a dot when multiplied by twenty (as indicated by the flag on top) allows easy visual representation of measurements of two hundred and three hundred. This is less cumbersome than the rows of dots normally used elsewhere. In general, the visual representation of measurements and the written text describing doña Luisa Juana's lands are in accord. However, from time to time the cadastral and the written text do not jibe. The questions are then which was more accurate and which did the officials accept as more accurate? Cadastrals had a long history in Central Mexico, but Nahuatl texts were a recent innovation. This suggests that native maps and cadastrals may have been accepted as more accurate descriptions. Often written texts merely describe in words what a pictorial shows.

Most fields were rectangular, but sometimes hilly terrain with ravines or other natural barriers prevented regular shapes. Chinampas might be distorted because of canals as shown, for instance, in the sixteenth-century map known as the Maguey Plan (Calnek, 1973). Descriptions for these irregularly shaped fields were fairly precise. Don Pedro de Suero had a "pointed field that is eight quahuitl at one end and just one quahuitl at the other, and is 160 in length" (TC 226,227).

In Culhuacan there were different zones of cultivation, chinampas at the lakeshore, level land, and the uplands on the Cerro de la Estrella. Also recognized were several types of soil as well as different terrains. Nahuatl has a highly developed vocabulary for soils, distinguishing them by texture, organic or chemical content, color, and topographic position (Sahagún, XI:250–58; Williams, 1976). Many Culhuacan testators indicated the soil type of their parcels, such as dry land [*teuhtlalli*] and level land [*tlalmantli*]. The various types of land allowed cultivation of different crops. Chinampa cultivation usually revolved around fresh vegetables, while upland soils permitted maguey cultivation.

Angelina's holdings of several parcels of chinampas were typical. Chinampas are artificially built-up extensions of farmland into Lake Chalco-Xochimilco. What are commonly known as chinampas are called *chinamitl* in the Culhuacan wills. *Chinamitl* is defined as a "woven structure or enclosure of reeds."[11] The term which passed into Mexican Spanish is *chinampa*,[12] although colonial Spanish documentation often calls them *camellones,* "ridges between furrows." Spanish land sales records of the 1580s mention *chinanpas*, and one of the Augustinians in Culhuacan, who presumably knew Nahuatl, called them *chinantles* (TC 92).[13] In the Culhuacan wills, testators usually list only the number of chinampas and do not identify them as such. For example, Pablo Huitznahuatl declared that "in Çacaapan there are eight [chinampas] which I give to Juan. . . ." (TC 166,169). The land is identified as chinampas by the context, and in this case a later clarification states that "the aforesaid eight chinampas are next to the field of the noble lady, my niece doña Elena Constantina" (TC 168,169).

From other historical and modern sources, we know that chinampa cultivation was (and is) not only intensive but also highly productive. According to estimates, one man can work between one half and three-quarters hectares of chinampa land with an estimate for the productivity of one hectare supplying the food needs of fifteen to twenty people.[14]

The fertility of the soil was maintained by mucking it with aquatic plants and mud and, in the colonial period, probably nightsoil as well (Armillas, 1961:266–67; Clavijero, 1976:229–30). The layout of the chinampas allows the root systems to have a continuous supply of water, and cultivation can be independent of rainfall. In Central Mexico the mild climate permits a continuous growing season (West and Armillas, 1950:180). Culhuacan's first chinampas are the earliest known, dating from the twelfth century (Blanton, 1970:333). Half of Culhuacan's estimated population of four thousand were dependent on chinampa agriculture in the fifteenth and sixteenth centuries (Parsons, 1976:242). Foodstuffs produced on chinampas throughout the southern lake region were transported to Tenochtitlan as tribute and as commodities for sale in the markets there. Possibly as early as the fifteenth century the chinampa zone expanded in response to the capital city's needs (Calnek, 1975).[15]

In one colonial report, Torquemada noted (1975:II,483) that "without much trouble [the Indians] plant and harvest their maize and greens, for all over there are ridges called chinampas; these were strips built above water and surrounded by ditches, which obviates watering." Chinampa construction was described by another colonial observer. "They make garden plots . . . carrying in canoes sod cut on the mainland, to heap it up in shallow waters, thus forming ridges from 3 to 4 *varas* wide and rise half a *vara* above the water" (Armillas, 1971:653). Sometimes complicated forms could result from what were previously separated mounds or small islands (West and Armillas, 1950:167), but in general chinampas were long, narrow strips.

The idea that chinampas were floating gardens—as in the "floating gardens of Xochimilco"—probably arose from errors in Spaniards' observations of an unfamiliar agricultural system. On the other hand, some Indians did use movable nurseries which were towed with "ropes from one place to another within the lagoon" (Armillas, 1971:653). Spaniards might have mistaken these movable nurseries for chinampas.

Since chinampas extended into the lakes and were not highly elevated above the water, they were subject to flooding. During the rule of the Tenochcan king Ahuitzotl (d. 1502), chinampas were flooded in Tenochtitlan by the rising lake level, perhaps owing to the construction of an aqueduct (Davies, 1973:194). Chinampas had been destroyed there a century earlier (about 1380) by overly abundant rainfall (Berlin, 1948:52). In the Uppsala Map of the midsixteenth century, Culhuacan is shown as an island (Linné, 1948), recording another period of flooding. In 1580, rising water levels were once again a problem in Culhuacan. Miguel de Santiago Ecatl ordered some of his chinampas sold "when the water has left [them]" (TC 118,119). He obviously was expecting the flooding to pass.

People only occasionally said how big their chinampas were; usually they just listed the number they had. The standard length seems to have been twenty matl long. Juana Tiacapan of Aticpac had "two chinampas that do not measure a full 20 matl each, but just 10 each" (TC 66,67). María Teicuh of Cihuatecpan had "in Acatzintitlan... four chinampas, each one 40 [units of measure] long and two small ones" (TC 230,231). That she mentioned their sizes is probably because they deviated from the standard. Angelina's cousin Bernardino Vázquez had chinampa land which was "in width, toward Mexico City [i.e., north] 45 [units of measure] and toward Coyoacan [i.e., west] 55" (264ff), but he does not say how many individual chinampas there were. For large plots of chinampa land this situation might be typical. Don Pedro de Suero (TC 226,227) had chinampa land measuring 300 × 20 [quahuitl]. María Salomé had chinampa land measuring 380 × 20 [matl].[16] María, like some other people (TC 26,27; 32,33; 40,41), had chinampas that she measured by the number of furrows [*cuemitl*] they contained, "the land at the edge of the water, five [chinampas], each with 15 furrows" (TC 26,27).

Chinampa land was the standard type that people owned. Among the Culhuacan testators almost a third of their chinampa holdings were in groups of seven. By the way some people refer to other groups of chinampas, it seems seven was some kind of ideal number. For instance, Tomás de Aquino had "some chinampas... which count as seven, and only with the land at the edge of the water do they come to be seven" (TC 64,65). Mariana, the wife of Juan Rafael Tlacochcalcatl, bequeathed some chinampas which would have been seven "when they are complete" (TC 130,131).[17] The trader Luis Tlauhpotonqui had only six chinampas in Motlauhxauhcan because "they stole one" (TC 138,139). Support for seven as an ideal number is found in the sixteenth-century map called the Maguey Plan, from an area under Atzcapolzalco's control (Calnek, 1972:190), in which each house site has seven chinampas.[18]

There seems to be some empirical reason for seven being the ideal number of chinampas, for seven is approximately the number needed to support one person for a year. As we have noted, an estimate of productivity of chinampas indicates one hectare supports fifteen to twenty people for a year. Taking the more conservative estimate of fifteen people, then 667 m² of chinampas land will support one person. In Culhuacan, chinampas seem to have standardly been twenty matl or 33.4 m long (one matl = 1.67 meters). Taking the average of the estimate of chinampas' width of three to four varas (one vara = .84 meter) we get that a chinampa was 3.5 varas or 2.9 m wide. The area of one chinampa is 97 m² and of seven chinampas 679 m². Thus the area of seven chinampas is very close to the estimate of 667 m² to support one person.

Chinampas often accompanied people's houses, and the two were often bequeathed together. Houses in Culhuacan may have been interspersed among chinampas as shown in the Maguey Plan and in plans of Mexico City house sites (Calnek, 1973;1974a). In Culhuacan the number of "house chinampas" varied from the canonical seven, from just two or three to five or six.[19] Angelina Mocel bequeathed a house "and all the chinampas which accompany it" to her nephew Juan Bautista (TC 180,181). When no number is specified, the amount of land remains a mystery. But Angelina's chinampas came from her father, Pablo Huitznahuatl, who had given her the house which "has seven chinampas at the border of the water" (TC 166,167). Some people referred to the chinampas near their houses as *atentlalli,* a word literally meaning "land by the edge of the water." This term is descriptive and seems not to have been a standard elsewhere; perhaps it was simply a Culhuacan toponym.[20]

Chinampas seem to have been the most common type of land attached to houses, suggesting that houses were near the shore line or canals. However, some people had *tlalmantli,* "level or leveled land," attached to their houses (TC 26,27). María Icnocihuatl's only possessions were her house and "the level land, only six matl of it, on which the house stands" (TC 78,79). In Sahagún's description of tlalmantli, he says, in fact, that "houses are there" (Sahagún, XI:252). Land which was tied to bequests of houses in some cases seems not to be directly adjacent to the houses, but someplace else entirely, and only attached in the legal sense (TC 256,257).[21]

Callalli, the Nahuatl word for house land (*calli,* "house"; *tlalli,* "land"), is not generally used in the late sixteenth century to describe the plot on which a house stood. In Culhuacan, one woman used the term callalli to describe chinampas attached to her house (TC 130,131). Sahagún includes this term in his listing of soil types,

Table 7 Toponyms Associated with Chinampas

Acalomac	Atotolco Atezcapan	Quaxochtenco
Acalotenco	Çacaapan	Quetzalapan
Acatzintitlan	Coatlantonco	Teccizco
Acoçac	Coltonco	Tecuitlaapan
Acpac	Cueptecco	Tlanepantonco
Ahuacatitlan	Cuicapantzin	Tepanecapan
Ayacac	Ecatitlan	Tequancuilco
Ayahualolco	Iyauhtenco	Tequixquipan
Amoxcuitlac	Ixtlapanco	Tlacatecco
Amoxentlac	Motlauhxauhcan	Tlacuexchiuhcan
Apilco (Tetla)	Nextitlan	Tlamaztonco
Atechcalcan	Petlacontitlan	Tolman
Atexcatenco	Quauhtenanco	Tomatla
Atlymopilohuaya	Quaxochco	Tonalecan
Atotocoyan		

saying that "this is the land on which a house has rested and also surrounding houses. It is fertile, it germinates" (Sahagún, XI:252). Soil around houses may have been especially fertile because of garbage and human wastes discarded there (Williams, 1976:117); however, people would want to build houses near good, fertile locations in the first place.

The Spanish word for houselot, *solar,* was in standard usage. In sixteenth-century Culhuacan, this is the only nonnative land term. The loanword solar had come into Nahuatl by 1550 (Karttunen and Lockhart, 1976:56).[22] The appearance may well have been related to the establishment of Spanish city forms (such as the cabildo and the physical rearrangement of Indian towns) around that time.

Sizes of houselots varied. Ana Juana's was large: fifteen matl by ten matl (around twenty-five by seventeen meters) (TC 80,81). Marcos Hernández described his houselot vaguely: it was only "8 matl toward Mexico City and toward the west it goes as far as the small water flowers" (TC 276ff). Angelina Mocel's cousin Bernardino Vázquez had a houselot which was probably large, but he, like Marcos Hernández, described it by its location. "And the houselot here is 45 [quahuitl] wide toward Mexico City, counted as far as where it reaches the edge of the water; and toward Coyoacan it just extends up to where my younger siblings exit [or where their land ends?]" (TC 264,265). It seems likely that Bernardino's houselot was from the division of an estate, since his land adjoins his younger brothers'.

Tlalmantli, level land, has been seen in the context of house land, but it was often just another type of agricultural land. The term for "level land" merely describes the topography and says nothing about soil types. Compound terms for land often include tlalmantli as an lexical element. For example, one testator owned *huehuetlalmantli* "patrimonial level land," (TC 214,215) and doña Luisa Juana owned *tequixquiçacatlalmantli* "nitrous soil with zacate which is level land."[23]

Tequixquitlalli, nitrous land, is described by Sahagún as "salty, corrosive, that which is leached...; unwanted undesirable. It is waste, disregarded.... It is abandoned; it lies useless" (Sahagún, XI:254). Despite this uninviting description, nitrous soil was useful for the manufacture of soap in the Texcoco area (Gibson, 1964:339). Doña Luisa Juana's nitrous soil had zacate growing on it.[24] Supplying Mexico City with zacate as fodder was one of Culhuacan's economic functions (Gallegos, 1927:172), so this land was doubtless not as useless as Sahagún's informants thought. One of the toponyms where chinampas were located was Tequixquipan "in the area of the nitrous [soil/land]" (TC 192,193).

Another type of land which was more typical of Culhuacan holdings was *teuhtlalli,* dry land (*teuhtli* "dust"; *tlalli* "land"). This was apparently a type of topsoil found on the upland slopes of mountains (Sahagún, XI:253). In the Culhuacan area, dry land was found in Huixachtlan, on the slopes of the Cerro de la Estrella, the mountain which dominates Culhuacan's landscape. The toponym comes from the Aztec name for the mountain, Huixachtecatl. In Culhuacan, the amount of dry land owned was second only to people's chinampa holdings.

Another category of land listed by testators is *tlalmilli* (*tlalli,* land; *milli,* field). Molina's 1571 *Vocabulario* (sec.2,124) gives "*tierras o heredades de particulares que están juntas en alguna vega,* etc." (lands or small farms belonging to individuals which are together in some fertile plain or the like); Siméon defines it more simply as cultivated land.[25] Gibson equates tlalmilli to calpulli lands (Gibson, 1964:267), but I suggest that our knowlege of tlalmilli is less clear-cut than this would indicate. Plots of Culhuacan tlalmilli were found in several different locations.[26] Some owners included men in Angelina Mocel's family, her father, Pablo Huitznhuatl, and her husband, Juan Velázquez.

Pablo Huitznahuatl owned some land he called *quauhtlalli* (TC 166ff). The term could derive from *quahuitl,* "trees," and be soil fertilized by humus of leaves or rotten wood that Sahagún described (XI:251). Or the term could derive from *quauhtli,* "eagle," and denote a civil category of land, a type of conquered land. For instance, quauhtlalli in Atlixocan was conquered land (Calnek, 1975:13). Someone else in Culhuacan who owned quauhtlalli was Juan Rafael Tlacochcalcatl. His was a type of patrimonial land (TC 144,145). The confusion about what the quauhtlalli was—a soil type or a civil category—is interesting because while the written Nahuatl is ambiguous, a glyph would have left no confusion. The old system of glyphic depiction in this one case is superior to the new system of description in Nahuatl.[27] Since both Pablo Huitznahuatl tecuhtli and Juan Rafael Tlacochcalcatl have traditional military titles as part of their names, I am inclined to think the Culhuacan quauhtlalli was a civil category of land, residual holdings of Aztec "conquered land."

The different types of soil in Culhuacan allowed several different crops to be cultivated or gathered. Maize and beans were the center of the native diet. They could be planted on any land with adequate water, such as chinampas. Plants growing on marshy land were gathered rather than cultivated. One such plant was *petlatolli,*[28] a type of reed used for matmaking (Sahagún, XI:195), and another was zacate, the grass used for fodder. Doña Luisa Juana had land with *tequixquiçacatl,* another type of reed which was rougher and coarser than zacate (Sahagún, XI:153).[29] On the upland slopes, magueys were grown.

Maguey cultivation was important because the plant had (and

Table 8 Toponyms Associated with Tlalmilli

Huixachtlan	Tepetlaixquac	Tomatla
Yahualiuhcan	Tlatepotzco	
Ocelotepec	Tochihuic	
Tepec Xallahuahco	Tocitlan	

has) multiple uses. Maguey [*Agave americana*] is an Arawak loanword into Spanish; the Nahuatl term for this plant is *metl*. They were (and are) used as boundary markers on fields while at the same time they prevent soil erosion. From other sources we know that the heart of the maguey, the stem and the thorns were all used. The fibre could be made into cloth or rope. Its most important use now is as the source of *aguamiel,* "honey water," from which the alcoholic pulque is fermented. Liquid accumulates when the plant is rasped, a process alluded to by Domingo Yaotl, who owned magueys. "I have six magueys here at the entrance [of the property, i.e. border]. I give them to my child named Andrés Ilpitoc. He is to scrape them [to get the juice], and it will be used for him" (TC 52,53).

A maguey reaches maturity, defined by the first production of aguamiel, in about seven years (Palerm, 1967). People in Culhuacan often mentioned the size of their magueys, giving a rough estimate of the plants' maturity. For example, Lucía Teicuh had a large field "with magueys that are not large yet because they have just recently been planted" (TC 124,125). Vicente Xochiamatl owned a number of different parcels with magueys. "I am distributing among my children my 20 magueys that are already big, part of them are to be sold to pay the tribute" (TC 112,113).[30] Magueys could be bequeathed or sold separately.

Although what Indians cultivated was largely unaffected by European imports, there were some exceptions. In the 1580s, European fruit trees were growing in Culhuacan. In the Texcoco region, these imports appear growing on nobles' lands, under sophisticated cultivation, as early as twenty years after the conquest (Cline, 1966:101). In Culhuacan one owner of fruit trees was a noble, doña María Juárez. She ordered that "my field in Coatlan, with peach trees on it . . . is to be sold in order to say masses for me. . . . No Spaniard is to buy [the field], but . . . only the citizens here" (TC 250,251). While doña María was hostile to the idea of her fruit trees passing into Spaniards' hands, another woman, Ana Tiacapan of Amantlan, was not, leaving open the possibility that the Spanish friars would get them. "The fruit trees, the pears and the figs that are in the patio are to be sold" for masses (TC 57,58). Apparently they were close to the house (which she also ordered sold) because she said, "Whoever buys the house will pay for all of it, but if the person buying the house doesn't come to agreement, the fruit trees will belong to the church and will be used for the friars" (TC 58,59). The Relación geográfica of the nearby town of Mexicatzinco reports that there were whole orchards of European fruit trees there in 1580 (Paso y Troncoso, 1979:198). Native fruit trees, such as the native cherry tree [*capolin; Prunus capuli*] that Juan Velázquez owned, continued to be cultivated (TC 204,205).

Another type of tree growing in the region was the native willow [*huexotl*], which people also bequeathed separately.[31] Willows grew on the banks of lakes and small pools and on the edges of chinampas, perhaps anchoring the soil (Paso y Troncoso, 1979:197; West and Armillas, 1950:173ff). They may also have acted as boundary markers, for Melchor de Santiago Ecatl describes them as being "at the entrance" of his property (TC 116,177).

In the cultivation of crops, Indians used a variety of fairly simple native tools, most of them being hand tools rather than those powered by feet (Rojas, 1984:176). The *huitzoctli* was a digging stick made of hardwood, whose tip was hardened by fire, used for making holes for seeds or upending soil (Rojas, 1984:178). Don Juan Téllez's huitzoctli was valued at a mere half a tomín (TC 40,41). Another tool was the *tlaltepoztli,* likely a hoe or spade with a metal base, which was more valuable than the huitzoctli, for Mateo Juárez paid six tomines for his (TC 74,75).[32] Another tool with metal components was the *tepozhuictli,* a hand and foot digging stick with a metal tip or blade,[33] which was used as the symbol of a tribute laborer (Rojas, 1984:184). The one that Juana Tiacapan of Coatlan owned was small [*tepozhuictontli*], perhaps scaled down because she used it herself (TC 108,109).[34] Some native women were involved in agricultural work, participating in planting and harvesting (Torquemada, 1979:II,481), although in Culhuacan this may not have been typical.[35] Despite the simplicity of the tools Indians used in agriculture, there were surpluses of crops which were rendered in tribute or sold in the market to support large populations of non-agricultural laborers.

In addition to the highly developed terminology to denote different types of terrain and soil, Nahuatl has many terms for civil categories of land which indicated distinct forms of tenure. Civil categories of land in Culhuacan show evidence of the general trends in the Valley of Mexico toward elimination of some prehispanic categories of land, shifts in categories, and new categories (Gibson, 1964:257ff). Prehispanic categories included land attached to the office of tlatoani [*tlatocatlalli*]; land devoted to the support of temples [*teotlalli*]; private lands of the nobility [*pillalli*]; lands attached to the *tecpan* or court [*tecpantlalli*]; and lands held by the calpulli [*calpullalli*].

Specific information on Culhuacan land tenure before the conquest is nonexistent, so this discussion relies on reports of land tenure from other regions. Regional variation in patterns is known to have existed, and for this reason, we cannot be sure that descriptions of what occurred elsewhere are valid for Culhuacan. The principal sources on land tenure are Alonso de Zorita for the Cuauhtinchan area (Baudot, 1976:451ff), and Alva Ixtlilxochitl and Juan de Torquemada for Tlaxcala or Texcoco.[36] Zorita cautions (1963b:86) that "if what I say here appears to contradict some other information, the cause must be the diversity that exists in all things in this province [i.e., Mexico]."

Late sixteenth-century Culhuacan still had land called by terms for prehispanic civil categories, but it also had other types not appearing in those sources. Some of these are inherited land [*huehuetlalli*], purchased land [*tlalcohualli*], and *cihuatlalli,* "woman land," all of which are found in other Central Mexican Nahuatl documention, suggesting that these were also fundamental.

In the late sixteenth century, the category of tlatocatlalli, ruler's office land, was considerably modified from its prehispanic tenure. According to prehispanic definition, office lands were held by the person who succeeded to the office of tlatoani (Alva Ixtlilxochitl, 1977:I,90), and were not personal property to be sold or bequeathed. In practice, the tlatoani's family would have benefited from the land over several generations, since the office of tlatoani itself was generally inherited. In late sixteenth-century Culhuacan, the only person known to hold ruler's office land, Miguel Cerón, was *not* a ruler, but a man who was awarded the land by court judgment (TC 62,63).

We know several things about Cerón's piece of office land: the size of the plot, the soil type, the toponym of its location, and how the land compared to his other holdings. The land in question was a seventy by twenty [matl?] plot of dry land [teuhtlalli]. Likely Cerón's award of office land was only a fraction of the original. The *Libro de las tasaciones* says that in 1552, Culhuacan Indians worked "in common" a four hundred by one hundred braza plot for the gobernador,[37] while in 1575 a plot was also worked for him, but the size is unspecified (González de Cosío, 1952:156). Records for other towns mention office lands measuring four hundred by four hundred or two hundred by two hundred brazas (Gibson, 1964:260). In Culhuacan the office land was in Tocititlan, a toponym of undetermined location, where some important people, including Pablo Huitznahuatl, had land.[38] All of Cerón's other land consisted of chinampas, so his acquisition of a plot of dry land represented a diversification of his holdings. Notably, Cerón's estate was quite small overall.

It is important the land retained the classification tlatocatlalli even though it no longer functioned to support the tlatoani. Probably the land was well-known as such, just as other land was known as church land. In addition, there was continued identification of land with dead owners, previously mentioned.

How Cerón acquired the office land is significant. It was awarded by court judgment [*justiciatica*].[39] However, the legal grounds on which the award was made were not given in the will. *Justicia* [justice] usually implies the Spanish courts, which would mean dispute, litigation, appeal, and settlement at a higher level. Likely then, the matter was not settled locally. In other places, tlatoque had successfully argued before Spanish courts that the office land was their personal patrimony (Gibson, 1964:260). Perhaps this happened in Culhuacan also. Although Cerón does not have the title tlatoani nor does he mention any connection to the family, likely there was some link.[40] The land may have passed into Cerón's hands because it had not been cultivated. Some office lands might have been converted to community lands [*sementeras de la comunidad*] prior to 1560. The Crown threatened sale or forfeiture of lands if they were not cultivated (Gibson, 1964:261). The fact that Cerón carefully noted that he had received the land by court judgment probably indicated the insecurity of his tenure.

By 1580, and probably earlier, Culhuacan "office lands" seem to have lost all resemblance to the prehispanic category. Cerón treated the land as his private property. He divided it, ordering part sold and bequeathing the rest to his chosen heirs. Unfortunately, no Culhuacan tlatoani's testament is known to survive, so it is not known whether all tlatocatlalli had undergone transformation in the sixteenth century.

In prehispanic Mexico, temples were supported by specific lands called *teotlalli*, "sacred lands." In colonial Culhuacan, there are references to *teopanmilli* [or *teopantlalli*], which apparently were lands connected with the Christian church. The similarity of terminology suggests a similarity of meanings: "lands to support religious activity." However, there are fundamental differences between the prehispanic temple lands and the lands called teopanmilli in colonial Culhuacan.

Although there are few references to church land, those that do exist provide considerable information about its complex status. Culhuacan church land was not residual temple land. This is consistent with findings for other Central Mexican localities, for, in general, prehispanic temple lands were not systematically taken over in the colonial period to support the Church (Gibson, 1964:258). The Culhuacan noblewoman doña María Juárez declared that "my field in Tlallachco is not to be sold, but is just to be rented out each year, and with the money that is acquired there, masses are to be said for us. This is all the land with which our souls will be helped. I mention, appoint, and request two people to speak for us, the executors Miguel García, [notary of the] church, and Martín Lázaro, deputy. If they die, new people are to be named to take care of it" (TC 250,251). She thus set up a perpetual trust for herself, putting Culhuacan officials in charge of it, and making provision for their replacement. The Church did not have direct control of the property, but it benefited from the income (as presumably did the soul of doña María).

Doña María did not herself call her land teopanmilli, but the testator Juan Rafael Tlacochcalcatl did. "This said [field] of mine borders with the field of the church that doña María Juárez left" (TC 144,145). Thus, the status of that particular piece of property was public knowledge.

One of the executors for doña María's church land was Miguel García, a notary, who listed church land in his own will. The status of his land is more complicated. Miguel had given most of his land to his nephew Gabriel Nentlamati and seems to have been putting Gabriel in charge of the church land as well. "And the seven [chinampas] that are in San Pedro Çacaapan also correspond to [are charged to?/the responsibility of?] Gabriel; they are our church land next to the chinampas of the late Francisco González" (TC 104,105). García had another parcel of church land, "in the land of Tlamacazco, there is also a church field of ours, 20 [units of measure] long and the same on all sides" (TC 104,105).

The legal status of Miguel's church land is less than clear. It is possible that the land he called church land was property whose revenues were set aside by him for support of the local church, with his family retaining control of the property. This would be somewhat similar to doña María's arrangement, except that in her case, she put non-kin in charge of the endowment. Doña María's scheme of land rental to aid her soul continuously is reminiscent of the Spanish institution of endowing masses from a lien on property, the *capellanía*, discussed previously.

Occasionally, property was deeded directly to a local religious institution, as in the case of Juana Martina. "And the level land that is at the entrance of Miguel Josef, deputy['s property], I assign to [the church of] our mother Santa María Magdalena" (TC 256,257), the church of her ward. In this bequest to her ward's saint, there were no strings attached, though presumably Juana would be rewarded in heaven. Angelina Mocel's great-uncle, Antonio Tlemachica, provided an endowment of land for religious purposes but the church was not in charge of it. He gave land to the "city elders, those in charge of Culhuacan" who might "raise a cross there or build something else there" (TC 98,99).

While the church lands were not residual temple lands, the practice of support of religious activity from specific land was a prehispanic tradition.[41] How do the prehispanic and postconquest lands to support religion compare? The general accounts indicate certain lands were owned by the temples. Other lands had a portion of their crop earmarked for delivery on a regular basis to the temples. The revenues from the lands seem to have been dedicated to the general support of the priests and festivals, apparently systematic support of religion.[42] On the other hand, church land in Culhuacan, to judge from the case of doña María Juárez's, was to generate income for masses for *individuals*. In other words, the income was primarily for personal salvation. The rent from doña María's land was a fee for service rather than generalized support of the clergy.[43] Church land in Culhuacan operated on a more piecemeal basis than the organized system of lands and tributes which supported prehispanic temples. In general, temple lands ceased to exist as a civil category after the Conquest, with the land usurped by Spaniards and Indians alike and diverted to secular use (Gibson, 1964:258). Church land in colonial Culhuacan was a new civil category beginning to develop.

Another prehispanic category of land is *tecpantlalli*, lands for support of the *tecpan*, the noble houses. Those who lived on the land and cultivated it were called *tecpanpouhqui* or *tecpantlaca*, "palace people." According to Torquemada, the palace people worked these lands in individual plots. Fathers could pass those plots on to their sons, but were not allowed to sell them. If a person died without heirs or moved to another place, his house and land remained in the hands of the tecpan (Torquemada, 1975:II,164). Palace people paid no tribute and had a higher status than commoners (Torquemada, 1975,II,164; Alva Ixtlilxochitl, 1977:II,91). We have nothing to corroborate these accounts for late sixteenth-century Culhuacan. This special category of commoners likely became absorbed in the general macehual population (Gibson, 1964:261).

In Culhuacan, the tecpan of the ward of Coatlan was involved in land matters with a resident of Tezcacoac, a Culhuacan ward. Melchor de Santiago Ecatl declared he had "patrimonial land [of the] tecpan of Coatlan that I was given, 60 [units of measure] and 60 wide" (TC 118,119). Melchor did not say why he got the land. In the town of Cuauhtinchan, the various lands of each *teccalli* [*tecpancalli*] taken together were called *huehuetlalli* ("patrimonial land") and included private lands of nobles and office lands (Reyes, 1978: 8). In Culhuacan the patrimonial land of the tecpan that Melchor had was to be sold for masses. The official who measured the land, Pedro de San Nicolás, knew about the proposed sale, so probably the tecpan was aware that the land was not reverting to it but was being alienated.

Some of doña María Juárez's land was connected to the tecpan of Caltenco. She alluded to another testament concerning the tecpancalli and then listed "all the house chinampas of the tecpan, the fields in Amaxac, and the "woman land" [*cihuatlalli*] in Huixachtlan, and the other [land] in Huixachtlan... and the (wet, sandy land? [*axalli*]) in Coatlan next to the field of don Juan Téllez who sows his part of it, and the cultivated land [tlalmilli] in Tomatla, and other lands in Tociçolco; all will go along with the tecpancalli" (TC 248,249). She seems to have had control over the land, since she listed it in her will, but perhaps she merely received the income from it. However, she ordered the sale of one of these parcels. "I mention again the piece [of land] in Tomatla. All the chinampas are to be sold in order to pay the 15 pesos which belong to Diego Ramírez, the inspector" (TC 248,249).[44]

Doña María seems to have had clearer title to other land of the tecpan, some of which she sold. "As to the house chinampas of the tecpan that the judge [*juez*] Juan de los Angeles declared to be its house chinampas, there are 20 of them, each one 20 [units of measure] long. I have divided them; 10 of them I alienated, as all the ward heads of Santa Ana Cal[tenco] know, and the other 10 still belong to me, for they are my property and inheritance" (TC 248,249). As with the owner of the ruler's office lands [tlatocatlalli], doña María received her land through the Spanish legal system. The relationship between the ward heads and the tecpan is unclear, but she seems to have been trying to forestall difficulties, perhaps with the ward heads themselves, about her sale of her tecpan land by noting their knowledge of the sale.

The status of Culhuacan tecpan land is murky. The examples found in the Culhuacan wills indicate a complex picture, not closely related to the descriptions found in the standard sources. Perhaps this is a case of regional variation of patterns, or the difference might be attributable to changes over time from prehispanic patterns. Clearly the Spanish legal system had some effect on the tenure of tecpan lands, with the award to doña María. But to what degree the other variant forms of tenure can be chalked up to direct Spanish intervention is not known.

Most sources on prehispanic land tenure include the category of *pillalli*, private lands which nobles controlled as individuals. This type of land contrasts with prehispanic tlatocatlalli, land attached to the office of ruler, described above. There were several types of prehispanic pillalli, some belonging to minor lords and descendants of kings and lords, while others pertained to lesser nobles (Torquemada, 1975:II,545–46). The important fact about this type of land was that some types could be sold. Although certain restrictions applied to the ownership of pillalli, these lands were the private property of the owners and could be bequeathed to multiple heirs or alienated.[45]

There was no identifiable pillalli in Culhuacan, although we have the wills of known elites, identified by titles, and know their landholdings were often extremely large. Examples are don Pedro de Suero (TC 224ff), doña María Juárez (TC 246ff), and doña Luisa Juana.[46] However, none of their land is called pillalli. Over the whole colonial period, there was a shifting and elimination of land categories. It is likely that with widespread private ownership of land by Indians—and extensive alienation of land—that there was simply no need specifically to distinguish pillalli from other private holdings.

Calpulli land [*calpullalli*] is the final general category of land found in the principal sources. As we have previously discussed, the calpulli is generally taken to be a fundamental unit of social organization, based on kinship or residence or perhaps some combination of the two. According to the report of the Spanish judge, Alonso de Zorita, the calpulli held title to the land, but the person who worked it could bequeath it to his chosen heirs. However, the land could not be alienated. If the land was not worked or if the holder had no heirs, it reverted to the calpulli for redistribution (Zorita, 1963b:107ff). Applying this description to all areas indiscriminately is inadvisable, since regional variation was rife, as Zorita himself noted.

In other sixteenth-century Central Mexican documentation, the term *calpullalli* appears. In Morelos, certain lands pertaining to the Marquesado del Valle were called calpullalli and subject to tribute (Reyes, 1979:28).[47] In Epatlan, Puebla, calpulli land was in effect land of the nobles (Reyes, 1979:26ff). Examples from Mexico City documents show calpulli to be temples, and the land called calpullalli was land pertaining to the cults (Reyes, 1979:42). Fray Diego Durán's account is in accord with this interpretation, saying that land was given "to each barrio, for the cult of the gods, and these lands are now called calpullalli, which is to say 'land dedicated to the barrios'" (Durán, 1967:II,83,50).

In early colonial documentation there are different definitions for the term calpulli and diverse meanings for calpullalli itself. The following is a description of what we *do* know about Culhuacan calpulli land. Of the several hundred parcels of land held by Culhuacan testators, only two plots were specifically labeled calpullalli.[48] Why more land is not called calpulli land is an interesting question. It might be that most land was, in fact, calpulli land, but not specifically called that because the meaning was understood. Another possibility is that the calpulli held title to the land and people therefore did not generally list it in their wills. I view this as unlikely since people mentioned other land they worked which they did not own.

Gerónimo Teuhcihuatl specifically identified only one of his parcels as calpulli land, while the rest are simply identified by their locations (TC 184ff). In the case of Juan Rafael Tlacochcalcatl, the calpulli land was only one of many parcels identified by civil category (TC 142ff). His other land included purchased land [*tlalcohualli*] and inherited or patrimonial land [*huehuetlalli*]. Just one of his parcels lacked identification by civil category. The term calpullalli might have been used in his testament to distinguish the land from the purchased land listed immediately before it. Juan Rafael Tlacochcalcatl said there were "seven chinampas that are calpulli land" (TC 144,145).

Both men who owned land specifically called calpulli land were residents of the ward of Coatlan. Neither parcel had a toponym indicating a location, so there is a good possibility that the land was also located in Coatlan. The fact that both men were Coatlan residents might have had a bearing on their identification of calpulli land, for the elders of the ward might have been more diligent in enforcing distinctions between calpulli land and other types.

Although there are only two cases of identified calpullalli, they provide information on ownership and bequest patterns. Both owners were male. Since Juan Rafael Tlacochcalcatl bequeathed his calpulli land to his daughter, however, we know females could own it. The land was "seven chinampas that belong to the house" (TC 144,145). The other parcel of calpullalli, owned by Gerónimo Teuhcihuatl, was twenty units long (no width specified) of dry land [teuhtlalli] with magueys on it.[49] Two different types of land, chinampas and dry land, were calpullalli, and the two parcels were doubtless in two different locations (perhaps within Coatlan). Both men bequeathed their land to their children; neither ordered it sold for masses. This is consistent with reports of prehispanic prohibitions on alienation of calpulli land. However, neither man ordered much of anything sold for masses. Gerónimo wanted one of his houses sold, but none of his land. Juan Rafael's only parcel ordered sold was a plot of purchased land. Thus, that they did not alienate calpulli land is not automatically significant. We must be aware of the possibility that these two identified pieces of calpullalli are a subset of other calpulli land, not specifically called by the Nahuatl term.

Zorita reported (1963b:108) that *calpulli* land reverted to the calpulli if there was no one to inherit it. In both cases of identified calpullalli, there were children who inherited it. However, occasionally property not called calpulli land reverted to the ward heads for reassignment (TC 68,69; 218,219). As discussed previously the land was given by testators who had heirs. However, for some reason—perhaps Christian charity or perhaps because the land was especially liable for tribute—they donated it to the ward heads to be assigned to poor people.

The question must be raised of how much control over land the calpulli had, even in prehispanic times. The amount of land owned by commoners certainly varied widely.[50] Significant variations in holdings suggest less than rigid control by the calpulli. In the colonial period people bequeathed their land to heirs and ordered it to be sold completely without reference to the calpulli. They obviously viewed their land as their personal property.[51] Since what the calpulli itself was is still unclear, how it functioned in relation to land is merely part of a much larger problem.

Unlike the categories discussed above which appear in some form in the standard sources on land tenure, there are other terms which appear standardly in local level Nahuatl documentation. These include *cihuatlalli*, "woman land"; *tlalcohualli*, purchased land; *huehuetlalli* and *tlalnemactli*, both types of inherited land; and *Mexicatlalli* "land of the Mexica." In the Culhuacan testaments, purchased land and inherited land are found with much greater frequency than "woman land" or "land of the Mexica."

Regarding "woman land," clearly it is in some way connected to women and occurs both at the imperial and local levels. In fifteenth-century Texcoco, Nezahualcoyotl gave eleven plots of land called cihuatlalli to his daughter upon her marriage.[52] This is clearly dowry land. In Cuauhtinchan about 1576, there was a type of pillalli called "furrows of female lords" [*tecuhciuacuemitl*] (Reyes, 1977:98). At the local level, cihuatlalli standardly occurs in Nahuatl documentation and appears to be a fundamental category of land. Cihuatlalli, "woman land," is found in a Nahuatl document from Xochimilco (1582) translated as *tierras... por bienes maternales*, indicating inheritance through the female line.[53] Cihuatlalli could be owned by both women and men. A man could speak of "his 'woman land'" [*icihuatlal*] (Anderson et al., 1976:28). As noted above, the only Culhuacan cihuatlalli seems to be land pertaining to the tecpan and apparently remaining with it after doña María Juárez's death. If it was dowry land or if it was inherited through the female line or both is not known. A Culhuacan toponym suggests there might have been more cihuatlalli. Luis Tlauhpotonqui owned a parcel of land in a place called Cihuatlalpan which can be translated "in the woman land" (TC 138,139); however, this may simply have been a toponym with no further significance. The term cihuatlalli must be seen in more contexts to clarify its meaning.[54]

Mexicatlalli, "land of the Mexica," is a land term which occurs in a variety of sources with different meanings. In the Culhuacan wills, the term appears in two different testaments, both times identifying chinampas. In Sahagún's work, the term is included in the listing of provinces, describing it as good land belonging to the city of Mexico and what belongs to the Mexican nation (Sahagún, XI:256). In the *Anales de Cuauhtitlan* (1975:31,50), Mexicatlalli is translated as "Mexican lands" [*tierras mexicanas*]. In Culhuacan, the term might have had a very local meaning, denoting land in Mexicapan, a place in or near Culhuacan. Other archival references to Mexicatlalli suggest various meanings for the term. Chinampas constructed in Atlixocan during Moctecuhçoma Ilhuicamina's reign were "classed simply as Mexicatlalli ... because it was acquired through land reclamation rather than conquest" (Calnek, 1975:13).[55] Nahuatl documents from Xochimilco also mention Mexicatlalli in Atlixocan, also calling it cihuatlalli. It is not specifically identified as chinampa land. The contemporary colonial translation given for Mexicatlalli is *"las tierras que están asia la parte de Mexico"* (lands that are toward the part of Mexico, i.e., facing Mexico City).[56] This rendering is somewhat dubious in my view, but possible.

The Culhuacan documents shed no light on the origin of the term Mexicatlalli, but we do know something about ownership and disposal of it. As just mentioned, Culhuacan Mexicatlalli was chinampa land. Both men and women owned it. In 1589, Diego Hernández listed seven chinampas of Mexicatlalli and bequeathed it along with most of his other land to his son Juan Melchor.[57] Another testator, Ana Juana (TC 82,83), owned three chinampas of Mexicatlalli which she willed to her son Juan Francisco. She said he already worked or paid tribute on it.[58] Mexicatlalli could be inherited, but whether it could be sold cannot be determined. As with a number of other land terms, Mexicatlalli needs to be seen in many other contexts to determine what it was.

One of the basic distinctions that developed in the sixteenth century and which continues today is between purchased and inherited land.[59] In the colonial period, two terms were used for inherited land, *tlalnemactli* and *huehuetlalli*. The distinction between the two is found in other Nahuatl documentation contemporary with the Culhuacan wills.[60] The first type, tlalnemactli, derives from the verb *(mo)maca,* "to give," and the noun *nemactli* means, in a general sense, "that which is given to someone, a portion." Tlalnemactli thus means "land received, a portion of land." A colonial Spanish translation of the term tlalnemactli gives *"tierras que vienen de derecho,"* (lands which come by right).[61] Pragmatically, this would boil down mainly to inheritance and dowry, but it could also apply to judicial apportionments. The other term, huehuetlalli, seems to have been a special category of inherited land. The term literally means "old land," but a better translation is "patrimonial land."[62] A Nahuatl document from Xochimilco renders the term *"tierras antiguas"* (old land).[63] The literal translation from Nahuatl has led to confusion of the civil category (a special class of inherited or patrimonial land), with a soil classification (old [exhausted] land).[64] This confusion has led to the translation "patrimonial land" used here.

Both men and women owned patrimonial land, men outnumbering women.[65] Some people stated that they got their huehuetlalli through inheritance. Juan Tezca, for instance, said "I have my patrimonial land which my grandfather Francisco... left me" (TC 32,33). As discussed previously, people tended to exclude their spouses from bequests of patrimonial land and leave it to lineal descendants—their children and grandchildren—who were the same sex as they, so Juan's bequest from his grandfather was not unusual. Melchor Santiago Ecatl's patrimonial land, given to him by the tecpan, has already been discussed (TC 118,119). Most patrimonial land, however, seems to have been received through inheritance from the testator's father or grandfather. As also noted previously, the tecpan's involvement with patrimonial land is interesting in light of evidence that lands of each tecpan in Cuauhtinchan, taken as a whole, were called huehuetlalli (Reyes, 1978:8–9). In general, however, huehuetlalli simply seems to have been a name for inherited land.

Patrimonial land could be chinampas or level land,[66] located almost anywhere, but several parcels were in Santiago Tetla.[67] Although most people knew precisely where their land was, as we noted already, the one parcel of land Juan Bautista did not know the location of was his patrimonial land (TC 34,35).

Regarding tlalnemactli, María Teicuh of Cihuatecpan declared that "in Cueptecco there are 15 inherited chinampas [*nochinannemac*] of mine that the judge, Juan de los Angeles, gave me" (TC 230,231). This same judge had given doña María Juárez ownership of tecpantlalli. Both doña María and María Teicuh seem to have been residents of their respective tecpans. Perhaps the land María Teicuh was awarded had also been part of the tecpan's holdings. Interestingly, María was one of the few women who also owned patrimonial land.

Even though we cannot make a sharp distinction between tlalnemactli and huehuetlalli, two names for inherited land, both terms were used as separate categories, indicating there was a distinction between them. Since both the way a testator acquired land and its civil category often affected its bequest, a distinction between huehuetlalli and tlalnemactli is probably more than simple terminology.

Tlalcohualli, purchased land, was often part of Culhuacan estates. In the colonial period, sales of land within the Indian community and between Indians and Spaniards were frequent. The existence of legal rules governing land sales indicates that transfers of property by sale was not a postconquest innovation (Alva Ixtlilxochitl, 1977: II,385). Sahagún lists tlalcohualli with other land terms (Sahagún, XI:251),[68] and states that land was sometimes sold when people were in financial straits (Sahagún, III:9). Land could be lost through gambling, a type of alienation (Sahagún, VIII:88). Very early colonial Nahuatl documents, such as the Tepoztlan census (about 1535), list purchased land.[69] The distinction between purchased land and other types is made in all types of local level Nahuatl documentation, indicating that purchased land was a fundamental civil category.

In Culhuacan, even when purchased land was inherited and in turn bequeathed by owners, the land retained the designation tlalcohualli. People continued to note who originally owned the land and the price paid by the purchaser. This was likely an attempt to establish clear title to the property. Other property retained old identifications, as seen with tlatocatlalli, office lands, but the case of purchased land might be different. If land was recognized as tlalcohualli, it could be bought and sold freely from then on, no matter how many times inherited. As previously noted, purchased land was often the only land a person ordered sold for masses, perhaps because it was clearly seen as alienable. As with patrimonial land in Culhuacan, purchased land was not generally willed to spouses.

There were several sources of land for sale. About half the testators ordered land sold to pay for masses. In addition, a number of Culhuacan nobles sold land, both to Indians and to Spaniards.[70] To all appearances, they did so *regardless* of its civil category. From the testamentary information, we know that don Juan de Aguilar, who was tlatoani in 1572, sold land to two Culhuacan citizens (TC 114,115; 236,239). And doña Juana de San Gabriel sold land to another citizen, Pedro Cano Acatl (TC 196,197). These sales were recorded in the testaments of the buyers or the buyers' heirs.

The parcels that people bought do not appear to follow any obvious patterns. If Indians were buying land to consolidate holdings in a particular place, it is not readily apparent. There is the general problem of knowing to what locations the toponyms referred, but none of the plots of purchased land were located in places with the same toponyms as their other holdings. Three different people purchased land in a place called Calpoltitlan, implying that it had a concentration of land available for sale. However, no one owned several holdings there.[71] Perhaps purchase of land in several places with different soil types was a conscious effort to acquire land with varying agricultural potentials.

Who owned purchased land? *Not* the largest landowners. Purchased land was generally part of medium-size estates, and the parcels of purchased land were often not large. While some people might have established residence through purchases of land and houses, one local merchant and money-lender, Antonio de Santa María, the father of Luis Tlauhpotonqui and María Tiacapan, seems to have bought land in the course of his general business activities (TC 134ff). Men who owned purchased land outnumbered women.[72] Some people inherited purchased land rather than buying it themselves, as was the case of Luis Tlauhpotonqui and his sister María (TC 134ff; 194,195); however, most of the men who owned tlalcohualli bought it themselves rather than inheriting it.[73] Several men (but apparently no women) owned more than one parcel of purchased land,[74] including Angelina Mocel's cousin Bernardino Vázquez (TC 264,265). Interestingly, Bernardino also sold land,[75] perhaps disposing of land he viewed as less useful and buying other parcels.

Some men who owned purchased land also owned purchased houses. Miguel Hernández (who had been a trader) bought both a house and land. He seems to have already held land in Culhuacan, but the house he bought was the only one he owned. The house used to belong to someone named Gabriel Acol. "We bought it, and there is a judgment about how [the purchase] is valid" (TC 274,275). From Antonio Tlemachica, Angelina Mocel's uncle, he bought a parcel for land for eleven pesos, quite a large sum of money.[76] "There is a written agreement of how it was bought" (TC 274,275). Unlike purchases of houses, where people often showed proof of payment [*carta de pago*] or listed witnesses to the transaction, this was generally not the case in purchases of land. Miguel Hernández's reference to a written agreement about the land is unusual. Land sales were probably not as much in question as house sales, which were more tied up with residence rights and therefore avoided claims less easily. Indians readily litigated over both houses and land, as the numerous lawsuits in the archives indicate.

Sales of land were not always straightforward. Pedro Cano Acatl bought some land belonging to doña Juana de San Gabriel and paid for it in cash and labor. "I gave her 10 pesos, 4 tomines for 60 [units of land], and to complete 80, 20 were just donated to me because sometimes I gave her obedience [i.e., I did things she ordered me to do]" (TC 196,197). Juan Bautista was not pleased about the way the sale of some of his land had gone. "I have seven chinampas in Acatzintitlan; Francisco Chimalquauh came to buy them from me, and he gave me 2 pesos, 4 tomines.... He just fooled me; another peso is to be given to me according to our agreement. If he does not want [to give it to me], let my chinampas be sold to someone [else]" (TC 34,35). Obviously Juan seems to have thought he retained some control over the property until the purchase price was paid. Whether he could exercise his rights without difficulty is a moot point.

While people generally noted the fact that they had purchased land, they also occasionally noted that they had sold land. María Teicuh of Cihuatecpan sold six chinampas to her *consuegros*[77] (TC 230,231). In this case, the buyers acted as witnesses to the wills, perhaps to assure the validity of the sale. As we have seen, Miguel

Hernández bought property from Antonio Tlemachica (TC 274, 275), but Antonio did not record the sale in his own testament (TC 96ff). It is certainly interesting and probably significant that sales of testators' land are recorded only in women's testaments. Women seem to have been minimally involved in the real estate market, and recording sales of their land may have been a way to assure the sales' validity. Women may have been in a more vulnerable legal position in general, for as we have seen, women's testaments seem to have been more open to challenge than men's.

It is difficult to gauge from the testamentary material the amount of participation of Spaniards in the Culhuacan real estate market. Since some Indians had thoroughly European names, it can be difficult to tell Indians from Spaniards. However, Spanish activity in the real estate market is alluded to by the noblewoman doña María Juárez. As we previously noted, she ordered some land sold, specifying that "Spaniards are not to buy these chinampas ... but only the citizens here" (TC 250,251). This restriction is important not only to indicate that Spaniards were acquiring Culhuacan land, but also that at least one noble viewed it as undesirable.[78] The land she ordered sold may have sat vacant for quite awhile for lack of a buyer. She made her will in 1577 and not until 1593 did the local friar certify that the land had been sold to other Culhuacan Indians.

Only four identifiable Spaniards bought Culhuacan testators' land. One Spaniard was Diego de Paz, the teniente for Culhuacan (TC 38,39). The sister and the brother-in-law of the prior of the Augustinian monastery, fray Juan Núñez, bought a house and enclosure.[79] The only other known Spaniard mentioned in the wills as buying land was Pedro Ortiz, who was married to an Indian noblewoman [*cihuapilli*] of Coyoacan (TC 196,197). He bought properties from several Culhuacan estates,[80] and seems to have been systematically acquiring land.

While Culhuacan testaments indicate some level of Spanish activity in the real estate market, records in Spanish of over one hundred Culhuacan land sales contemporary with the testaments confirm that activity.[81] The significance of the land sales documents is twofold. First, the sellers were the Who's Who of Culhuacan. Unlike doña María Juárez, nobles were *not* generally reluctant but were actively engaged in selling large quantities of land to Spaniards. Second, the acquisitions were by a single Spanish official who was buying up land in a few concentrated areas of Culhuacan. These consolidated holdings were the foundation of the hacienda complex which was beginning to develop there. The timing of the first large Spanish land acquisitions in Culhuacan, the late sixteenth century, and the people engaged in selling land, the Indian *principales,* are both typical of hacienda development in the Valley of Mexico.[82] The Indian population was in decline and had less need for land. At the same time, the population of Spanish cities was growing, as was their need for food, and Spaniards were becoming actively involved in agriculture. They acquired Indian land by grant, purchase, and usurpation.

The locations of parcels bought by Spaniards are given on occasion, often general descriptions such as "on the big hill." At other times specific place names are given, such as Ayatongo (Ayauhtonco), Ayltitlan, and Xalpan. These toponyms recur often in both the Culhuacan wills and the Spanish land sales records.

The purchases were not being made in random places but were concentrated in a few areas. Most were probably on the Cerro de la Estrella. Although chinampa agriculture was the dominant type in Culhuacan, the uplands of the mountain were likely used for less intense agriculture. Areas not under cultivation might well have been a source of firewood and small game. Removal of marginal land from peasants' access or control has often had deleterious side-effects, as has been noted for early modern England (Tawney, 1967).

Some chinampas were also sold to Spaniards. Don Diego de Motecuhçoma's estate contained chinampa land measuring one thousand by five hundred brazas (about 140 hectares).[83] Doña Apolonia Coronado's only sale was a 180 (× 20?) braza plot of chinampa and nitrous land (*tierras salitres*).[84] Chinampa land tended to remain in Indian hands (Gibson, 1964:406), so the huge amount of chinampa land sold from don Diego de Motecuhçoma's estate may have been anomalous.

The value of land in the Spanish land sales records varied. In a given location, the amount of land a peso would buy differed considerably. There is no explanation in the land sales records of what determined price. The amounts paid to the Indian sellers were consistent with the prices in the Culhuacan native testaments, however. Few plots of land sold for more than twenty pesos, although individual sellers often sold more than one plot, bringing in considerably more money. Don Francisco Flores sold nine plots for ninety-eight pesos and Alonso Jiménez, another principal, sold five for fifty-eight pesos. Two of Angelina Mocel's cousins sold land: doña Elena Constantina and her husband, Juan de San Miguel, sold a small amount of land; Bernardino Vázquez sold about three hectares of land.[85] In the Spanish land sale records, the Indian sellers were mainly men, but there were also women. They included the noblewomen doña Elena Constantina, just mentioned, doña Juana Téllez, doña María Teicuh, doña Luisa Motecuhçoma,[86] and doña Juana de San Gabriel, who also sold land to Indians. From her sales to Spaniards, doña Juana received almost one hundred pesos.

Overall, there are records of nearly twelve hundred hectares of Culhuacan land passing into Spanish hands in the late sixteenth century. Most individual plots sold were small, but certain nobles sold several plots, and the total amount was large. The largest single sale was in 1588, a sixteen hundred by eight hundred braza parcel (about 357 hectares) from the estate of don Diego Motecuhçoma, a grandson of the Aztec ruler Moctecuhçoma.[87]

Not only did Indians generally own land, but some also rented it (Zorita, 1963b:107). In Culhuacan there are isolated instances of rental. Although Miguel Huantli owned several parcels of land (including purchased land), he sowed two others that he did not own. "There is a chinampa that I cleared but which doesn't belong to me; I only cultivated it [with the permission of] someone else. I declare that I give what is planted on the chinampa to Ana Tiacapan, my older sister.... And in another place there is also [a chinampa] that I sowed in amaranth. It isn't my chinampa either, rather also someone else's. I declare that the amaranth that is sown there belongs to my older sister" (TC 200,201). Thus, the crops belonged to him, but not the land. Those who owned land and rented more probably needed more, perhaps for some kind of commercial enterprise.[88] Children, as we have seen, were often allowed to plant on their parents' land, but did not thereby gain ownership of it.

Land could be acquired in a number of ways. Standard legal methods were inheritance, purchase, court judgment, donation, and rental. Another method was usurpation. Spaniards usurped Indian land (Gibson, 1964:406), but there is evidence that Indians also usurped it. In Culhuacan, Luis Tlauhpotonqui did not have the canonical seven chinampas, as we have seen, because "they stole one" (TC 138,139). Who the thieves were is not known. In another case, Bernardino Vázquez, Angelina Mocel's cousin, essentially admitted to usurping land. "Here is what I explain so that God our lord doesn't punish me: there is a chinampa... and the child [of the owners], a young woman, lives in Mexico City, and it is her property" (TC 266,267). Bernardino seems to have taken advantage of her absence to use the land.[89]

Another aspect of land tenure is taxation. In the prehispanic and early colonial periods, tribute was originally paid according to the amount of land each possessed (Harvey, 1984:88). Officials seem to have kept land registers with this fact in mind (Williams, 1984:115). Particular parcels of land may have been specifically liable for tribute. In the prehispanic era, there were types of land such as office land and land to support the temples in which crops went entirely to the office or institution. Seemingly there were parcels in sixteenth-century Culhuacan held by individual citizens where the crops were taxed. Agustín Tepanecatl willed one parcel to his children. "There they will produce its tribute [*itlacalaquil*] when I have died, the tribute of the dead [*miccatlacallaquilli*]" (TC 254, 255).[90] After Miguel Huantli had died, his "maize that is planted... is all to be picked, from it will be taken our half fanega of maize[91] and the tribute [*tlacallaquilli*]. Let [the ward heads] take it because it is our tribute as subjects" (TC 200ff). Other property might have specifically been subject to taxation, but the phrasing in Nahuatl is ambiguous. The Nahuatl word *tequitl* can mean either "tribute" or "duty, work." The phrase in Ana Juana's testament *nicmacatiuh y notelpoch y Ju⁰ Fran^co caneye*[91] [sic] *ipan tequiti,* the gloss can be "I give [land] to my son Juan Francisco because he already works on it" or "... because he already pays tribute on it." However, other things she says suggest that *tequitl* should be glossed "tribute." She had some land which she gave her son so that he could do his public works duty [*cohuatequitl*], give his zacate tribute [*cohuaçacatl*], and his various other tributes [*ixquich nepapan tequitl*] (TC 82,83).[93] As mentioned previously, some people who made donations of land to the ward heads so that it would be redistributed to the poor gave land that seems to have been especially liable for tribute (TC 68,69; 218,219).

Since land was the major form of property that testators willed to their heirs, we know the most about this form of wealth. From people's descriptions of their own holdings, we can see that land tenure in Culhuacan underwent a number of changes in the colonial period, with the elimination of some prehispanic categories, shifts in prehispanic patterns, and the development of new forms of tenure. Continuity in the system also existed, for land continued to be identified in terms of native toponyms, native soil categories, and native measurements. Land retained civil designations even though the tenure changed. The development of a full-scale real estate market is probably the most important change from the prehispanic period, but the fact that there were prehispanic precedents for sales of land shows that it was not foreign to Indians' conceptions of land tenure.

9 / CONCLUSIONS

The period when the Culhuacan wills were made was a time of great change in Central Mexico. The sixteenth century was when things fell apart in the Indian world. Conquest destroyed the superstructure of the Aztec empire, epidemic disease reduced the Indian population, and religious evangelization transformed old beliefs or sent them underground. Despite these cataclysmic changes, Indian culture showed tremendous resilience.

Culhuacan in the sixteenth-century was a typical Indian town in the Valley of Mexico. Although it had a long and distinguished history, the town had already declined by the late prehispanic era. In the colonial era, the town's status as an altepetl was translated into cabecera status. After a brief period as an encomienda of the capital Mexico-Tenochtitlan, Culhuacan passed into the hands of a typical encomendero family, the Oñates, which held it until the late seventeenth century. The Culhuacan Indians who made wills in the late sixteenth century made no mention of the town's encomendero, a distant figure who received a private income from their labor. With the Crown's establishment of a system of rule of Indian towns, Culhuacan was given the lowly rank of pueblo and functioned like other Indian towns in New Spain.

Changes in town structure occurred as a result of Spanish colonial rule. The process of change in Culhuacan was completely consistent with those occurring in other Indian towns. The town's highest official became the juez-gobernador, a newly created office separate from that of tlatoani. In the early sixteenth century, the same person often held both offices, but the two usually came to be held by different separate people. In Culhuacan by the late sixteenth century, the two offices were separate and that of tlatoani had declined, with some of its land being transferred to a non-tlatoani. A Spanish-style cabildo with elective offices was created, probably in the midsixteenth century, and was smoothly functioning in the 1580s. The officeholders were elite men who rotated to different offices. Among the functions of the town government were tax collection and maintenance of order.

The function most clearly seen in the Culhuacan wills was estate administration. This process included the town's notaries recording its citizens' final statements, preservation of those documents in a central repository, and acceptance of money for delivery to the church. In cases of complicated but undisputed divisions of estates, the highest governmental officials carried out the partitions. In disputed cases of inheritance, town officials functioned to render judgment and impose penalties on those contravening their decrees.

It is difficult to gauge to what extent Spanish colonial policies affected the way estates were administered. However, there were differences in the ways Spaniards' and Indians' estates were dealt with, indicating that perhaps there were prehispanic precedents for Indians' methods. Executors of Spaniards' estates were chosen by the individual testator, while executors of Indians' estates were officials of the town government. These officials called themselves topileque, as often as not, rather than by the loanword title albacea. Supervisions of the sale of property and responsibility for delivering money to the friars were in the hands of government officials. The final bequests of testators were thus not private matters dealt with privately but formal, public transactions. This public aspect is consistent with prehispanic legal practice of important acts being done before witnesses.

The reshaping of native culture under Spanish rule is notable in the realm of religion. Augustinian friars were the apex of the religious hierarchy, replacing the native priesthood, yet elite Indian men helped oversee functions of the new Christian religion. By the late sixteenth century, the Indians of Culhuacan had adopted the outward forms of piety. Indians owned Christian religious objects, such as crucifixes and religious books, made charitable donations to the poor, calculated time by the Christian calendar, and were cognizant of important Christian feastdays. At death, they made testaments and followed the European practice of requesting masses, candles, and burial in the church. We cannot determine how profound an understanding Indians had of Christian doctrine, but they embraced the public manifestations of Christian piety. Because testaments were considered religious as well as civil documents, and because all the religious formulas were routinely observed, using testaments to estimate Indians' piety may distort religion's importance among colonial Indians. There is a tendency for us to impute greater religious fervor to people of previous eras.

In colonial Mexico, the Church actively promoted the making of testaments not only for the sake of their Indian parishioners' souls, but also because the Church was practically guaranteed some portion of the estate. Especially prominent in Indian wills is the large amount of property destined to be sold for masses, a clear change of bequest patterns from the prehispanic period.

Significant changes occurred in Indian populations due to the Spanish conquest. With waves of epidemics, the population declined precipitously, and, by the late sixteenth century, there were significantly fewer Indians. The Indians of Culhuacan were aware of life's fleeting nature, for even as testators chose their heirs, they realized some would not survive them long and testators made alternative bequests. The dying attempted to take care of their surviving dependents through bequests and instructions to caretakers. Survival of the family was important. Often the survivors remarried and took other steps to stabilize their family situations. Doubtless the enthusiastic adoption of the Spanish institution of fictive kinship, compadrazgo, in which godparents could assume some of the roles of parents, is an example of this.

The citizens of Culhuacan exhibited a whole range of social behavior. Personal relations were not static or determined by ritualized behavior, despite the exhortations about proper conduct recorded in the standard sources, such as Sahagún. Certain figures are recognizable to us: the wicked stepmother, the stingy husband, the dutiful daughter, the loving son. The formal texts describe the desirable and undesirable behavior of kin, and the people of Culhuacan inadvertantly illustrate it. The formal structure of kinship divided kin from non-kin, but could not enforce harmonious social relations among relatives.

Bequests to some relatives and disinheritance of others were ways to show the strength of social bonds. Both men and women divided their estates among a number of heirs, but differences between men's and women's bequest patterns emerge from the

Culhuacan wills. Both men and women tended to leave significant amounts of property to their children and to a lesser extent spouses, nieces and nephews. However, women seem to have been much more ready to have their houses sold for masses than to pass them on to their heirs. Men seem to have assumed much more responsibility for providing for their surviving families. In addition, men seem to have defined their responsibility more broadly to include godchildren and stepchildren, while women generally excluded them from inheritance.

Serious disputes between kin over property occurred, and people resorted to the Spanish courts to resolve them. Justice was dispensed according to Spanish notions of proper inheritance, which may have prompted changes in native bequest patterns. Those not wishing to have their wills disputed may have made bequests which they knew were not likely to be challenged. The effect of this might have been to de-emphasize lateral ties to siblings, which seem to have been important in the prehispanic era, and to promote the importance of lineal ties to children and grandchildren, links which were more congruent with the Spanish system. There is clear evidence that people who disinherited kin who might logically have been their heirs made the effort to explain the exclusions. Testators may well have been anticipating the arguments that disgruntled relatives would possibly have made in court.

Another possible effect of Spanish law on Indian inheritance was to widen the distribution of property within the nuclear family. Spanish law guaranteed equal portions to sons and daughters, as well as a share for the surviving wife, which may well have put more property in the hands of colonial Indian women.

Depopulation probably also contributed to women's holding large amounts of material wealth, including land. In the immediate preconquest era, the population of the Valley of Mexico was dense, and resources were likely restricted. Although there is evidence that noblewomen owned land as dowry and possibly also through inheritance, commoner women seem not to have had dowries, nor did they seem to share standardly in bequests of land, the major productive resource. However, with depopulation in the colonial era, resources were much more abundant, and commoner women may have shared in estates to a greater extent than they had previously. It is obvious from the Culhuacan wills that women received portions of estates not only as custodial heirs, holding their children's property in trust, but also as full heirs.

It is difficult to assess the effect that women's status as full heirs would have had on the overall status of native women, but systems in which women inherit property in their own right are certainly different from those in which women are excluded (Goody, 1976). Colonial Aztec women could receive all types of property, land, houses, and movable goods from male and female donors, and likewise pass it on to heirs of their choice. Ownership of property often translates into power, and we should not underestimate the importance of women holding wealth in their own right. While there were cultural constraints on the behavior of ideal wife, daughter, or sister, making women to some extent submissive to male kin, nonetheless, it is clear from colonial testaments that this did not preclude the Culhuacan women from standing up to their husbands, engaging in commercial activity on their own, and managing their property as they saw fit. Widows did not yield ownership of their own property to their children, but retained ownership and thus some form of control over their potential heirs.

Some have argued that the status of Aztec women was falling in the immediate preconquest era, citing as evidence the de-emphasis of female deities and relaxation of restrictions on extramarital intercourse for men (Leacock and Nash, 1977; Nash, 1978). However, it would seem that the Spanish conquest opened up new opportunities for Indian women. Marriage to Spaniards was one option for Indian women generally not open to Indian men. Colonial Indian women may also have been the beneficiaries of depopulation, an unforeseen consequence of conquest which produced an abundance of resources. This may have allowed potential rights to inherit translate to reality. (This occurred in Europe after the Black Death where women acquired property in the absence of men [Hilton, 1975].) Studies of inheritance patterns among seventeenth- and eighteenth-century Mexican Indians need to be undertaken, but my guess is that when population pressures reasserted themselves, women were again excluded from inheritance of land. If sixteenth-century Indian women were excluded from inheritance, they took their cases to the Spanish courts, a new avenue of acquiring property, where they had an excellent chance of winning if they were the plaintiffs.

Women's productive role seems to have declined in the colonial economy. In the prehispanic era, they produced cloth for domestic use, for rendering in tribute, and for use as a medium of exchange. In the colonial era, Spanish money replaced cloth as a medium of exchange, and tribute was generally rendered in money by the late sixteenth century. In addition, as the Spanish colony grew, Spaniards set up textile factories to supply the needs of the urban population. Indian women continued to weave for the market, but the value of their goods may well have declined. Weaving equipment and partially finished cloth were movable goods frequently appearing in their estates, and details about the completion of projects shows a spirit of cooperation among Culhuacan's weavers.

Culhuacan men were beginning to dress like Spaniards. An index of cultural assimilation was clothing styles, and in this respect, Indian men seem to have been much less conservative than women. The changes in styles had been initiated by the Spanish friars who viewed native men's clothing as immodest. Spanish pants and shirts replaced loincloths and capes. Native women's garb of skirts and huipils was fairly modest and there would have been no compelling reason for the Spanish friars to impose Spanish styles as rigidly. However, Indian noblemen went beyond the basic peasant attire. In the prehispanic period, clothing was a marker of status, and this likely continued in the colonial era also. In general Indian noblemen tried to emulate the styles of their Spanish rulers.

Naming patterns are another aspect of colonial native culture which show differences between men and women. All baptized Indians acquired a Christian given name, but in Culhuacan the inventory of women's names was smaller than men's. In addition, the second names men and women had were markedly different. Women tended to have stereotyped Nahuatl birth-order names, while men had much more varied and some quite colorful surnames. This may have another example of cultural conservatism with respect to women. Adoption of a full Spanish surname seemed to have been linked to status. While both high status men and women had typical Spanish surnames, a greater number of men had them. Patronymics were not generally used but may have been adopted by very high status nobles. In addition, high nobles adopted Spanish noble titles of don and doña.

Hispanization was a slow process and language is to some extent an index of it. The names of new concepts which were deliberately imposed, such as those connected with the Spanish legal system and the Christian religion (including the Christian calendrical system), were found in loanword form. More informal exchanges with the Spanish world are evident in the inventories of Culhuacan estates. Indian men and women owned things introduced by Spaniards—new plants such as fruit trees; new animals such as horses, mules, and chickens; tools such as axes, knives, and swords; furniture such as chests and tables; and books such as breviaries and other religious texts.[1] In addition, Spanish money replaced native media of exchange, and it appears in a number of estates.

Culhuacan was not a closed, static native community. Its traders had connections stretching from the Valley of Morelos to the colonial capital of Mexico-Tenochtitlan. There was movement of money, goods, and people. Nontraders also had contact with other places and people. Townspeople went to the capital to pursue lawsuits. People from other towns married Culhuacan citizens and moved there. Non-Indians, such as the Spanish friars and possibly some officials of the corregimiento, lived in the town. Ordinary Spanish citizens, such as the prior's relatives, also took up residence there. Some outsiders were disruptive and were banished, such as the black assailant of Diego Sánchez.

Culhuacan society was marked by varying degrees of wealth. There were several forms of wealth in Culhuacan, primarily land, and to a lesser extent houses and movable goods. Some high nobles had extremely large estates, far more than they could ever work themselves, while some humble citizens had no land whatsoever. Wealth did not necessarily correlate with class, for there were poor nobles and rich commoners.

A fundamental question is whether Spanish concepts of property altered those of Indians. One function of wills was to give wealth to chosen heirs. Indian men and women speak of "my house," "my land," and "my movables," and acted as if they had the absolute right to dispose of them. Although movable property does not seem to have been as valuable as other types, it was bequeathed to specific heirs. Houses, which were possibly more liable to claims by heirs, were often given as shared bequests, and the practice of dismantling houses was likely to satisfy multiple heirs. Land was held by men and women who knew the precise number of their parcels, their size, soil type, location, civil category, and from whom they had originally received them. In all cases, testators clearly acted as if the land was their property, for they gave it to chosen heirs or ordered it sold. Whether they had the right to do so or not is unclear, but listing of property in testaments was definitely a way to assert property rights.

Land tenure in Culhuacan shows evidence of considerable change from the prehispanic period. Overall, the most important development was a full-scale real estate market. Large quantities of land passed into the hands of Spaniards, sold by Indian elites. With some exceptions, most of it was not chinampa land, the most typical kind of land the people of Culhuacan owned. The sales were of the uplands of Culhuacan, for they were suitable for Spanish agriculture. With a large number of Culhuacan people ordering land sold for masses, land tenure was destablized. Land could be bought by Indians who previously might not have had much, and by Spaniards who were now interested in running their own agricultural enterprises.

I suggest that the demographic crisis merely accentuated trends which were already present. Sale of land was not a postconquest innovation, but it was an option exercised by a greater range of people in the colonial period. The amount of control that the calpulli had in the prehispanic period must be questioned. Clearly, in the late sixteenth century people were treating their property as if it were theirs to bequeath or to sell at will, virtually regardless of its civil category. Rental of land by individual Indians may have been a colonial innovation, but it seems not to have been widespread in late sixteenth-century Culhuacan.

A number of continuities from the prehispanic patterns are evident. The retention of the names of prehispanic civil categories of land despite its changed tenure and identification of fields by deceased owners' names does seem to be an attempt to keep order in the system. Other retentions from the prehispanic period were toponyms locating land, terms for cardinal directions, and terms for classifying soil types. Land was measured in native units, despite Indians' knowledge of Spanish units. There was no reason to change any of these native patterns. The retentions are important but do not alter the fact that land tenure in the colonial period was substantially different from that in the prehispanic era.

The noblewoman doña María Juárez clearly saw the acquisition of land by Spaniards as undesirable. It was not sale of land she objected to, but sale to Spaniards. She was the only person in Culhuacan to make an explicit comment about sales to Spaniards, but her sentiment was echoed by another Indian noblewoman (from Xochimilco) in 1582. Some Culhuacan testaments record sales to people known to be Spaniards but not identified as such. Although doña María's stricture is isolated, it is nonetheless generally true that Indian noblewoman sold much less land to Spaniards than Indian noblemen did, as shown by land sales records. Perhaps this is another example of women's cultural conservativism.

In the end, doña María was right. The permanent loss of Indian land to Spaniards threatened the economic base of the peasant economy. In general, when the Indian populations recovered some of their numbers in the seventeenth century, much of the land needed to support them was in the hands of Spaniards. In Culhuacan chinampa land was the dominant type and as such was much less desirable to Spaniards. But the alienation of the uplands of Culhuacan was permanent and likely had deleterious side-effects on the Indians.

Information about sixteenth-century Indians of any given town is fragmentary at best. In *The Testaments of Culhuacan,* we have one of the best sources from the people themselves. The insights we have into people's lives give us the sense of dealing with real personalities. Diego Sánchez, who lay dying from a knifewound inflicted by a black man, tried to take care of his brothers and sisters. Ana Juana attempted to protect her son's inheritance against her good-for-nothing third husband. Luis Tlauhpotonqui made a futile effort to collect debts owed to his deceased, wheeler-dealer father. Doña María Juárez was worried about the sales of land to Spaniards. These are not merely interesting anecdotes. When placed in context, they illustrate dynamics of social relations and the process of cultural change.

The Culhuacan wills in the aggregate provide a picture of life in a late sixteenth-century Indian town. Rather than being a static, posed picture, it is an action shot of people going about their business. The purpose in reconstructing the picture has not been to pile datum upon datum but to analyze the dynamics of late sixteenth-century Indian society at a level scarcely undertaken before. Sixty years after the Spanish conquest, Culhuacan was still clearly an Indian town, but it was also clearly a *colonial* town. There were obvious continuities from the prehispanic era, but also distinct and irreversible changes brought about by Spanish rule.

Indians made wills for many reasons: to fulfill the requirements of the Christian religion, to assure that masses would be said for the salvation of their souls, to bequeath their wealth to their chosen heirs and exclude other claimants, to give instructions about the care of their minor children, to repudiate some debts and arrange for the payment or collection of others, to justify their own behavior, to praise worthy relatives, and to vilify unpleasant and disagreeable kin. Wills were the final words of the dying, but even as death neared, some thought of the future. Doña Luisa Juana had one very human wish, "May you not forget me."[2]

APPENDIXES

Appendix 1 / Prices / 173
Appendix 2 / Spanish Loanwords / 177
Appendix 3 / Testament of Cristina Tiacapan / 183
Appendix 4 / Division of doña Luisa Juana's estate / 189

1 / PRICES ABOUT 1580

Movable goods—furnishings
bed [*tlapechtli*] TC 41 — 6 tomines
bed TC 257 — 1 tomín
5 old mats [*petlaçolli*] TC 41 — half real
2 seats of wood [*quauhicpalli*] TC 41 — half real

Movable goods—tools
digging stick [*huitzoctli*] TC 41 — half real
tepozhuictli TC 75 — 6 tomines
tlaltepoztli TC 75 — 5 tomines
scissors [*tijeras*] TC 43 — 2 tomines
knife [*cuchillo*] TC 207 — 1 tomín

Movable goods—storage
basket, small reed TC 43 — 5 cacao beans
basket, wooden w/handle TC 43 — 1 tomín
basket, small, round, covered TC 43 — 20 cacao beans
chest [*caja*], with lock TC 43 — 10 tomines
chest, closable w/lock TC 103 — 1 peso

Movable goods—for food preparation, serving, and storage
bottle [*limeta*] TC 43 — 1 tomín
cup [*taza*] TC 105 — 3 tomines
jícara TC 41 — 1/2 tomín
jícara TC 43 — 10 cacao beans
jícara, old TC 43 — 15 cacao beans
jug [*botija*] TC 41 — 1/2 tomín
metate TC 153 — 3 tomines

173

plate & bowl, tin TC 41 — 6 tomines
tecomate, Michoacan-style TC 41 — 2 tomines
tecomates, 3 broken TC 41 — 1 tomín
tecomate, 1 broken TC 43 — 15 cacaos
tecomates, 5 TC 45 — 2 tomines
tecomate, 1 painted TC 103 — 1 peso
tecomate, 1 painted TC 103 — 3 tomines
tecomate, 1 painted TC 103 — 4 tomines

Movable goods—miscellaneous

blanket TC 89;TC 91   [*asked 3 pesos*]   2 pesos [got]
boots, old TC 43 — 2 tomines
cloth, striped with rabbit fur TC 41 — 1/2 tomín
crucifix TC 257 — 1 tomín
drum TC 119 — 5 tomines
drum TC 207 — 3 tomines
drums, 1 upright, 1 log TC 213 — 1 peso
flute TC 207 — 1 tomín
skirt, new TC 89;TC 91   [*asked 4 p^{o}s 6 t^s*]   2 pesos [got]
stone, chalchihuitl TC 75 — 3 pesos

Animals

2 ducks TC 153 — 4 tomines
1 old duck TC 153 — 1 1/2 tomines
1 horse TC 105 — 8 p^{o}s, 4t^s
1 horse TC 137 — 10 pesos
1 horse TC 155 — 8 pesos
1 horse TC 189 — 6 pesos +/−
1 horse TC 189 — 15 pesos
1 horse TC 275 — 16 pesos

Houses

house and enclosure T–58–4 — 40 pesos
house, small, old TC 23 — 3 pesos
house TC 39 — 3 pesos
house TC 61 — 9 pesos 4 t^s
house, small TC 77 — 2 pesos 5 t^s
house TC 93 — 15 pesos
house TC 115   [*asked 9 p^{o}s*]   8 pesos [got]
house TC 165 — 6 pesos

house TC 197   [*asked 10 p°s*]   9 pesos [got]
house, small TC 205   6 pesos
house TC 273   [*part payment*]   3 pesos

Land

chinampas, 7 TC 35   2 pesos 4 t^s
chinampas, 5 TC 99   2 pesos 4 t^s
chinampas, 12 TC 115   8 pesos
chinampas, 12 TC 197   3 pesos 4 t^s
chinampas, 7 TC 211   2 pesos 4 t^s
chinamps, 5 + level land TC 275   11 + pesos
land, size not known TC 39   9 pesos
land, small piece TC 111   2 pesos 4 t^s
land, size not known TC 139   20 pesos
land, small piece TC 143   1 peso 4 t^s
land, size not known TC 163   3 pesos
land, 80 × ? TC 197   10 + pesos
land, 40 × ? TC 213   8 pesos

Miscellaneous

bail, two people, offense unknown TC 79   1 peso
bail, 1 person, assault of alguacil mayor TC 137   3 pesos
labor, masons to build walls TC 95   4 tomines
mass, 1 solemn high TC 111   2 pesos 4 t^s

2 / SPANISH LOANWORDS

From *The Testaments of Culhuacan*

Spanish/English	**Nahuatl**
abril "April"	abril TC 246
agosto "August"	agostos, agustos TC 54,62
albaceas "executors"	aluceas, albaçeasti, alvaçias, aluçiasme, albaceasme TC 20,54,236,120,262
alcaide "jailor"	algayte TC 54
alcalde "judge"	allde TC 62,278
alguacil "constable"	alguacil, alhuacil TC 62,278
alguaciles "constables"	alguaciles, alguacilesme TC 54,62
alumbre, "alum"	alonbra TC 72
ángel "angel"	noangel "my angel" TC 66
ánima "soul"	animan; nanima "my soul" TC 20
años "years"	anos TC 18
azadón "hoe"	anzaron TC 52
botas "boots"	botasçolli "old boots" TC 42
botija "bottle"	botixa TC 40
breviario "breviary"	nobreviario "my breviary" TC 104
caballo, cavallo "horse"	cavallo, cavallome, nocavallo, nocahuayo "my horse" TC 136,192,154,154
caja "chest, box"	caja, caxa, casa, cassa, nocasaçol "my old chest" TC 44,42,96,22,128
camisa "shirt"	camixatli TC 274
candela(s) "candles"	cantella, candellas TC 182,206

Spanish/English

carta de pago "receipt"

castillan "Castile"
cerrojo "bolt"
chaqueta "jacket"
compadre "co-parent"
compañía "company"
concierto "agreement"
coro "choir"
crucifixus "crucifix" (*Latin*)
cruz "cross"
cuartillo "quarter of a tomín"
cuchillo "knife"

diciembre "December"
dios "God"
dieszmo "tithe"
diputados "deputies"

doctores "medical doctors"
doctrina "[book of] doctrine"
domingo "Sunday"
don [noble title, male]
doña [noble title, female]
duraznos "peach trees"
enero "January"
escalera "ladder"
escobilla/escudilla "brush/ bowl"
escoplo "chisel"
escribanía "writing desk"
escribano "notary"

escritura "writing desk" or "scripture"
esencia "essence"

espíritu "spirit"

Nahuatl

carta de paco, carta te vaco TC 236,194

castilan TC 104
zeroso TC 102
xaquetaçolli "old jacket" TC 88
icompadre "his co-parent" TC 172
copania TC 274
concierto T–58–4–9r
coro TC 150
crucifixus TC 98
cruz TC 154
quartillapan TC 116
cochillo; nocochilo "my knife"; onechcochillohui "he knifed me" TC 206,220

deçienbre TC 106
dios, d. TC 20,92
tiesmo TC 118
dibotados, depodados, dipotato TC 278,174,220

dodortin TC 220
doctrina TC 244
domingo TC 94
don TC 16
dona TC 42
toraznos TC 250
enero TC 186
escallera TC 44
yscouila [not clear what is meant] TC 40
yscobo TC 104
escriuania TC 102
s^o, esc^o, escrivano, es^{r}no TC 86,52,52,18
escritura TC 44

excencia, ensecia, esçençia, heseçia TC 20,50,96,100
Espu TC 66

Spanish/English	Nahuatl
espada "sword"	esbata TC 44
español "Spaniard"	espanol TC 250
estaño "tin"	ystaya TC 40
et cetera	e^{tca}, et^c, et^a TC 132,160,220
fanega [Spanish measure]	anecas TC 260
febrero "February"	hebrero TC 220
firma "signature"	tofirmas "our signatures"; firma, nofirmas [sic] "my signature" TC 52,94
fiscal "fiscal"	fiscal, fixcal TC 42,72
folio "folio"	folio TC 206
fray "friar"	fray TC 44
frezada "blanket"	breçada, freçada, freçata TC 88,136,278
gobernador "governor"	go^r, gobernador, gouernador, gou^{or} TC 28,222; T–58–4–7v, 5v
hacha "axe"	acha, hacha TC 42,104
higos "figs"	icos TC 58
(h)oras "[book of] hours"	oras TC 104,244
(h)ospital "hospital"	ospital TC 220
iglesia "church"	iglesia, yglessia TC 20,240
imagen "image"	inmase TC 94
jueves "Thursday"	juebes, jueues, jubes, jueves TC 80,254,254; T–58–4–5r
juez "judge"	juez, xoez TC 122,230
julio "July"	Julio, Julios, jullio TC 42,52
junio "June"	Junio TC 150
juntera "plane"	xontera TC 104
juramento "oath"	juramento T–58–4–7v
justicia "justice"	susticiatica "by means of justice"; yjus^{a}stzin "its justice" TC 62,118
letras "letters"	letras T–58–4–2v
libro "book"	llipro TC 222
licencia "license"	inlicencia "his license" T–58–4–5v
limeta "glass bottle"	limeta TC 40
lunes "Monday"	llunes TC 86
macho "male (mule)"	macho TC 274

Spanish/English	Nahuatl
mandamiento "order"	madamiento, mandamiento TC 226; T–58–4–3v
martes "Tuesday"	martes, mardes TC 86,228
marzo "March"	março TC 130
mayo "May"	mayo TC 158
mayor "principal, chief"	manyor, mayor TC 62,62
mayordomos "majordomos"	mayordomosme TC 118
medio "half (a tomín)"	m°, medio, mediopan TC 88,42,44
mes "month"	mes TC 278
mesa "table"	mesa TC 44
miércoles "Wednesday"	miercolles TC 164
misa "mass"	misa, missa TC 94,18
nombrado "appointed"	nunbrado, nonbrado TC 54,206
noviembre "November"	nouie, novienbre, nobienbre TC 18,84,278
octubre "October"	octobre, otobre TC 90,198
original "original"	original TC 212
padre "father"	pe TC 44
patos "ducks"	patos, batos TC 150,152
pena "fine, punishment"	pena T–58–4–10v
peras "pears"	peras TC 58
persona "person"	çe persona "one person" TC 134
peso [Spanish coin]	p°s, pesus, p°stica TC 22,140,272,136
pintura "pictorial document"	pintura T–58–4–3v
plato "plate"	plato TC 40
pleito "lawsuit"	preydo TC 260
pobre "poor person"	bople TC 260
posesión "possession"	posesion, possession T–58–4–4r, 3v
prenda "pawn"	frenta, brenta TC 138,72
prior "prior"	prior, priyor, por, pror TC 42,64,72,146
público "public"	bopligo TC 272
puerta "door"	puerta, poerta, boerta, poertaçolli TC 22,132,132
purgatorio "purgatory"	purcatori TC 24
regidor "town councillor"	regidor, resitor TC 62,90

Spanish/English	Nahuatl
sacristán "sacristan"	sachristan, sachristiame TC 118,118
santísma "most holy"	sanctissima TC 24
santo/a "holy, saint"	santa, sancto TC 20,226
señor "sir, lord"	senor, sennor, s^{or} TC 18,82; T–58–4–2r
sentencia "sentence, ruling"	sentencia, sentençian TC 226,274
septiembre "September"	setienbre TC 202
sierra "saw"	siera, xera TC 42,104
solar "houselot"	xolar, jolar; nosolar "my houselot", xollar, jolarpan, isolaryo "its houselot" TC 156,176,208,38
taza "cup"	tazça TC 104
teniente "lieutenant"	teniente T–58–4–2r
testamento "testamento"	testamento, testamiento, testamen, techtamendo, textamento TC 90,222,80,228
testigos "witnesses"	testigos, testigosme, testigostin, testicoti, testicos, testicosmen TC 212,76,54,86,118,88
tijeras "scissors"	dijeras TC 42
tomines "coins, money"	t^s, tomines, not^s "my money"; t^{s}tzin TC 40,138,154,244
traslado "copy"	traslado TC 212
trinidad "trinity"	drinidada, trinidad, drinidad TC 200,20,142
vaqueta "leather"	vaqueta TC 42
vara [measure of length]	vara TC 172
viernes "Friday"	viernes, fiernes TC 72,42
vigilia "vigil"	vigilia TC 24
visitador "inspector"	visitador TC 248
zapatos "shoes"	çabatos TC 42
zaragüelles "pants"	noçallahueras "my pants" TC 206

3 / TESTAMENTS OF CRISTINA TIACAPAN

As part of a lawsuit preserved in the Bibliothèque Nationale of Paris (Manuscrit Mexicain 110) is the Nahuatl testament of Cristina Tiacapan. The lawsuit was brought by Cristina's stepdaughter, Marta Petronila, who ultimately won. This Nahuatl testament is the only Culhuacan will with a contemporary colonial translation to Spanish, apparently made for the lawsuit. The transcription of the Spanish translation was done by James Lockhart, who believes that the translation was made by a native Nahuatl speaker. I made the English translation presented here directly from the Nahuatl text.

Testament of Cristina Tiacapan
Translation from the Nahuatl

—In the name of God the Father, God the Son, and God the Holy Spirit, just one true God, I begin my testament; know all who see and read this document that I, named Cristina Tiacapan, whose home is here in San Juan Evangelista Culhuacan, belonging to the ward of Santa Ana Tepanecapan, if I die, let my God and ruler forgive me. And here is what I have possessed on earth, that my late husband Miguel Huitznahuatecatl gave me. And I say now:

—Three [chinampas], each of 40 [units of measure] long, (which is equivalent to) six [of 20 units?], in Amaxac, are to be sold in order for masses to be said for me.

—Also I declare that three [chinampas] in (Atiçacal)titlan, each one 90 [units of measure] long are to be sold in order for masses to be said for me.

—In addition, I give 40 [units of measure of land] in Yahualiuhcan and 20 in Tlatepotzco and 40 in [Santiago] Tetla, and 20 in Ayauhtonco to Juan Ecatl and his wife Martina Tlaco; no one is to claim it from him. And I declare that Baltasar Amaro is to take 20 [units of land], also in Ayauhtonco where I mentioned, with which it comes to 40 [units of measure of land].

—Also I give three chinampas with little bits of level land, four in all, to Juan de Santa Ana. No one is to claim it from him.

—And in Tlanepantlatonco, together with what I already mentioned that I gave to Juan de Santa Ana, there are three [chinampas], each one 20 [units of measure], which extend up to the field of Pedro de (Salba) Tlacatecatl.

—And in Apilco I give five [chinampas], each one 20 [units of measure] long, and two in Quauhtenanco, each one 20 [units] long, to Juan Ecatl. And Juan Ecatl is to take the house where I lie, with the little house, all of it together. No one is to claim it from him.

—And the land at the edge of the water, the chinampas of (the house) that go around it, will all belong to Juan Ecatl.

—Done before the witnesses Marcos Mauhtli, Juan Ecatl, Baltasar Amaro, Juan de Santa Ana, Juan, the little boy, son of the invalid; Juana Teicuh, wife of Juan Lázaro; Ana Tiacapan, wife of Agustín Ahuilizcatl; and the wife of Juan Ecatl, named Martina; Ana Xoco, widow of Juan Tlanencauh; and the wife of Pedro Chantli, named Marta Teicuh. Before these Cristina Tiacapan gave her orders. Today, Sunday, the 4th of the month of November of the year 1576; I, Baltasar Amaro, wrote it.

—And I, the notary of the church, wrote the testament by order of don Lorenzo de San Francisco, and as is the original and just as it says in the testament, not one letter nor anything else was omitted; rather, the copy was made perfectly like [the original]. And in order to verify it, the lord fiscal put his signature here.

Don Lorenzo de San Francisco, fiscal.

Miguel Jacobo de Maldonado [appointed notary].

Bibliothèque Nationale de Paris
Manuscrit Mexicain 110 f.6
Testament of Cristina Tiacapan

—In ica ytocatzin dios tetatzin d. tepilzin, d. Espu sto çan çe huel nelli dios nicpehualtia yn notestamento ma quimatican yn ix-

quichtin yn quittazque yn quipohuazque ynn amatl yn nehuatl
notoca xpina tiacapan nican nochan s^t Ju^o Evangelista Colhuacan
oncan nipohui yn ipan tlaxillacalli s^t ana tepanecapan yntla
ninomiquilliz ma quimotlapopolhuiliz yn noteouh yn
notlatocatzin Auh ca yz catqui ynn onicnopielli tlalticpac
onechmomaquillitia yn nonamic catca miguel huitznahuatecatl
catca auh niquitohua ynn axcan
—In 3 tetl ohompohualhuiyac vi tetl ynn oncan amaxac
monamacaz yc missa nopan mitoz
—Ihua niquitohua 3 tetl nanapohualhuiyac ypan matlatlactli ynn
ompan (...)(yl?)titlan monamacaz yc missa nopan mitoz
—No yhuan ompohualli yahualiuhcan yhuan tlatepotzco
çenpohualli tetla ompohualli yhuan ayauhtonco çenpohualli
nicmaca yn Ju^o ecatl yhuan ynamic mina tlaco ayac quixtoquilliz
yhuan niquitohua cenpohualli quicuiz yn bal^{ar} amalo yn çanno
oncan ayauhtonco onicteneuh yc onaçi yn ompohualli
—No yhuan 3 tetl chinamitl tlatlamantontonti yn ye mochi
nauhtetl nicmaca yn Juo d s^t ana ayac quixtoquilliz
—yhuan ynn oncan tlanepantlatonco çan çentemi ynn onicteneuh
ynn onicmacac Ju^o de s^t ana yetetl cecenpohualli ymiltitech ymiltitech huallaçitica p^o de (salba?) tlacatecatl
—yhuan ynn o(n?)can apilco çecenpohualhuiyac macuiltetl yhuan
ontetl çeçenpohualhuiyac quauhtenanco Nicmaca yn Ju^o Ecatl
yhuan yn calli ynn oncan nihuetztoc yhuan yn caltepiton mochi
quiçencuiz yn Ju^o Ecatl ayac quixtoquilliz
—yhuan in atentlalli yn ichinayo quiyahuallotica çan mochi ytech
yez yn Ju^o Ecatl
—Imixpan omochiuh testigos marcos mauhtli yhuan Ju^o Ecatl
bal^{ar} amallo Ju^o de sanctana Ju^o piltontli ypiltzin yn cocoxcatzintl
[sic] ynamic Ju^o laz^o Ju^a teycuiuh ana tiacapan ynamic augustin
ahuillizcatl yhuan ynamic Ju^o Ecatl ytoca mina ana xoco ynamic
catca Ju^o tlanencauh yhuan ynamic p^o chantli ytoca martha
teycuiuh Izquintini yn imixpan otlanahuati xpina tiacapan axcan
domingo yc iiii dias del mes de nobienbre de 1576 anos
onitlacuillo nehuatl bal^{ar} amallo
auh yn nehuatl Escri^o della yglesia ytencopatzinco ynic
oniquicuillo testamento don lurenço de s fran^{co} auh yn iuh ca
original yn huel ipan teneuhtica testamento atle çentetl letra
yhuan atle opolliuh ynan huel yuh ca ça huel yuhqui yn itech

omocopin auh ynic oquimoneltilili yn yehuatzin senor fiscal
nican oquimotlallili yfirmatzin

don luren^(c)o de   Miguel Jacobo
s^(t) fra^(co) [fiscal?]   [de Mal^(do)...]

BNP Manuscrit Mexicain 110 f.5r,v
Testament of Cristina Tiacapan
Colonial Spanish Translation, ca. 1590

—En el nonbre de dios padre Hijo y espiritu s^(to) vn solo dios todopoderoso este mi testamento todos quantos vieren y leyeren como yo cristina tiacapan [soy natural ?] de san ju^(o) evangelista si de pres^(te) me muriere que dios nuestro s^(r) me perdone en quantas ofensas le he cometido y digo que lo que yo e tenido y tengo me lo dexo mi marido que dios aya en gloria miguel huiznavatocatl y esto digo con toda mi voluntad

—que de tres a quarenta brazas en largo e seis en el pago de amaxac se an de uender para que se digan misas por mi

—yten mas digo tres a ochenta brazas en largo e dies braças en el pago atiçacaltitlan tanbien se an de vender para que digan las misas por mi

—yten a quarenta yavaliucan y en tlatepuzco veynte tetla quarenta y en ayavhtonco v^(te) lo doy a ju^(o) ecatl e a su muger martina tlaco nadie se las tome

—yten digo v^(te) a de tomar baltasar amaro en ayavhtonco donde tengo dho en cunplimi^(o) de quarenta a de tomar baltasar amaro en el mesmo ayavhtonco

—yten digo tres chinamitl en pedaços (que) todo quatro le doy a ju^(o) de sancta ana tres a v^(te) lindan con tierras de pedro de salba tlacatecatl

—y en el Pago de apilco v^(te) en largo cinco pedaços y dos a v^(te) en largo en quautenango lo doy a ju^(o) ecatl

—y en la casa donde estoy hechada con la casilla todo lo doy a ju^(o) ecatl nadie se las tome

—y en atentli con sus chinantles que le cercan todo a de ser para Ju^(o) Ecatl

Hizose delante de t^(os) marcos mauhtli y ju^(o) ecatl baltasar amaro ju^(o) de sancta ana ju^(o) piltontli y Hijo del enfermo [sic] su marido ju^(o) lazaro ju^(a) teycuh ana tiacapan muger de agustin avilicatl y a

su marido ju⁰ ecatl llamada martina ana xoco mug^er que hera de
ju⁰ tlanencauh e su marido pedro chantli llamada marta oyeronlo
todos estos delante dellos paso lo que m^do cristina tiacapan oy
domingo a quatro dias del mes de novienbre de mill y qui⁰s e
setenta e seis a⁰s yo lo escreui baltasar amaro /f.5v/ yo el escriu⁰
de la yglesia por mandado escreui testamento don loreço de san
ffran^co asi como esta el original del testamento no le ffalta letra
nada ffalta (assi) como esta lo trasunte y anssi lo conffirmo el
ffiscal y lo ffirmo de su n^e don lorenço de san ffran^co ffiscal
xacobo maldonado nonbrado
—ba sierto y berdadero este traslado sacado y coRegido con el
original a todo mi saber y entender y asi lo juro a dios y a esta
cruz y lo firme de mi nonbre
ju⁰ mendez de sotomayor

4 / DIVISION OF DOÑA LUISA JUANA'S ESTATE

Preserved in the Archivo General de la Nación, Mexico (Tierras 58-4) are the records concerning the estate of doña Luisa Juana, a member of the Motecuhçoma family. When doña Luisa Juana died, she left her estate to her father, Juan de San Miguel. Her land, which came from her late grandmother's estate, had apparently continued to be held undivided with her mother's sister, doña Luisa Isabel. The death of doña Luisa Juana prompted the division of the estate.

The ten folios contain the text in Nahuatl and cadastrals of the land under discussion. The documentation is not in perfect order. For instance, the testament of doña Luisa Juana begins on folio 1 and its continuation is on folio 7r. The following list summarizes what is contained in these records.

Folio 1r,v. The first part of the will of doña Luisa Juana, done 15 June 1580.
Folio 2r. Cadastrals showing the inheritance of doña Luisa Isabel, the sister of doña Luisa Juana's mother.
Folio 2r,v. Certification of the copy of doña Luisa Juana's will, done 12 December 1594.
Folio 3r. Cadastrals showing the inheritance of Juan de San Miguel, doña Luisa Juana's father. [See Fig. 4].
Folio 3v. Presentation to the cabildo of the agreement by Juan de San Miguel and his sister-in-law, doña Luisa Isabel, done April 1581.
Folio 4r. Writ of the juez-gobernador to the alcalde to give Juan de San Miguel possession of his land, done 25 April 1581.
Folio 4r,v,5r. Act of giving possession of the land to Juan de San Miguel by the alcalde, done 27 April 1581.
Folio 5r,v. Request by Juan de San Miguel to sell to Spaniards the

190 / APPENDIX 4

house and enclosure belonging to his late daughter, doña Luisa Juana, dated 19 April 1581.

Folio 6r,v. Payment of money to Juan de San Miguel for his daughter's house and enclosure, done 1 May 1581.

Folio 6v. Continuation of folio 2r. of cadastrals showing the land belonging to doña Luisa Isabel.

Folio 7r,v. Continuation of doña Luisa Juana's will, done 15 June 1580.

Folio 7v,8r,v,9r,v. Appearance before the cabildo of Juan de San Miguel and his sister-in-law doña Luisa Isabel (the two called here "the children of don Diego de Motecuhçoma") to divide land, done 5 November 1580.

Folio 9v,10r. Validation of the agreement between Juan de San Miguel and his sister-in-law doña Luisa Juana and the setting of penalties for violation of the agreement, date not entirely certain, possibly 1 November 1580.

Division of the Estate of Doña Luisa Juana
Archivo General de la Nación, Mexico.
Ramo Tierras Volume 58, Expediente 4

/f.1r/ In the name of our lord Jesus Christ and of his precious mother, the noblewoman, Saint Mary, forever a very true virgin, know all who see and read this document that I, doña Luisa Juana, whose home is here in San Juan Evangelista Culhuacan, belonging to the ward of Coatlan, even though I am ill, nonetheless my spirit and memory are undisturbed and sound, and I very truly believe in the Holy Trinity, Father, Son, and Holy Spirit, three persons of just one power and essence, and I believe all that the Holy Church of Rome believes, and I strongly vow that I will always live and die in the true faith. Let our lord God not ordain that he should abandon me, so that the devil will not cloud my judgment, and [as I am not very ill?] when I die, or if I continue living that at some time I not do something which would be counter [to the good?] ... now I confess ... with my deeds ... and now I retract my statement and say that I will also do thus [follow the right path?]. For this reason, now with invocation and supplication of our lord God I make and order my testament that I will ordain with my last will.

—First I say that I place and leave and give my spirit and soul entirely into the hands of our lord God, because he came to redeem it with his precious blood here on earth. Let him deign to come to take my soul. And my body I give to the earth because from earth it came. And when I die I will be buried inside the church before [the image of] the noblewoman Saint Mary.

—May you hear me, you who are here with me, now in your presence I give my orders to my father, Juan de San Miguel and to the lady, my mother, doña Elena Constantina. I say and state that concerning the grant made by my lady, my deceased grandmother doña Juana de Motecuhçoma, /f.1v/ that all the lands and fields that she gave me in the place called Nextitlan I give and assign to you, my father, and to my lady, your wife.

—And you, my progenitors, Juan Itzpancalcatzintli and Juan Tlacochcalcatzintli, speak well in favor of my declaration: I say that my deceased grandmother left us in charge of our dear father, prior fray Juan Núñez, to divide [our inheritance] between us. And I say that I also leave it up to him: may he promptly do [determine] all my inheritance.

—First I declare concerning the house that is in Acpac, that the lady my deceased grandmother divided between my aunt, doña Luisa [Isabel], and me. [The house], whose back part faces toward Ixtapalapa, will be sold, and the proceeds in money that result will be delivered to the church in order that masses be said for both of us, my mother doña María de Motecuhçoma and me... [with] however much the price is in money. Miguel Vázquez will show people my inheritance, because he knows where it terminates.

—Second, I declare that concerning the grant that my lady made, my deceased grandmother doña Juana de Motecuhçoma, the lands that she gave in all the locations that my aunt doña Luisa and I have not divided, in Tochihuic, in Tlallachco, in Apilco, in San Lorenzo, in Santiago [Tetla], and in Huixachtlan, all [of them] I am giving to you, all will belong here [to our family] because it is the inheritance of your late wife, my deceased mother, doña María de Motecuhçoma, and it is truly my property. For this reason I give it to you, because you are my father. Miguel Vázquez will show people all the places where my inheritance is. [testament continues on folio 7r].

/f.2r/ The inheritance in Santiago Tetla of doña Luisa Isabel
—a narrow field
—in Axomolco
—in Aztahuacan

—in Apilco
—in Ocelotepec, forty [wide]
400 long it is still as it has been [unplanted? unworked?]
—in Tlatlauhquitepec; it is to remain as it is
[continues on /f.6r/]

—Here in the city of Culhuacan, the 12th day of the month of December in the year 1594, by order of the very honored lord teniente here in the said city of Culhuacan, whose jurisdiction reaches to Mexicatzinco, I made [I copied] this testament that doña Luisa Juana ordered. She mentioned the house and the fields as are seen in the testament. And the house and fields were sold and a bill of sale was made. I made the written copy, not a word was lost nor a letter omitted. And the very honored lord teniente, Francisco Alemán, in order to verify it, placed here his signature. [Done] before me the appointed notary, and I affirm /f.2v/ all the things that were mentioned; it is a true copy of the original and in order to verify it I place here my signature, the 12th day of the month of December of the year 1594.
Francisco Alemán, teniente. Before me [Gabriel Jiménez?], appointed notary.
/f.3r/ The fields of the inheritance pertaining to Juan de San Miguel
—in Tochihuic   all the chinampas are [uncounted?]
—in Nextitlan   240
—the inheritance of Juan de San Miguel in San Lorenzo Tetzonco:
    petlatolli   zacate   tequixquitl
—the inheritance of Juan de San Miguel in Santiago Tetla, first in the place named
—Tlatozcac
—in Xalpan
—in Axomolco
—in Aztahuacan

/f.3v/ Here in the city of Culhuacan the ... of the month of April of the year 1581, [before] the lord don Juan Marcos [de Velasco], juez-gobernador, here in the said city, before me, Miguel Jacobo [de Maldonado], appointed notary, Juan de San Miguel declared that he had come to present a notarized statement of agreement concerning the partition, because the two of them, he and his sister-in-law, doña Luisa Isabel, divided all the houses and lands and fields as in their declaration of accord and as it is in the pictorial. And accordingly Juan de San Miguel and his sister-in-law doña Luisa Isabel presented their declaration of partition. Juan de San Miguel wishes to take possession of all the fields that pertain to him and that he inherited so that no one at some time should take them from him or contend with him in the future, because [the agreement] will always have value and he will do on [the land] whatever his heart desires, so that it will truly appear to be his property. Having seen the declaration of accord of Juan de San Miguel and his sister-in-law doña Luisa Isabel, and as it appears in the pictorial, the juez-gobernador said that he gave orders for a writ, to be made that possession be given Juan de San Miguel. And Lorenzo de San Francisco, alcalde here in the said city, is to go to give it to him. Thus spoke and ordered the lord juez-gobernador, and in order to verify it, he placed here his name and signature. Don Juan Marcos, gobernador. Before me, Miguel Jacobo de Maldonado.

/f.4r/ I, don Juan Marcos [de Velasco], juez-gobernador here in the city of Culhuacan, order you, Lorenzo de San Francisco, alcalde here in the said city, that when you see this my writ, then go to give Juan de San Miguel possession of all his inherited fields, as appears in the declaration of accord between him and his sister-in-law doña Luisa Isabel. And if someone says something counter to it and disputes the possession, let him be brought before me so that I will hear his declaration, and I will do him justice. Done the 25th day of the month of April of the year 1581. Don Juan Marcos [de Velasco], gobernador. Before me, Miguel Jacobo de Maldonado, appointed notary.

The lord Lorenzo de San Francisco [alcalde] here in the city of Culhuacan, in order to effect the writ of the lord juez-gobernador, thereupon went to all the places where the inherited fields of Juan de San Miguel were. First he gave him possession in the place called Santiago [Tetla] where in Tlatozcac there are fields of 40 [units of measure] wide and 80 long. When they arrived there, the lord alcalde took Juan de San Miguel by the hand, and to give him possession he went taking him from one place to another on [the land]. And with a wooden digging stick [Juan de San Miguel] dug in the four corners in order to show that he took possession of all his land. In the second place [in Santiago Tetla], Xalpan, [there is land]

140 [units of measure] long and 20 wide. In the third place, called Axomolco, /f.4v/ [there is land] 140 [units of measure] long and 40 wide. And in the fourth place, named Aztahuacan, [there is land] also 140 [units of measure] long and 40 wide. And in all the said fields, Juan de San Miguel dug in the corners with a wooden digging stick to demonstrate that he had taken possession of all his inherited lands. And the lord alcalde said, "In peace and safety I give you possession of all your inherited fields." No one there disputed it or impeded it. There are inherited fields of Juan de San Miguel in another place, named San Lorenzo Tetzonco, in length 800 [units of measure], and in width, toward Mexico City, 80, but toward Xochimilco, 40, with all [the land] of reeds and grasses and tequesquite. In all the places mentioned, the lord alcalde also gave Juan de San Miguel possession calmly and happily. And also in each place he dug in all four corners with a wooden digging stick to demonstrate that they were his inherited fields. And in the third place, Juan de San Miguel was given possession, in the place named Nextitlan [of land that was] 240 [units of measure] long and 40 wide. And in the place called Tochihuic [there is land] 67 matl long and 30 matl wide. In all the said places he likewise dug in the four corners with a wooden digging stick as mentioned above, and calmly and happily Juan de San Miguel was given possession. And the lord alcalde said, "Keep in tranquility all your fields of which you were given possession." And neither did anyone /f.5r/ dispute with or impede him in all the places where he went along taking him, so that everywhere he designated the inherited fields of Juan de San Miguel. [Done] before the witnesses: don Juan Ramírez, don Juan García, Agustín Jiménez, alguacil mayor; Gregorio de Alvarado, regidor; Pedro de San Bernardino, official in charge of the land, Juan Bautista Quenitoloc, land measurer. Today, Thursday, the 27th day of the month of April in the year 1581. Before me, Miguel Jacobo de Maldonado, appointed notary.

Here in the city of Culhuacan, the 19th of the month of April of the year 1581, before the lords don Juan Marcos [de Velasco], juez-gobernador, and the alcaldes here in the said city, and before me, the appointed notary, appeared Juan de San Miguel, whose home is here in the said city, and he said and declared to the lords that he has a/some houses[s] with an enclosure that were the property of his deceased legitimate daughter named doña Juana Luisa, whom our lord God carried away. And this house and enclosure were given to her by her late grandmother named doña Juana Motecuhçoma, whom our lord God also carried away. And it also appears in the testament that the said house and enclosure were given to the daughter of Juan de San Miguel who was named doña Juana Luisa; and when the young woman /f.5v/ died, she made her testament concerning her inherited house and enclosure; all of it was to be sold, and with the proceeds in money masses were to be said for the both of them, her and her mother, doña María Tiacapan, whom our lord also carried off. And all the time after doña María Tiacapan died, the late wife of Juan de San Miguel, and their daughter named Juana Luisa died, masses have not yet been said to help their souls, because no citizens here in Culhuacan have appeared who want to buy the house and enclosure, because they are worth a lot of money. Therefore now Juan de San Miguel brought it before the lords, the governor and the alcaldes, and asked of them that they give him their license and legal power so that some Spaniard can buy the whole house and enclosure. And with the proceeds in money, masses will be said for his wife and for his daughter, for the aid of their souls, as it is in the testament. And having heard the petition of Juan de San Miguel, lord, the governor and the alcaldes, said and ordered that they give license to Juan de San Miguel so that he can sell all the house and enclosure of his daughter named doña Juana Luisa. And as she said in her testament, with [the proceeds] masses will be said for the both of them, her and her mother named doña María Tiacapan, for the aid of their souls, because there is need of it. Thus they ordered, and in order to verify it, they placed here their signatures and names. Don Juan Marcos [de Velasco], gobernador. Lorenzo de San Francisco, alcalde. Juan Téllez, alcalde. Before me, Marcos Jorge, appointed notary.

/f.6r/ I, Juan de San Miguel, say that I truly take and receive 40 pesos in money from the hand of Sr. Diego de San Román and from his wife, Elvira Núñez, with which they are paying for the house and enclosure that are in Acpac. And it is mentioned in the testament how it will be sold, and with the proceeds in money masses will be said for the two of them, already mentioned, for my legitimate wife, who was named doña María Tiacapantzin, and for my daughter, whom our lord God carried away. With [the money] will be said masses for the aid of their souls. In order to verify it, I place here my

name and signature. Done today the first day of the month of May of the year 1581. And afterward Juan de San Miguel, when he had received the money, the 40 pesos, for which he sold the house in Acpac, as it is written in the testament[s?] of the deceased, his deceased legitimate wife, doña María Tiacapan, and his deceased legitimate daughter, doña Juana Luisa, Juan de San Miguel immediately divided the money in order that masses be said for the redemption of their souls. Thirty [pesos] he gave to our dear father, fray Juan Núñez, in order that he say masses for the said deceased, because he was named their executor. And the 10 pesos remaining Juan de San Miguel took to be spent on himself, because he previously aided his legitimate wife and his legitimate daughter, mentioned above; for ten masses were said /f.6v/ and [ten?] vigils with which he aided the souls of the deceased. And concerning the 10 pesos he is taking, in order to verify it, he set down his signature before the witnesses of how he gave the money [to fray Juan Núñez] and took 10 pesos for himself: the juez-gobernador, don Juan Marcos [de Velasco], and before Miguel Jerónimo, Francisco Maldonado, Diego Elías, executor, and Miguel Jacobo [de Maldonado], notary of the church.
/f.6v/ Done today, Tuesday, the 17th of the month of May of the year 1581. Don Lorenzo de San Francisco, alcalde. Before me, Miguel Jacobo de Maldonado.

[continuation of the pictorial of the lands of doña Luisa Isabel from folio 2r]
—In Tochihuic
—In Nextitlan
—The inheritance of doña Luisa Isabel in San Lorenzo Tetzonco:
reeds   grass   tequesquite

[continuation of the testament of doña Luisa Juana from folio 1r].
/f.7r/ because many times in my presence my lady, my grandmother notified him [where it was]. I request my dear father the prior that he take the oath of Miguel Vázquez not to lie. This is all I order you. May you not forget me. Before the witnesses who were especially summoned and she herself sought out, Juan Itzpancalqui and Juan Tlacochcalcatl. And those there who were caring for the invalid also heard it: Andrés Juárez, Diego de la Cruz, and Juana Teicuh, widow of Francisco Temilo. Today, Tuesday, midnight, the day of the Holy

Cross, the 3rd day of the month of May of the year 1580. I wrote it by order of doña Luisa Juana, the invalid, I, Marcos Jorge, official in charge of the choir. In order to verify it, the witnesses placed their names here: Juan Rafael [Tlacochcalcatl]. But Juan Itzpancalqui does not know how to write, and in order to verify it, he made a cross [to show he is] a true witness.

/f.7v/ The 15th day of the month of June of the year 1580, before the lord don Juan Marcos de Velasco, juez-gobernador of the said city, appeared this testament that doña Juana Luisa ordered. And when he saw it and understood it, he said that he ruled this testament valid, and no one is to violate it. And to verify it, he put down his name and signature. Don Juan Marcos de Velasco. Before me, Alonso Dávila de Santiago, appointed notary.

Here in the city of Culhuacan, the 5th day of the month of November of the year 1580, before the lord don Juan Marcos de Velasco, juez-gobernador, here in the said city appeared Juan de San Miguel and doña Luisa Isabel, children of don Diego de Motecuhçoma, whom our lord carried away, and they informed him that their deceased father, the late don Diego de Motecuhçoma left them his lands and fields; first in Santiago Tetla, in Texalpan, second, a narrow field [in Santiago]; third, in Tlatozcac; fourth, in Xalpan; fifth, in Axomolco; sixth, in Aztahuacan; seventh, in San Lorenzo Tetzonco; eighth, in Tochihuic; ninth, /f.8r/ in Amimintitlan; tenth, in Apilco; eleventh, in Quauhtitlan; twelfth, in Ocelotepec and Tlatlauhquitepec. And they came to show him all the places where the said fields are, as they appear in the pictorial, with the agreement and approval and common will of Juan de San Miguel and doña Luisa Isabel [by which] both of them agreed to divide the fields that belonged to don Diego de Motecuhçoma in all the different places. And so that their statement of agreement as to how they want to divide the fields of their father, for that reason Juan de San Miguel and doña Luisa Isabel have come before the lord juez-gobernador and shown their will before the judge. He said that Juan de San Miguel takes 60 [units of measure] of the fields that are in Santiago Tetla, 40 [units of measure] in Tlatozcac, and 20 [units] in Texalpan, which [makes] 60. And doña Luisa Isabel likewise takes 60 [units of measure] of the fields in Santiago Tetla, 40 in Texalpan, and 20 of the narrow field, which [makes] 60. And all of it goes together, [the land of] each one 80 units of measure long. And secondly, there are fields they are dividing in the place named Axomolco. Doña Luisa Juana is taking 40, and Juan de San Miguel is also taking the same [amount], 40 [units of measure] long. [The fields] go together and are each 140 [units of measure] long. Third, there are fields they are dividing in the place named Aztahuacan, 80 [units of measure long]. Doña Luisa Isabel is taking 40 [units of measure] and Juan de San Miguel is also taking 40. [The fields] go together [and are] 140 each, each equal. And fourth, there are fields they are dividing in the place named San Lorenzo Tetzonco, 160 [units of measure]. Doña Luisa Isabel is taking 80 [units], Juan de San Miguel is also taking 80. And [the fields] go together and are, each 800 [units of measure] long. /f.8v/ And there is level nitrous land where there are fields with reeds on them. The nitrous field and all that belongs to it they are dividing in half. Fifth, there are fields that they are dividing in the place named Tochihuic. Juan de San Miguel is taking 30 [units of measure], and the other 30 doña Luisa Isabel is taking. The fields go together and are each 67 matl long. Sixth, there are fields they are dividing in the place named Amimintitlan, 40 [units of measure] wide, and in length 207 matl. And Juan de San Miguel and his sister-in-law doña Luisa Isabel have agreed that [the fields] will not pertain to either but will be in common, and if some debt in money [owed by the estate] appears from somewhere and is fully acknowledged, the wherewithal to pay it will come from there. For this reason they place it in common and are not assigning it to anyone. Seventh, in Apilco there are chinampas that are 40 [units of measure] wide and 300 [units] long, and by the common accord of Juan de San Miguel and doña Luisa they are assigning them [in such a way that] they also divide them between them. Juan de San Miguel is taking 20 [units], and doña Luisa is also taking 20. Eighth, there are chinampas in the place named Quauhtitlan Tlallachco, 70 wide and 1800 long; Juan de San Miguel and his sister-in-law doña Luisa Isabel said that just for the sake of our lord God [for charity] they give them and to don Francisco Xiloman and doña Juana Tiacapan, illegitimate children of don Diego de Motecuhçoma. Without any dispute they leave them the said chinampas in Quauhtitlan, the illegitimate children /f.9r/ of don Diego de Motecuhçoma are to take them. And if they do not accept the chinampas they have granted them in Quauhtitlan, Juan de San Miguel and his sister-in-law [doña] Luisa Isabel will take them and divide them between them. Ninth, there are fields in the places named Ocelotepec and Tlatlauhquitepec, and with the common agreement of Juan de San Miguel and of his sister-in-law doña Luisa Isabel they declared that the fields in both the said locations are to belong to doña Luisa Isabel alone. This is all their agreement about how Juan de San Miguel and doña Luisa Isabel divided their fields and chinampas that their late father don Diego de Motecuhçoma left them.

—And when they came to present their declaration of agreement, all of the above mentioned, before the lord juez-gobernador, Juan de San Miguel and his sister-in-law doña Luisa Isabel asked that he confirm for them all the items of their declaration of agreement by which they divided their fields and chinampas in order that no one sometime should contend with them or dispute or violate their declaration of accord, their written agreement, and in order that it be fully valid, they came before the lord juez-gobernador to confirm it for them through his office of justice. And when Juan de San Miguel and his sister-in-law doña Luisa Juana came to show their written agreement and accord, it was done before the alcalde, Martín Cano and the alguacil mayor, Miguel de Ribas, don Juan Ramírez, don Juan García, Miguel Gerónimo, Antonio de Galicia, Francisco Cihuatecpanecatl, regidor mayor; the witnesses whose names are mentioned above are the ones before whom the written agreement and statement of accord of Juan de San Miguel and doña Luisa Isabel was done, and they verify it with their signatures and names. Juan de San Miguel. Doña Luisa Isabel. /f.9v/ Martín Cano, alcalde. Miguel de Ribas, alguacil mayor. Don Juan Ramírez. Don Juan García. Miguel Gerónimo. Before me, Miguel Jacobo de Maldonado, appointed notary.

And when the lord juez-gobernador of the said city here saw and understood all the declaration of agreement of Juan de San Miguel and his sister-in-law doña Luisa Isabel to divide their fields and chinampas in all the places where they are, that their deceased father don Diego de Motecuhçoma left them, [the juez-gobernador] said and ruled, "Let it be observed and validated how Juan de San Miguel and his sister-in-law doña Luisa Isabel distributed and divided their fields and chinampas between themselves, so that they have distributed to each the same amount of fields and chinampas as his own. Let them keep them in peace and tranquility; by means of justice I make the [lands] their property and inheritance, and I give them possession of them when the /f.10r/ alguacil mayor has gone to put stakes to show the lands which belong to each one as his or her property, so that no one will ever violate the written agreement and statement of accord of Juan de San Miguel and his sister-in-law doña Luisa Isabel. Now in the name of his majesty I order that the penalty for anyone who wishes to violate or dispute this agreement; he will be confined in jail for ten days and will receive 100 lashes in the marketplace, and will be exiled for six months, and will pay 10 pesos that will belong to the chamber of his majesty." Thus he ordered and judged, and to verify it he placed here his signature and name. Likewise done the 1st day of the month and year mentioned above. Don Juan Marcos, juez-gobernador. Done before me, Miguel Jacobo de Maldonado, appointed notary.

AGN Ramo Tierras 58, expediente 4

/f.1r/ Testamento de d^a Luisa Juana, Yndia Comun [in a hand later than that of the text]

Yn ica ytocatzin in tote° Jhro yhuan yn itlaçonantzin Cihuapilli Sancta Maria in mochipa huel nelli ychpochtli Ma mochintin quimatican yn ixquichtin quittazque in quipohuazque ynin Amatl in nehuatl Dona luysa ju^a Nican nochan S^t. ju° euag^{ta} Clhcan honcan nipohui yn ipan tlaxillacalli Cohuatlan Maçoyhui y ninococohua yece in noyollo in notlalnamiquiliz Aquen ca çan pactica Ca huel nelli melahuac ynic nicnoneltoquitiya in SS^{ma} Trinidad tetatzin tepiltzin yhuan SS° yn ey Personas çan ce yn ihuelitzin yn iyelitzin yhuan mochi nicneltoca yn ixquich quimoneltoquitiya in Sta yglia Romana yhuan ninocennetoltiya ca mochipa ypan ninemiz yhuan ypan nimiquiz in melahuac tlaneltoquiliztli Auh in tote° dios Macamo quimonequiltitzino Macamo nechmomacahuilitzino ynic amo nechtlapoltiz [sic] in tlacatecolotl yhuan ynic amo huey cocolizt. . a yn iquac ye nimiquiz intla noçoc nonnemiz ynic amo quenmaniyan ytla nicchihuatiuh in quixnamiqui . . . axcan Nicnocuitiya . . . notlachihualiztica . . . titiuh niman Axcan niccuepa y notlatol niquitohua no yuh nicchihuaz Auh ypampa yn axcan yn inotzaloca ytlatlauhtiloca in tote° dios nicchihua nictecpana in Notestamento in ça tlatzaccan notlanequiliz ynic nictecpanaz Ynic centlamantli Niquitohua y noyolliya in naniman ymactzinco

nocontlaliya noconcencahua nicnomaquiliya in tote° dios ypanpa
ca ytlaçoyezyotica hoquimomaquixtilico in nican tpc Auh ma
quimonequilti ynic quihualmaniliz yn naniman Auh y nonacayo
nicmaca tlalli ypanpa ca tlalli ytech quiz yhuan yn iquac nimiquiz
honpa nitocoz in calitic teopan yyxpa^{co} cihuapilli Sta Maria Ma
xicmocaquitican y notlan Ancate ynic amixpan nicnonahuatiliya in
notatzin ju° de san Migl yhuan in Cihuapilli y nonatzin dona
Elena Constantina niquitohua Nictlaliya y notlatol yn
intetlaocolilitzin in notecuiyotzin y noçitzin moyetzticatca Dona
Ju^a de motecuhcçoma /f.1v/ yn ixquich nechmomaquilitiya in
tlalli in milli yn itocayocan Nextitlan namechnomaquilitiuh
Amotechtzinco nicpouhtiuh in tinotatzin yhuan y notecuiyotzin y
monamitzin [sic]
ii—Auh yn amehuantzitzin yn annotechiuhcahuan
Namechnonahuatiliya ju° ytzpancalcatzintli yhuan ju°
tlacochcalcatzintli Ma huel ipan Amotlatoltizque y notlatol
Niquitohua in yehuatzin nocitzin moyetzticatca ytechtzinco
techmocahuiltiuh in totlaçotatzin p^{or} fray ju° Nunes ynic
techmotlaxexelhuiliz Auh in nehuatl niquitohua çanno ytechtzinco
niccauhtituh Ma yçiuhca quimochihuiliz yn ixquich nonemac
iii—Achtopa Niquitohua in caltzintli yn onpa mani Acpa [sic] in
techmixtlapanilitiuh yn nahuitzin in dona luysa in tlacatl in
Cihuapilli in nocitzin moyetzticatca yn itztapalapanpa tepotzeticac
in calli monamacaz yn ipatiuh mochihuaz in to^s Calaquiz Teopan
yc Missa topan mitoz tomextin ... nonatzin in dona Maria de
motecuhcçoma yp. ... az in quexquich yp. ... mochihuaz in to^s
yehuatl quiteytitiz in nonemac in Migl Vazquez ca quimati yn
oncan tlantica Nonemac
—Ynic ontlamantli Niquitohua yn itetlaocolilitzin y notecuiyotzin
in nocitzin moyetzticatca in dona ju^a de motecuhcçoma yn
ixquich nechmomaquilitiya yn izquican yn ayamo tictoxexelhuiya
in nahuitzin in dona luysa in tlalli in tochihuic yhuan in tlallachco
yhuan yn apilco yhuan in s^t lorenço yhuan yn santiago yhuan
huixachtlan Mochi nimitznomaquilitiuh Mochi nican pohuiz
Canel ynemactzin yetiuh in monamictzin catca in dona Maria de
Motecuhcçoma y nonantzin moyetziticatca Ca huel naxca ypanpa
in nimitznomaquiliya Canel tinotatzin yehuatl quiteytititiyaz yn
izquican caca nonemac in Migl [see f.7r].
/f.2r/ -Santiago tetla ynemac dona luysa ysabel
—milpitzactli

—Axomolco
—Aztahuacan
—Apilco
—Ocelotepc tlatlauhquitpec
honplli cen-
tzonhuiyac
çanoquiuhca ... c no yuhca

Yn nican ypan Altepetl Clhcan a doze dias del mes de Di^e mill y quinientos y noventa y quatro anos yn yehuatzin in cenca mahuiztililoni s^or te^e yn nican ypan Altepetl homoteneuh Clhcan yc açi yn iJuridicion in Mexicatzinco ytenpan^co yn onicchiuh ynin Testamento yn oquitlalitiya dona luysa ju^a hoquiteneuhtiya in calli yhuan in Milli yn iuh neztica yn ipan testamento Auh in Calli yhuan in Milli homonamacac homochiuh Carta de Venta Nehuatl honicchiuh in traslado Atle cencamatl hopoliuh yhuan Atle centetl Letras homocauh Auh in yehuatzin in cenca mahuiztililoni s^or teniente fran^co de Aleman yc oquimoneltilili Nican hoquimotlalli yfirma Nixpan yn nehuatl escri^o nobrado Nicneltiliya /f.2v/ yn izquitlamantli homoteneuh huel melahuac ynic omocopin yn itech Original yc nicneltiliya Nican nictlaliya nofirma a doze dias del mes de Di^e de mill y quinientos y noventa y quatro a^os fran^co aleman teniente Nixpan (a^l xi^ez?)
Escri^o nonbrado

/f.3r/ -Ju^o de san migl ymilnemac ytech pouhqui
—tochihuic
—Nextitlan yn tlahapilli
in mochi
chinamitl
10^a plli ypan ii plli
—Sant lorenço tetzonco ynemac ju^o de san Miguel

       Petlatolli   -çacatl   -tequixquitl

—Sanctiago tetla ynemac ju^o de s. migl ynic cecni mani ytocayocan
—tlatozcac
—Xalpan
                        Ryes [later hand]

—Axomolco
Aztahuacan
[In a late hand, it seems to be trying to confirm that the space below does not count.]

/f.3v/ -Yn nican ypan Altepe......... mani Metztli Abril de 1581 anos yn yehuatz.. senor don ju⁰ marcos gou^or juez in nican ypan Altepetl hoteneuh nixpan in nehuatl Migl Jacobo escri⁰ nonbrado hoquito in yehuatl ju⁰ de s. migl yhuan hoquimixpantililico ce escriptura de concierto yn itech pohui tlaxexeloliztli ypanpa yn ixquich in calli in tlalli in Milli yn oquimoxexelhuique yn innehuan yhuepol in dona luysabel [sic] yn iuh ca yn innenonotzaliztlatol yhuan yn iuh catqui yn ipan yn pintura Auh ynic oquimixpantililique yn intlaxexeloliztlatol in ju⁰ de s. migl yhuan yn ihuepol in dona luysa ysabel yn ixquich ytech pouhqui yn imil in ju⁰ de san miguel yn inemac homochiuh quinequi yn ipan yn ipan [sic] yxquich Conanaz Possession ynic amo quenmaniyan Aca quicuilitiuh Anoço ypan quixnamiquitiuh in ye honpa titztihui Auh yeyca ca cemicac ypan chicahuatiyez yhuan quichihuaz in tleyn ypan quinequiz yyollo ynic huel neçiz ca ye yaxca ca ye ytlatqui Auh in yehuatzin in senor gou^or juez yn oquimottili yn innenotzaliztlatol in ju⁰ de s. migl yhuan yn ihuepol dona luysa ysabel yhuan yn iuh neztican yn ipan Pintura hoquimitalhui ynic omotlanahuatilli Mochihuaz Mandamiento ynic macoz Possession in yehuatl ju⁰ de san Migl Auh yehuatl quimacatiuh in lorenço de s^t fran^co Allde yn nican ipan Altepetl homoteneuh yhui yn yn oquimitlahui ynic omotlanahuatili in senor gou^or juez yc oquimoneltilili nican homotlalili yfirma yca yn itoca
Don Ju⁰ Marcos gou^or Nixpan Migl Jacobo de Mal^do

/f.4r/ -Yn nehuatl don ju⁰ marcos gou^or juez y nican ypan Altepetl Colhuacan Nimitznahuatiya in tehuatl ti lorenço de sant fran^co allde y nican ypan Altepetl homoteneuh yn iquac tiquitaz ynin notenahuatillamauh Niman xiyauh xicmaca in possession yn yehuatl ju⁰ de san Migl yn ipan yn ixquich ymilnemac yn iuh neztica yn ipan yn innenonotzaliztlatol yn ihuepol in dona luysa ysabel Auh intla haca ytla quitoz in quixnamiquiz in possession Ma nixpan hualaz ca niccaquiliz yn itlatol yhuan nicchihuiliz just^a yc 25 mani Metztli Abril de 1581 anos
Don Ju⁰ Marcos gou^or Nixpan Migl Jacobo Mal^do escri⁰ nonbrado

—Yn yehuatzin senor lorenço de sant fran^co y nican ypan
Altepetl Clhcan ynic oquimoneltilili yn itenahuatiltzin senor juez
gou^or Niman honpa hoya yn izquican mani yn imilnemac in ju^o
de s. miguel ynic ceccan hoquimacac Possession ytocayocan
sanctiago tlatozcac yn oncan mani milli ynic patlahuac honplli
Auh ynic huiyac 4 plli Auh yn iquac yn oncan hohonacic in senor
allde Niman ymatitech conan in ju^o de san migl ynic oquimacac
Possession honcan ypan hoquihuihuicatinen yhuan nauhcanpa
hoquinanacaztatac yca in quauhhuictli ynic oquinezcayoti yn
ixquich yc conana yn itlal yn ica Possession ynic ocan xalpan ynic
huiyac 7 plli Auh ynic patlahuac cenplli Auh yniquexcan
ytocayocan Axomolco ynic huiyac 7 plli Auh ynic tlahuac [sic]
/f.4v/ honplli ynic nauhcan ytocayocan Aztahuacan ynic huiyac
çanno chiconplli Auh yni patlahuac honplli Auh yn izquican
homoteneueh Milli No yzquicanpa oquinanacaztatacac yca
quauhhuictli ynic oquinezcayoti yn ixquich y conana yn
itlalnemac yn ica Possession Auh in senor allde hoquito yhuiyan
yocoxca nimitzma [sic] in Possession yn ipan yzquican Mani in
momilnemac Ayac honcan hotlachalani yhuan Amonoac honcan
ypan hoquitlacahualti Auh ynic ocan mani yn imilnemac in ju^o de
s. migl ytocayocan sant lorenço tetzonco ynic huiyac hontzontli
Auh ynic patlahuac in Mexicopa 4 plli Auh in xochmilcopa
honplli yhuan yn ixqui in petlatolli yhuan in çacatl yhuan in
tequixquitl yn izquican homoteneuh çannohuiyan [sic] yocuxcan
pacca yn o ypan quimacac senor allde in Possession in yehuatl
ju^o de san Migl Auh ^canno yzquicanpan Nauhcanpa
hoquinanacaztatac yca yn quahuictli ynic oquinezcayoti yn
imilnemac Auh ynic yexcan homacoc Possession in ju^o de s.
miguel ytocayocan nextitlan ynic huiyac 10^ac plli yhuan honplli
Auh ynic patlahuac honplli yhuan in itotocayocan [sic] tochihuic
ynic huiyac 3 plli ypan chiconmatl Auh ynic patlahuac cenplli
ypan matlacmatl yn yzquican homoteneuh çanno yzquican
nauhcanpa hoquinanacaztatac yca yn quahuictli yn iuh tlacpac
homoteneuh çanno yhuiyan pacca yocuxca yn omacoc Possession
in yehuatl ju^o de s migl Auh in yehuatl senor allde hoquimitalhui
Ma yhuiya yocuxca xicmopiyelli yn ixquich momil yn ixquich
ypan hotimacoc Possession yhuan Amo no haca honcan /f.5r/
hoquichalani Anoço hoquitlacahualti yn izquican honcan ypan
hoquihuihuicatinen ynic nohuiyan hoquimachiyoti yn imilnemac
in ju^o de san Miguel ymixpan testigos don ju^o Ramirez don ju^o

garcia Augustin xiez Alguazil mayor gregorio de Aluarado
Regidor pedro de sant Bernardino tlaltopille ju⁰ Bapᵗᵃ quenitoloc
tlalpouhqui Axcan jueves yc 27 Mani Metztli Abril de mill y
quinientos y ochenta y vn anos
Nixpa Migl Jacobo de Malᵈᵒ escri⁰ nonbrado

—Yn nican ypan Altetl [sic] Colhuacan yc 19 mani Metztli Abril
de 1581 anos in yehuantzitzin senores tlatoque don ju⁰ marcos
gouᵒʳ juez yhuan alldes y nican ypan Altepetl omoteneuh
ymixpantzinco honecico in ju⁰ de s. miguel Nican ychan yn ipan
Altepetl omoteneuh ymixpantzinco honecico in ju⁰ de s. miguel
Nican ychan yn ipan Altepetl homoteneuh nixpan in nehuatl
escri⁰ nonbrado hoquito in ju⁰ de s. miguel ynic
oquinmononochilli in tlatoque ca quipiya calli yhuan tepancalli
yyaxca catca ytlatqui in teoyotica yychpoch catca ytoca dona juᵃ
luysa hoquimohuiquili in toteᵒ dios Auh in yehuatlyn in calli
yhuan in tepancalli quimacatiya yn içitzin catca yn itoca catca
dona juᵃ motecuhcçoma catca ho no quimohuiquili in toteᵒ dios
Auh ynin ca ypan neztica in testamento yn iuh macoc in calli
yhuan in tepancalli yn omoteneuh yn iychpoch ju⁰ de s. migl yn
itoca catca dona juᵃ luysa Auh yn iquac Momiquili yn i /f.5v/
chpochtli oquichiuhtiya ytestamento yn ipanpa yn icalnemac
yhuan yn ix [sic] ytepancalnemac Mochi monamacaz Auh yn
ipatiuh yez in toˢ Missa yquinpan mitoz yn innehuan ynantzin
dona Maria tiyacapan ho no quimohuiquili in toteᵒ dios Auh yn
ixquich cahuitl homomiquilique in dona Maria tiyacapantzin yn
inamic catca ju⁰ de san Migl yhuan yn iychpoch ytoca dona juᵃ
luysa Ayayc ceppa ynpan mitohua Missa yn ipanpa yn ipalehuiloca
imAnimas yeyca camo ac neci yn aquin quicohuaz in calli yhuan
in tepancalli in nican Altepehuaque Colhuaque yehican ca miec
toˢ ypatiuh ypanpa yn axcan in yehuatl ju⁰ de s. migl ynic
oquimotlayxpantillico in tlatoque gouᵒʳ yhua alldes
hoquinmotlaytlanilili ynic quimomaquilizque yn inlicencia yn
ihuelitzin ynic huell aca espanol quinamaquiltiz yn ixquich in
calli yhua in tepancalli Auh yn ipatiuh yez in toˢ Missa yn quipan
[sic] mitoz yn inamic yhuan yn iychpoch yn ipanpa yn
ipalehuiloca mochihuaz yn iManimas yn iuh ca yn ipan
testamento Auh yn o yuh quimocaquitique in senores gouᵒʳ yhua
in senores alldes in tlatoque yn itlaytlaniliz in ju⁰ de s. migl
hoquimitalhuique ynic omotlanahuatilique ca quinmomaquiliya

Licencia in juº de s. migl ynic huel quinamacaz yn ixquich yn ical yhuan yn itepancal yn iychpoch yn itoca catca dona juᵃ luysa yn iuh quitotiuh yn ipan ytestamento in Missa ypan yc mitoz yn innehua ynantzin yn itoca catca dona Maria tiyacapan yn ipapa yn ipalehuiloca yn iManimas yehica ca yuh monequi yhui y ynic omotlanahuatilique ynic oquimoneltilique Nican hoquimotlalili yn infirmas yhua yn intoca

don Jhoan marcos gouᵒʳ   lorenço de s. francº allde
Juº tellez allde   Nixpan Marcos Jorge escriº nonbrado

/f.6r/ -Yn nehuatl Juº de s. migl Niquitohua ca nelli niccui nicceliya yn onplli pºs toˢ ymacpatzinco in senor diº de sant Roman yhuan yn inamictzin Elbira Nunez yn ic quimopatiyotiliya in calli yhuan in tepancalli yn oncan ma [sic] Acpac yn ipan teneuhtica in testamento ynic monamacaz Auh yn ipatiuh mochihuaz in toˢ Missa yquinpan mitoz yn omentin yn omentin [sic] homoteneuh in teoyotica y nonamic yn itoca catca dona Maria tiyacapantzin yhuan yn teoyotica nochpoch yn oquinmohuiquilli in toteº dios yc missa ynpan mitoz yn ipanpa yn inpalehuillo [sic] yn iManimas ynic nicneltilliya Nican nictlaliya notoca nofirma Axcan homochiuh yc cemilhuitl mani Metztli Mayo de 1581 anos
—Auh çatepan Yn yehuatl juº de s. miguel yn o yuh quicelli in toˢ yn onplli pºs ynic oquinamac [sic] in calli Acpac yn iuh ca yn ipan yn intestamento in mimiccatzitzintin in teoyotica ynamic catca in dona Maria tiyacapantzin in teoyotica yychpoch catca in dona juᵃ luysa in yehuatl juº de s. migl ynic Missas inpan mitoz yn ipanpa yn inmaquixtiloca yn imanimas Auh niman hoquixello in toˢ cenplli on matlactli hoquimomaquilli in totlaçotatzin fray juº nunez ynic yehuatzin Missa quimochihuiliz yn inpanpa homoteneuhque mimiccatzitzintin ypanpa ca ymalbaceatzin mochiuhtica Auh in 10ᵃᶜ pºs hoconmocuilli in yehuatl juº de s. miguel ytech monequiz yehica ca hachtopa honquinpalehui in teoyotica ynamic yhuan in teoyotica yychpoch yn omoteneuhque tlacpac ca matlactli /f.6v/ Missa homito yhua yᵃᶜ [iiᵃᶜ??] vigilia homito ynic oquinpallehui ymanimas in mimiccatzitzintin Auh ypanpa in 10ᵃᶜ pºs conmocuilliya ynic oquimoneltilli nican hoquitlalli yfirma ymixpan testigos ynic oquitemacac tomines yhuan yn oconmocuili 10ᵃᶜ pºs in toˢ in don juº Marcos juez gouᵒʳ ymixpan Miguel Hierᵐᵒ francº Malᵈᵒ diº elias Albacea

Miguel Jacobo escri° yglia /f.6v/ Homochiuh Axcan Martes a 17 dias del mes de Mayo de 1581 anos
Don lorenço de s. fran^{co} allde Nixpan Migl Jacobo de mal^{do} escri° nonbrado

—Tochihuic
—Nextitlan
—Sant lorenço tetzonco ynnemac dona luysa ysabel

        Petlatolli   -çacatl   -tequixquitl

/f.7r/ [continues from f.1v]
Vazquez ca miyecpa nixpan quimonahuatili yn notecuiyo in noçitzin Nicnotlatlauhtiliya in notlaçotatzin p^{or} Ma juramento quimomaquiliz ynic amo yztlacatiz in Migl Vazquez ca ye yxquich ynic namechnonahuatiliya Macamo annechmolcahuilizque ymixpan in huelli ypanpa honotzaloque yn oquintemotiya yyomatca testigos ju° ytzpancalqui ju° tlacochcalcatl Auh yn oncan homoquicuitlahuiyaya in cocoxcatzintli ho no tlacaque Andres xuarez diego de la cruz yhuan ju^a teycuhc ynamic catca fran^{co} temilo Axcan Martes yohualnepantla ypan yylhuitzin sancta cruz yqueylhuitl mani Metztli Mayo de 1580 anos
Honitlacuilo ytencopa in dona luysa ju^a in cocoxcatzintli Nehuatl Marcos Jorge Cor[o?] topille
ynic oquineltilique nican hoquitlalique yn intoca in testigos ju° Rafael Auh in ju° ytzpancalqui Amo quimatin tlacuiloz Auh ynic tlaneltilia hoquiquetz cruz ynic nelli testigo
/f.7v/ -Yc caxtolilhuitl mani Metztli junio de mill y quinientos y ochenta Anos in senor don ju° Marcos de Velasco gouernador juez yn ipan homoteneuh Altepetl yyxpantzinco honez ynin testamento yn oquitlalitiya dona ju^a luysa Auh yn iquac hoquimottili yn oquimocaquiti hoquimitalhui ynic omotlanahuatili Ma chicahuatiya [sic] ynin testamento Ayac quitlacoz Auh ynic oquimoneltilili nican hoquimotlalili ytoca yfirma
Don Jhoan marcos de Velasco
Nixpan Al° dauila de santiago escri° nonbrado
—Yn nican ypan Altepetl Colhuacan yc 5tl mani Metztli Nouiembre de 1580 anos in yehuatzin senor don ju° Marcos de Velasco gouernador juez y nican ypan homoteneuh Altepetl

yyxpantzinco honecico in yehuantin in ju° de san Migl yhuan
dona luysabel [sic] ypilhuan in don di° de motecuhcçoma yn
oquimohuiquili in tote° dios ho yuh quimononochilique ca yn
yehuatzin yn intatzin catca in don diego de moctecuhcçoma catca
quinmocahuililitiuh ytlaltzin ymiltzin ynic ceccan mani s.tiago
texalpan ynic ocan Milpitzactli yniquexcan mani tlatozcac ynic
nauhcan xalpan ynic macuilcan Axomolco ynic chiquaceccan
mani Aztahuacan ynic 7 mani s^t lorenço tetzonco ynic 8can mani
tochihuic ynic /f.8r/ 9can mani Amimintitlan ynic 10can Apilco
ynic 11quauhtlan [sic] ynic matlaccan homome hocelotepec
yhuan tepetl tlatlauhcan yn izquican mani milli yn omoteneuh
hoquimixpantililico yn yzquican mani Milli yn iuh neztica yn ipan
Pintura innenonotzaliztica yhuan intlaquallitaliztica yhuan in
cepantlanequiliztica in ju° de s migl yhuan in dona luysa ysabel
homononotzque yn imomextin quimoxexelhuizque yn izquican
Mani milli yn imiltzin catca don di° de Motecuhcçoma Auh ynic
chicahuatiyez yn innenonotzaliztlatol ynic quimoxexelhuiznequi
yn imil yn intatzin ypanpa yn ixpan^{co} hohuallaque in senor
governador juez in yehuantin in ju° de s. migl yhuan dona luysa
ysabel hoquinextique yn intlanequiliz yn iyxpan^{co} juez hoquito in
yehuatl ju° de s. migl concui heplli in milli yn onpa mani
santiago tetla honplli tlatozcac yhuan cenplli texalpan
yquepohualli Auh in dona luysa ysabel çanno yxquich concui yn
eplli in milli in çanno honpa mani in santiago tetla texalpan
honplli milpitzactli cenplli milpitzactli yqueplli çan ce yauh çan
mochichixquich Nanapohualli ynic huihuiyac Auh ynic ocan mani
milli in quimoxelhuiya ytocayocan Axomolco honplli concui in
dona luysa ysabel No ixquich yn onplli in concui in ju° de s. migl
ynic huihuiyac chichiconplli çan ce yauh çan mochichixquich
yniquexcan mani milli in quimoxelhuiya ytocayocan Aztahuacan
Naplli onpohualli concui in dona luysa ysabel no honpohualli
concui in ju° de s. migl chichicohnplli [sic] ynic huihuiyac çan
cenyauh çan mochichixquich Auh Auh [sic] ynic nauhcan mani in
quimoxelhuiya in Milli ytocayocan s^t lorenço tetzonco chicueplli
Napohualli Concui in dona luysa ysabel no naplli concui in ju°
de s. migl Auh ynic huihuiyac ohontzontli çan cenyauh çan mochi
/f.8v/ chixquich Auh in tequixquiçacatlalmantli yhitic ca in
petlatolmilli çan yc cenmani yhuan in tequixquimilli Mochi
quimotlacoxelhuiya ynic macuilcan quimoxelhuiya in milli
ytocayocan tochihuic cenplli honmatlactli concui in ju° de s. migl

no cenplli onmatlactli concui in dona luysa ysabel ynic huihuiyac
eheplli ypan chichicohonmatl çan cenyauh çan mochichixquich
Auh ynic chiquacecan mani in quimoxelhuiya milli ytocayocan
Amimintitlan ynic patlahuac honplli Auh ynic huiyac Matlacplli
yhuan chiconmatl ho yuh mononotzque in yehuantin ju° de s.
migl yhuan yn ihuepol in dona luysa ysabel Ayac ytech
pouhquiyez çan nepantlayez Auh intla ytla canapa neçiquiuh in
netlacuilli in tomines in huel macho honcan ytech quiçaz ynic
moxtlahuaz ypanpa in çan nepantli quitlalliya yn amo ac ytech
quipohua Auh ynic chicocan mani chinamitl honplli ynic
patlahuac Auh ynic huiyac 15plli oncan in temi Apilco in
yehuatlyn in chinamitl incepannenonotzaltica in ju° de s. migl
yhuan yn dona luysa ytech quipohua no quimonepantlaxelhuiya
Cenplli concui in ju° de s. migl no cenplli concui in dona luysa
Auh ynic chicuexcan temi chinamitl ytocayocan quauhtitlan
tlallachco ynic patlahuac 3 plli onmatlactli Auh ynic huiyac
4tzontli yhuan 10ac plli ho yuh quitoque in ju° de s. migl yhuan
yn ihuepol dona luysa ysabel çan icatzinco in tote° dios
Quinmaca quintlaocoliya in don franco xiloman yhuan in dona jua
tiyacapan ycalpanpilhuan yetihui in don di° Motecuhçcoma
yhuiyan yocoxca quincahuiliya yn omoteneuh chinamitl onpa
temi quauhtitlan Quicuizque /f.9r/ yn icalpanpilhuan yetihui in
don di° motecuhçoma Auh intlamo quicelizque yn intlaocoliloca
mochihua in chinamitl in quauhtitlan temi çan concuizque in
yehuantin in ju° de s. migl yhuan yn ihuepol in dona luysa ysabel
quimonepantlaxelhuizque Auh ynic 9mani milli ytocayocan
hocelotepec yhuan tlatlauhquitepec ynnenonotzaliztica in ju° de
s. migl yhuan yn ihuepol in dona luysa ysabel ho yuh quitoque
çan icel ytech pouhquiyez in dona luysa ysabel in milli yn
occanixti yn omoteneuh yxquich in yn innenonotzal ynic
oquimoxexelhuique yn inmil yhuan yn inchinan in yehuatin ju°
de san miguel yhuan dona luysa ysabel yn quicahuilitiuh yn
intatzin catca in don di° motecuhçoma Auh ynic onextico yn
innenonotzallatol yn ixquich tlacpac homoteneuh ymixpanco
senor juez gouor Auh in yehuantin ju° de s. migl yhuan yn
ihuepol dona luysa ysabel no yuh quimotlaytlanililique ynic
quinmotlachicahuililiz yn ipan yzquitlamantli yn
innenonotzaliztlatol ynic oquimoxexelhuique yn inmil yhuan yn
inchinan ynic amo quenma.... n Aca quimixnamiquitiuh
quichalanitiuh yn anoço quitlacotiuh yn innenonotzalliztlatol yn

inConcierto Auh ynic huel chicahuatiyez ypanpa yn ixpan^co
hohuallaque in s^or gou^or quinmotlachicahuililiz yn ica
yjust^atequitzin Auh in yehuantin in ju° de s. migl yhuan yn
ihuepol in dona luysa ysabel ynic oquinextico yn inConcierto yn
innenonotzal ymixpan homochiuh allde Min Cano yhuan Alguazil
Mayor Migl de rribas Don ju° Ramirez don ju° garcia Migl Jer^mo
Antonio de galicia fran^co cihuatecpanecatl Regr Mayor Auh in
yehuantin testigos in tlacpac homotocateneuhque ynic ymixpan
omochiuh in Concierto yn innenonotzaliztlatol in ju° de s. Migl
yhuan in dona luysa ysabel ynic quineltiliya yn infirma yn ica
yntoca
Ju° de san Migl   Dona luysa ysabel [notarial hand]
/f.9v/ Min cano Allde   Migl de rribas alguazil mayor
Don ju° Ramirez   Don Ju° Garcia   Migl Hier^mo
Nixpan Migl Jacobo de Mal^do escriuano nonbrado

—Auh yn iquac ho yuh quimocaquiti in senor juez gouernador
in nican ypan Altepetl homoteneuh yn iquac hoquimottili yhuan
yn oquimocaquiti yn ixquich yn innenonotzalliztlatol in ju° de s.
migl yhuan yn ihuepol in dona luysa ysabel ynic
oquimoxexelhuique yn inmil yhuan yn inchinan yn izquican
mani yhuan yn izquican temi in quincahuilitiya yn itatzin catca yn
don di° Motecuhçoma hoquimitalhui ynic omotlanahuatilli Ma
yn mopiya Ma yuh chicahuatiye ynic omotlamamacaque ynic
oquimoxexelhuique ynin yn inmil yn inchinan in ju° de s. migl
yhuan yn ihuepol in dona luysa ysabel ynic cecenme ymixcoyan
quexixquich milli yhuan chinamitl yn oquimomamacaque Ma
yhuiyan yocoxca quimopiyelican yca just^a niquimaxcatiya
Niquimnemactiya yhuan ypan niquinmaca Possession yn iquac
estaca quiquequetzatiuh /f.10r/ Alguazil Mayor ynic
quinezcayotituh ynixixquich intlal yn intech popouhtica yn
imiyxcoyan ynic amo quenmaniyan Aca quitlacotiuh yn
inConcierto yn innenonotzallatol in ju° de s. migl yhuan yn
ihuepol in dona luysa ysabel yn axcan ycatzinco su mag^d nictlallia
pena yn aquin quitlacoznequiz ynin Concierto yn anoço
Quixnamiquiz Matlaquilhuitl ylpitiyez yn teylpiloyan yhuan
macuilplli yc mecahuitecoz yn oncan tiyanquizco yhuan
chiquacen Metztli totocoz yhuan Matli [sic] p°s yc tlaxtlahuaz
ytech pohuiz in iCamara su mag^d yhui yn yn omotlanahuatilli
ynic omotlatzontequilli ynic oquimoneltilili Nican hoquimotlalili

yn ifirma yca yn itoca homochiuh in çanno yehuatl ypan
cemilhuitl yhuan yn Metztli yhuan in xihuitl in tlacpac
omoteneuh
Don ju⁰ Marcos gouernador juez
Nixpan Miguel Jacobo de mal^(do) escri⁰ nonbrado

Sato Ryes   [later hand]
De 159^(ta) y 4 Ano

NOTES

Chapter 1

1. Presently Culhuacan is part of the Mexico City urban sprawl. Some prehispanic and colonial sites are still evident, but the description in this chapter is the situation in the late fifteenth and sixteenth centuries.

2. Dyckerhoff (1984:237) following Sullivan (1976) gives *-hua'can* as "place of where owners of X are." According to the Relación Geográfica of Culhuacan, the name means "twisted ridge" (*cerro corbado*) (Gallegos, 1927:171). The glyphic representation of Culhuacan is a mountain with a twisted top. The glyph has some phonemic content. "The mountain in name glyphs serves one of three functions: (1) as a medium to express shape or color; (2) as an indication of a settlement (*in atl in tepetl* 'the water, the mountain' is a metaphor for settlement); (3) as a picture word which indicates *tepetl* 'mountain.' In the case of Culhuacan, the mountain serves as the object utilized to express curvature. [It] appears to be phonetic, the coltic giving the initial syllable of Colhuacan [Culhuacan]" (Dibble, 1971:328).

3. Technically it is a basin since it has no natural outlet.

4. The dates for the foundation of Culhuacan are in dispute.

5. See Chapter 8 on land for a fuller description of chinampas.

6. Davies (1977;1980) has done extremely interesting work on the Toltecs, including the problems of Tollan's relation to Culhuacan. I have generally followed his interpretation.

7. See Chapter 4 for a fuller discussion of Spanish administration.

8. The *Libro de las tasaciones* gives the Culhuacan population in 1552 as 771 married Indians and 311 widowed people (*viudos*) (González de Cosío, 1952:156). The *Descripción del arzobispado de México en 1570* gives the number of tribute payers as 1,030 (cited in Cook and Simpson, 1948:8). For the year 1572, the *Relación de los pueblos de yndios que los religiosos de Sant Agustín tiene a su cargo,* written by fray Juan Adrián gives the figure of one thousand tribute payers (cited in Cook and Simp-

son, 1948:7). The Relación geográfica of Culhuacan (Gallegos, 1927:172) says that in 1580 there were nine hundred "whole" tribute payers, explicitly not counting young men. Each "whole" tribute payer was explicitly said to be two persons. All of these figures are based on partial counts. Blanton (1970:339–40) sets the population density of Culhuacan (a site he estimates at sixty-five hectares) at twenty-five to fifty persons per hectare with a total population of 1,625–3,250. Parsons (1976), taking Blanton's data, has rounded it off to about four thousand.

Chapter 2

1. León-Portilla (1976) published a description of the corpus and two preliminary translations. Another description of the wills appears in the introduction to *The Testaments of Culhuacan* (Cline and León-Portilla, 1984).

2. Kellogg's study (1979) of inheritance patterns of Mexico City Indians is based on wills randomly preserved in lawsuits. All the cases are, by definition, disputes; the bequest patterns she discerned are likely skewed.

3. There is some evidence that her father's wife, Bárbara Tlaco, was not Angelina's mother. If that is true, then the relatives through Bárbara are not as close kin.

4. Don Diego de Motecuhçoma of Culhuacan is identified as Motecuhçoma's grandson in AGN–T–1739–5–15r. He is related in some unclear way to the other Motecuhçomas in Culhuacan, who were Angelina Mocel's relatives by marriage.

5. AGN–T–58–4. See Appendix 4.

6. There is some evidence that Cihuatecpan and Tezcacoac were only one ward with a dual structure. Thus twenty wills may have come from just one ward.

Chapter 3

1. Angelina may have been Bárbara Tlaco's stepdaughter. Her name *mocel* means "only," and she never actually calls Bárbara her mother.

2. See Chapter 1, note 8 on population figures. Nahuatl: *cocoliztli,* "sickness."

3. Examples of formulas in other Nahuatl wills can be found in Anderson et al., 1976.

4. We are concerned with outward forms. It is very difficult to chart the extent of personal belief.

5. AGN–T–58–4–6v.

6. Vovelle's work (1978) is interesting and persuasive. While formulas

for testaments may reflect only the notaries' shifts in beliefs, the number of masses, candles, and religious things requested by testators do reflect changing beliefs. In the eighteenth century, there were fewer flowery invocations and less money spent on pious requests.

7. Doña Luisa Juana was related to Angelina Mocel by marriage. Doña Luisa Juana's stepmother, doña Elena Constantina, was Angelina Mocel's cousin. See Table 2.

8. AGN–T–58–4–1r.

9. Both occasions when "noon," *nepantla tonatiuh*, "the middle of the sun," was specified, it was a Sunday. Perhaps there was some special reason why the time was noted on Sundays.

10. AGN–T–58–4–7r.

11. The notary or the testator might have got the saint's day wrong. I have been unable to discover a Saint Catherine whose day was November 21.

12. Church burial: TC 20,21; 24,25; 46,47; 48,49; 64,65; 100,101; 256,257; 267,268; 270,271. "At the church" could mean burial in the churchyard, but some specify "inside the church," leaving no doubt.

13. AGN–T–58–4–1r.

14. Oscar Lewis described the Day of the Dead observances in the Nahuatl-speaking town of Tepoztlán. There in the late 1940s food was offered for the dead, along with the appropriate prayers. A separate observance was held for dead children (Lewis, 1951:462).

15. AGN–T–58–4–7r.

16. Wakes in the modern Nahuatl-speaking town of Tecospa do not include meat. "Tecospans say it is evil to eat meat at a wake, for that would be like eating the corpse" (Madsen, 1960:209).

17. See the discussion of land connected to the church in Chapter 8.

18. The physicians are identified by the Spanish loanword *dodortin* [*doctores*]. The Augustinian friar, Agustín Farfán, who spent some time in Culhuacan in the 1580s (TC 262,263), wrote a text for friars to use when no doctors were around, *Tratado breve de medicina.*

19. See extensive discussion of the executors in Chapter 4.

20. "And such a testament as this must be made before seven witnesses who are called and requested... by the maker; and none of these witnesses should be a *siervo* [serf, slave, servant]: nor less than fourteen years old: nor a woman: nor a man of bad reputation.... Moreover, we say,... that each one of them must write his name at the end of the testament, saying thus: I, so-and-so, am witness of this testament, that such a man made it, naming him, I being before him. And if some of them don't know how to write, any of the others can do it... at his direction. And besides this, all the witnesses must place their seals with pendant cords on the paper of the testament. And if someone of them does not have a seal, he

can do it with the seal of another.... Moreover, we say that the maker of the will must write his name at the end of the paper, saying thus: I so-and-so, declare that I made this will in the way that it is written in this paper. And if he doesn't know how or is not able to write, another can do it for him ... at his direction" (Markov, 1983:442, her translation from the 1555 edition of the *Siete Partidas*).

21. AGN–T–58–4–7r.
22. BNP 110–3r.
23. It could be the head of the testator.
24. TC 32,33; 36,37; 76,77; 114,115; 174,175.
25. There are only a few cases in *The Testaments of Culhuacan* of a woman being named as the owner of an adjoining field, one being Pablo Huitznahuatl, who named his niece doña Elena Constantina as a neighbor (TC 168,169).
26. AGN–T–58–4–1r.
27. BNP 110–6r. These phrases are formula and are echoed in other Nahuatl documents.
28. Indian notaries' handwriting was often much clearer than the scrawls of the Spanish friars.

Chapter 4

1. See the discussion of the Oñate family in Chapter 1.
2. There is a reference to a Juan Gallego, a judge who awarded some land to an Indian (TC 148,149). There is a remote possiblity that this was Gonzalo Gallegos the corregidor.
3. Much of this discussion closely follows Gibson (1952, 1964).
4. However, in the Nahuatl documentation, Culhuacan is never called a cabecera.
5. AGN–V–279–1–19r.
6. Nahuatl typically says the same thing in two different ways.
7. The following information is known about Culhuacan tlatoque and juez-gobernadores. Don Juan de Aguilar was called tlatoani in 1572 and ex-gobernador in 1581; don Pedro de Suero was tlatoani before 1580; don Juan Ramírez was tlatoani in 1580 and gobernador in 1585; don Juan Marcos de Velasco was juez-gobernador in 1580–1581, and called one of the *"señores-tlatoque"* (lord rulers) in 1581.
8. See the discussion on the tlatoani's lands in Chapter 8.
9. There was a high bail, probably because of the rank of the victim.
10. AGN–T–58–4–4.
11. Often the punishment was the same—death—but the method of inflicting it varied by rank.
12. See Appendix 2 for loanword lists.

13. The change to the Gregorian calendar can be seen because notaries often put both the day of the week and the date.

14. TC 210,211; 224,225; 268,269; 272,273.

15. He may have been a newly promoted notary for his handwriting and spelling are just awful. Notaries probably went through a period of apprenticeship, learning to write Latin letters and spell. Most of the notaries had polished hands and relatively invariant spelling. This notary's hand is untutored and his spelling quite unusual.

16. Lockhart et al. (n.d.) discuss the situation in Tlaxcala where discipline of officials remained in the hands of the cabildo. Spaniards on occasion removed tlatoque who were not serving their needs (Gibson, 1964:177).

17. The transactions listed in Miguel García's estate may simply have been those left undone at the time of his death.

18. Farriss (1984:337) indicates that among the colonial Yucatecan Maya, the choirmaster was the highest Indian religious official.

19. AGN-T-58-4-7v.
20. AGN-T-58-4-9r.
21. AGN-T-58-4-9r.
22. AGN-T-58-4-3v.
23. AGN-T-58-4-3v.
24. AGN-T-58-4-3v.
25. AGN-T-58-4-3v.
26. AGN-T-58-4-4r,v.
27. AGN-T-58-4-4v.
28. AGN-T-58-4-5r.
29. AGN-T-58-4-5r.
30. AGN-T-58-4-5r.
31. AGN-T-58-4-5r.

32. This was part of a well-meaning but largely futile attempt to create "two republics" in the New World, one of Indians, the other of non-Indians (Mörner, 1963:45ff).

33. AGN-T-58-4-5r.

34. Residence of these Spaniards in Culhuacan is not surprising, for a typical pattern of immigrants was to settle where they had relatives. Fray Juan was already in Culhuacan and likely had brought his sister and her family over.

35. AGN-T-58-4-6r.
36. AGN-T-58-4-5v.

37. This might suggest that she was their stepmother rather than their mother.

38. BNP 110-13r.
39. BNP 110-2r,3r.

40. BNP 110–45r. In error I have stated that the outcome of this case is not known (Cline, 1984b:49).

41. See Chimalpahin's 8th Relación. See also extended discussion of terms by Reyes (1975, 1979). A doctoral dissertation by Susan Schroeder (1984b) presents an exhaustive analysis of Chimalpahin's usage of sociopolitical terms.

42. The usage of the term tlaxilacalleque in the Culhuacan documents does not make it absolutely clear that the people referred to are the ward elders or the ward people. In one case, we have translated the phrasing *yn tlaxilacaleque hiyauhtenco tlaca,* "the ward heads, those of Iyauhtenco" (TC 68,69). An alternative translation is "the ward people, those of Iyauhtenco." [In *The Testaments of Culhuacan* we have mistakenly put Iyauhtenanco rather than Iyauhtenco (TC 69)]. In another case, we have translated the phrase *yn tlaxillacalleque chaneque sta ana* "the ward heads, the citizens of Santa Ana" (TC 268,269), but it could be "the ward people, the citizens of Santa Ana."

43. With testators of the same name, the ward affiliation helps distinguish one from the other.

44. Santiago Tetla may have been viewed as a barrio of Culhuacan, but it seems to have had subdivisions itself, which is consistent with sujeto status.

45. Farriss (1984:206) notes that among the colonial Yucatecan Maya, changes in residence might have been prompted by attempts to escape payment of debts. New jurisdictions would accept immigrants because they were then liable for local taxation.

46. Women elders [*huehuetque*] are mentioned by Chimalpahin (Schroeder, 1984a).

Chapter 5

1. Angelina Mocel never mentions her father's wife, Bárbara Tlaco, nor does she leave her any property. Bárbara may have been Angelina's stepmother. Another explanation is that Angelina and Bárbara were not getting along at the time of Angelina's death. Bárbara acted as witness to Angelina's will, however. If Angelina were not Bárbara's daughter, then her relation to María Tiacapan and Antonio Tlemachica are step-relations not distinguished by a kin term.

2. Intercourse with an unmarried woman or concubine was fornication; adultery was a serious crime, punishable by death. See Offner, 1983, for a full discussion of prehispanic marital law.

3. Namictli may be a colonial usage (Schroeder, 1984a).

4. The legitimacy of the marriage would affect the legitimacy of the offspring. In the prehispanic period when men of the high nobility would

have multiple wives and concubines, the strength of the bond affected the sons' accession to office and position.

5. Carrasco (1961) indicates for a sixteenth-century community in the Texcoco area that there was a tendency toward ward endogamy, especially in the largest wards, but that there were no prohibitions against exogamy.

6. Quoted from Lockhart (1980:25) citing Gonzalo Gómez de Cervantes, *La vida económica y social de la Nueva España al finalizar del siglo xvi,* México, 1944:135. Lockhart's article discusses a land transaction in which a woman takes the dominant role. Gibson (1964:152,505) cites this passage of Gómez de Cervantes as one of the "peculiar features of Indian life" which "struck Spaniards as inappropriate or bizarre."

7. The quotation starts with a singular subject and ends with a plural. Whether this is scribal error is unclear.

8. Six out of twelve widowed men, ten out of fifteen widowed women.

9. There were special reasons for disinheriting her children, discussed below in the main text.

10. AGN-T-58-4-8v,9r. Perhaps these children received other land in addition to this donation. We do not have the will of their father don Diego, only the record of the estate division.

11. BNP 110-13r. Juan de San Miguel notes his daughter doña Luisa Juana was legitimate (AGN-T-58-4-5r). See Kellogg (1979:88) for a note on legitimacy.

12. I prefer this gloss, proposed by Offner (1983:197), which indicates the net-like linkages of kin. The gloss "lineage" unduly emphasizes the lineal aspect of the tlacamecayotl.

13. Kellogg (1979:173,179) suggests this, taking the notion from Clara Millon.

14. Offner (1983:193) argues that terms could be polysemous, referring to collaterals as well as lineals, but Kellogg notes that in archival notations collaterals are often marked by the saying the relations were "distant," Nahuatl *huecapan;* Spanish *lejano/a* (Kellogg, 1984:37).

15. I think that María Tiacapan and Luis Tlauhpotonqui were cousins who use sibling terms for each other. See note 32 below.

16. María Salomé and Petronila, Angelina's sisters-in-law, are called *ichpochtli,* "maidens," probably indicating unmarried status. This leads me to believe that the two were younger. [In *The Testaments of Culhuacan* the term *ticuiuhtzin* is mistranslated as "older sister" (TC 185,186)].

17. The great grandmother's role in the tlacamecayotl is, however, emphasized. "The good great grandmother [is] worthy of praise, deserving of gratitude. She is accorded glory, acclaim by her descendants. She is the founder, the beginner [of her lineage]" (Sahagún, X:5).

18. AGN-T-58-4-1.

19. BNP 110.

20. In periods of epidemic disease, old people were likely to be more vulnerable to sickness. Although Nahuatl has an elaborate set of kin terms for generations above grandparent, not surprisingly, no Culhuacan testator lists such a term.

21. The Spanish words for godchild, *ahijado/a,* were not taken into Nahuatl as loanwords in Culhuacan around 1580. Rather, the terms *teoyotica conetl* (female speaking) and *teoyotica piltzintli* (male or female speaking) for "godchild" were used. The modifier *teoyotica* "godly" or "in the church" was often used to indicate legitimacy through church sacrament. Thus as we have seen *teoyotica omonamicti* would be "married in the church" or legitimately married. However, it is clear that the terms teoyotica conetl and teoyotica piltzintli refer to godchildren and not to legitimate children because testators noted who the child's father was (TC 64,65; 156,157).

22. Five people mention godchildren, all of them godsons (TC 64ff, 112ff. 154ff; 80ff 146ff). Just one woman mentioned her own godchild, Juana Tiacapan (TC 146), and we know that Ana Juana's son was the godchild of don Francisco Flores, but she does not list a godchild of her own. The Libro de bautismos of Culhuacan (1588) lists goddaughters (Gorbea Trueba, n.d.:3), so the testamentary data are skewed in some way. Perhaps though the ties to godsons were more important than to goddaughters.

23. Among the colonial Maya, godfathers were more important than godmothers (Farriss, 1984:258–59).

24. Whorf (1937:274) says that /t/ and /tl/ were not phonologically distinct in Uto-Aztecan, and that the distinction developed later in Central Mexico. Thus tatli, "father," and tlatli, "uncle," derive from the same term.

25. This could be "uncle and aunt."

26. His namesake Cacama was a king of Texcoco, the successor of Nezahualpilli.

27. I am curious who Bárbara Tlaco was identified with, her uncle Antonio Tlemachica or her husband Pablo Huitznahuatl. The answer to this will likely never be known.

28. Notecuiyotzin may be a standard form of address used by women for uncles. Doña Luisa Juana used the term for her stepmother (AGN–T–58–4–1r).

29. Only men gave property to aunts and uncles but I think this is due to the smallness of the sample.

30. The tlacamecayotl given by Sahagún only discusses the elder brother, *teachcauh,* and is silent on the possibility of a sibling term being used for a cousin.

31. They almost never receive the bulk of an estate.

32. The term for older brother María Tiacapan uses is *noquichtihua-*

tzin rather than the more usual *noteachcauh*. I think there is evidence that Luis and María are cousins. Luis calls Antonio de Santa María, his father, by the standard kin term tatli, María calls the same man "my lord" and mentions her father, who is *not* Antonio.

33. I speculate that this strong affirmation of the tie to her brother-in-law might have been due to her being possibly his wife in a polygynous situation with her sister (sororal polygyny), a pattern seen in modern Tlaxcala (Nutini, 1965).

34. Lorenzo de San Pablo, Juana's husband, seems to be from Mexico City, likely taking his name from the ward of San Pablo, where his brother-in-law Hernando García is known to have been resident (TC 68,69).

35. These younger sisters are not mentioned in Luis's will, perhaps because they were in fact younger cousins. See note 32 above.

36. Dowry is another standard way property could be passed on but, there is little evidence of it in the Culhuacan wills.

37. In *The Testaments of Culhuacan* we have glossed *inemac* as "their inheritance". Nemac[tli] denotes "portion" and generally means inheritance, but also *inter vivos* donations.

38. Kellogg (1979) has longitudinal data on a number of sixteenth-century native families of Mexico City.

39. María Salomé's testament is a lengthy fragment. In the missing section, she might have bequeathed her daughter a house, but the general pattern is to list the house first.

40. Kellogg (1979:59), using wills from Mexico City, posits daughters and granddaughters as preferred heirs to women's houses, but there is no evidence in the Culhuacan data confirming this.

41. It is ambiguous whether she means that Cuitlahuac is her home or the house in question is her home. Presumably, it was the latter, since it seems to be a justification of the bequest.

42. The pattern of female preference is seen by Kellogg (1979:59) for sixteenth-century Mexico City.

43. Kellogg found one Mexico City native woman who gave a house to her brother (1979:76).

44. Kellogg (1979:68) suggests uniform exclusion of husbands among Mexico City native women.

45. A pattern found in Mexico City (Kellogg, 1979:67).

46. The passage is not entirely clear.

47. Tomás's will is a fragment. It ends immediately after his saying, concerning this bequest, "or if he dies..." (TC 66,67). Presumably he would have made a contingency plan, such as ordering the house sold for masses.

48. The "orphan" might have been an illegitimate child. Equally likely is that he was a poor relative of some kind. Censuses of the sixteenth

century show a number of households with seemingly unrelated people (Carrasco, 1964; Offner, 1984).

49. Faith (1966), however, notes that in medieval England, peasants had a great emotional attachment to the land.

50. See further discussion on patrimonial and purchased land in Chapter 8.

51. We only have a long fragment of her testament. She received this land by inheritance.

52. The case is made by Kellogg (1979). The evidence that she uses to discern these patterns are lawsuits over property. By definition they are the disputed cases and the data in them skewed. The Culhuacan wills are the undisputed cases (with the exception of Cristina Tiacapan (BNP 110).)

53. BNP 110.

54. In the modern Nahuat-speaking town of Yaonahuac daughters now inherit land as well as sons. Taggart (1983:44ff) traces this to changes in Mexican law under Porfirio Díaz in the late nineteenth century. Married couples were considered a single legal entity, so that wives gained rights over their husband's property. Even if the husband received the property from his parents, the wife must consent to its sale. Taggart believes this gave women influence over how property was bequeathed, and that daughters have subsequently received more land.

Chapter 6

1. Offner (1980) indicates that the productivity of some of these publicly worked lands was quite low. See discussions of labor in Hicks (1974, 1984).

2. See the chapter on land for further discussion of calpulli land and other civil categories of land.

3. Calnek (1972:111) quoting William T. Sanders estimates 500 square meters of chinampa land will support one person for a year. By my calculations, seven chinampas have about that area. According to Sanders, one man can cultivate about a half hectare of chinampa land by himself (quoted in Parsons, 1976:244), while Parsons suggests three-quarters hectare per man (Parsons, 1976:245). See Chapter 8 for the calculation.

4. Textile workshops for wage labor may have existed in Tenochtitlan (Calnek, 1974b:191), but if so, the women laborers might not have been highly paid, forcing them to supplement their income. According to Sahagún's informants, "embroiderers lived in great vice and became terrible whores" (Sahagún IV:7).

5. What he was going to do with it is unclear. Regarding husbands whose wives wove, an early sixteenth-century report implies that one of the principal reasons Indian men married several wives was to benefit

from them economically by the sale of their woven goods (Motolinia, 1950:149,191).

6. Sahagún, X, illustrations 119, 120,122–27; 129,133. Interestingly, the English translations of the Nahuatl text often indicate these as male traders, but the illustations show females.

7. Offner (1983:280) discusses collateral and interest as found in Zorita and other sources.

8. The large number of sales of Indian land to Spaniards may have been prompted by the need for cash.

9. See the auction of the estate of don Juan Téllez, discussed below, where most prices for goods are quite low.

10. Where these places were cannot be determined. They seem not to have been in Culhuacan.

11. The term derives from the Spanish word *justicia,* "justice," and the Nahuatl affix *-tica,* "by means of."

12. In the prehispanic period, debtors were thrown in jail until debts were paid by him or his family, and if not paid, the debtor was enslaved (Offner, 1983:280). Indian slavery was abolished by Spaniards in the midsixteenth century. It is interesting that the jail was where money for a debt owed a Culhuacan citizen was held.

13. This description appears as part of the introduction to Luis Tlauhpotonqui's will (TC 134,135). My thanks to James Lockhart for helping unravel this passage.

14. Thompson (1978:176) notes that in the eighteenth century, Mayan wives were willed horses because it was an effective way of providing support.

15. One of his horses may have been a mule. He calls it *nocahuallo macho,* which could mean "my male horse," or "my mule." *Macho,* "male," was a common Spanish way of denoting a mule.

16. Unfortunately, we do not know if this Martín Cano was the same person who was alcalde at one point and who was involved in insuring a debtor's payment to the trader Luis Tlauhpotonqui (TC 136,137).

17. She is called the widow of Juan Aca[tl] in both wills. Very likely she was Joaquín's sister, since she was the first witness listed. His sister Juana Tiacapan was in charge of administering his estate, and it would have been very likely that she acted as witness. If Luis Tlauhpotonqui's debtor was another trader's sister, it would seem that money was available to members of the merchant community.

18. The distance between Culhuacan and Yecapixtla was about one hundred kilometers. Ana's move to Yecapixtla might suggest that her husband was a trader from there and married her on one of his expeditions. She maintained ties to Culhuacan despite the move.

19. The Nahuatl reads *yn oras i tetl yhua nobreviario i tetl yhua iii tetl*

nahuatlatolli yhuan i tetl cofessionario. What exactly the *nahuatlatolli* (writings in Nahuatl) were is an intriguing question. They might simply have been breviaries in Nahuatl as our tentative gloss suggests. Likely they were on a religious theme, since those were virtually the only books available at the time.

20. Although twenty pesos was a large price, Antonio seems to have had large amounts of cash on hand. The largest amount of land that Spaniards buying land in Culhuacan in the 1580s could buy for twenty pesos was about one hectare. One plot of that size would not have put Antonio in competition with large land owners such as Pablo Huitznahuatl.

21. On a 1982 visit to the chinampa town of Xochimilco, I photographed Indians transporting zacate in boats.

22. See Chapter 8 for a discussion of Indians' concepts of direction and space.

23. See Appendix 1 on prices.

24. Kellogg (1979:271,273) citing litigations from AGN ramo Tierras.

25. AGN–V–279–1–6v,32r.

26. *Centetl çan tepiton amo huey*, is typical Nahuatl phrasing, saying the same thing in two different ways.

27. Molina gives "corral" for tepancalli. In English this term generally refers to pens for animals, which is not the primary function of the enclosures in Culhuacan. Although in *The Testaments of Culhuacan*, we have followed Molina and used "corral," I now prefer "enclosure."

28. María Teicuh willed something to the mother-in-law of the gobernador and that woman was a witness to the will, so likely there was some type of connection through kinship.

29. Two-story houses are still associated with wealthy people, according to ethnographic evidence. Among French peasants, a second story was "a step up in the hierarchy and success even if the builder left it empty and unused" (Weber, 1976:159).

30. Tlapancalli is described in Sahagún as a "flat-roofed house" (Sahagún, X:271). A Nahuatl document from Coyoacan was accompanied by a contemporary Spanish translation, which gave *altos*, "upper parts," as the translation. Anderson et al. (1976:56) note that *tlapancalli* "could by its roots equally mean 'flat-roofed house' or 'upper room.'"

31. Tlecopatl, according to Molina (1970:147), means "office or room where something is kept." Etymologically it may mean "in the direction of the fire." This may have led to the Spanish translation of *cocina*, "kitchen," in a Coyoacan document (Anderson et al., 1976:56).

32. Madsen (1960:60) notes that corncribs made of wood are still in use in a Nahua-speaking town.

33. Oquichpan derives from *oquich[tli]* "man" and *-pan*, locative.

There is a corresponding term, *cihuapan,* described by Sahagún (XI:270–71) in the description of the tecpancalli.

34. See the discussion of cihuacalli, below in the main text.

35. Lewis (1951:363ff) gives a description of the modern use of temazcalli which is remarkably close to prehispanic and colonial reports.

36. TC 56,57; 60,61; 166,167; 180,181; 270,271.

37. Madsen (1960:63–65) has an ethnographic description of shingle-making. According to him, well-cared for shingles last twenty years, but only two years if neglected.

38. A loanword from Spanish which indicates it is a new introduction.

39. In the Carolingian period in Europe, wooden houses were often dismantled and the parts used for new structures. Bavarian law provided fines for burning portions of houses, the highest fines being for columns supporting the roof, and lesser ones for interior supports and corners (Riché, 1979:107). In thirteenth-century England, peasant houses were not elaborate and were easily built and dismantled. "The posts and beams were the only materials which were costly enough to be worth moving" (Homans, 1960:208).

40. Loanwords are an index of the encroachment of Spanish material culture. See Appendix 2.

41. Kellogg (1979:83) found Mexico City native women listing more movable property than men. I suspect this is *not* because women owned more but because they owned less land than men. Wanting to bequeath something to their heirs, the women gave what they had, which was movable property, whereas men had land, and they bequeathed that, not bothering to mention the movable goods which were worth less.

42. See Appendix 1 on prices.

43. Even today, papers are kept at home and constitute a kind of family archive (Diskin, 1979).

44. The Nahuatl says *yscouila no ystaya* (TC 40). It is unclear whether the Spanish loanword is *escobilla,* "brush," or *escudilla,* "bowl."

45. The Nahuatl says *taça chichiltic yetetl yhuan peyotl,* "three red cups with *peyotl.*" *Peyotl,* a mushroom producing hallucinogenic effects if eaten, is the primary meaning of this word. In *The Testaments of Culhuacan,* we have tentatively suggested "with covers?"

46. *Botasçolli* "old boots" is composed of the Spanish loanword, *botas,* "boots," and the Nahuatl word for old, *çolli.* This combination of Spanish loanword and Nahuatl modifier is common.

47. I wonder how high his status was, given that the sword was broken.

48. Diego Sánchez was stabbed by one. In the Culhuacan wills, there is only one instance of a Spanish loanword noun being incorporated in a Nahuatl verb, *onechcochillohui* "he knifed me" (TC 220,221).

Chapter 7

1. He does not call himself tecuhtli in his own testament, but is identified as such in Antonio Tlemachica's will (TC 100,101). The debate on the role of tecuhtli has been longstanding. Rounds (1977) suggests that the office was unspecialized and included several roles. He argues that the various roles: judge, soldier, administrator, religious leader, etc., reported in the sources are typical functions of rulers in traditional, pre-state societies.

2. See the discussion below on names and status.

3. María Inés is likely (but not necessarily) also a relative of Angelina Mocel, but the linkages are unknown.

4. See Chapter 3.

5. The passage identifying him says *matheo xuarez nicnotl* (TC 74) which could be glossed "Mateo Juárez, I am an orphan," but the other possible translation is "poor person."

6. Schroeder (1984a) has evidence from Chimalpahin of a rich macehualli in the prehispanic period whose wealth was coveted by a nobleman, who got access to it by marrying his daughter to the man.

7. Motolinia was the name which the Franciscan Toribio de Benavente took.

8. Six and a half fanegas is about nine and three-quarters bushels.

9. The subject is actually plural, referring to him and his wife, but I have simplified the passage for reasons of style.

10. Hellbom (1967:235) indicates that it has been supposed that women took part in the cultivation of edible plants and fruit, but she also says commoner women worked professionally in horticulture. Peasant women's role in agricultural work varies. Boserup (1970) gives extensive evidence in Asia and Africa of female participation and sometimes dominance in the agricultural sector. She postulates that population pressure forces the adoption of plow agriculture and that men assume the bulk of the work when that happens. See Burton and White (1984) for a modification of her theory. Lewis (1951:98) reports that in the 1940s that "Tepoztecan women are not expected to work in the fields, and Tepoztecans of both sexes look down upon the women of the neighboring villages who do agricultural work" and other men's jobs.

11. The Nahuatl reads *ynpanpa ca civatzintli que quichivatitiuh*. There is some possibility that civatzintli could mean "little female," taking the *-tzin* as a diminutive rather than an honorific. This would change the sense of the translation to: "because she is a little girl, how is she going to work it?" However, the more usual way of indicating diminutives is *-ton[tli]*. I believe the translation we have given in *The Testaments of Culhuacan* is the correct interpretation of the passage.

12. Kellogg (1979:66), using data from Mexico City, postulates that people tend to have movables consistent with their gender, that is cooking equipment for women, agricultural tools for men.

13. In *The Testaments of Culhuacan,* we have translated cihuatlatquitl as "women's things," which is close to the etymology. However, I have now come to think that "woman's weaving equipment" is closer to the meaning. There is a corresponding word, *oquichtlatquitl,* mentioned by Pablo Huitznahuatl, "all my men's things, a boat, a chest, a tecomate, my bed, and the small planks" (TC 168,169). It is not clear if he means just "men's things:" and the list following, or if oquichtlatquitl had a specific meaning the way cihuatlatquitl refers to weaving equipment, or whether it was another item on the list.

14. What he would do with the weaving equipment is unclear, since it is unlikely he would have used it himself.

15. The terminology having to do with weaving is unclear. The ellipsis glides over several terms which cannot be translated with accuracy.

16. Sometimes offerings of yarn were presented to the church. Juana Tiacapan of Coatlan had "thirty-six spindles with yarn" in her estate (TC 108,109), which she ordered sold for masses. Apparently the executors could not get rid of them all, for a month after her death, fray Juan Núñez certified the receipt of "some little spindles of yarn, seven or eight" as part of the goods to pay for masses (TC 110,111).

17. It is commonly felt in modern Mexico that Indian men more readily adopt western clothing because they will be paid less if they dress like Indians.

18. The word camisa is one of the few which became fully assimilated to Nahuatl, taking the absolutive ending *-tli* (Karttunen and Lockhart, 1976:21).

19. Citing Chimalpahin, Carrasco (1984:43–44) discusses a case in prehispanic Chalco in which a woman seems to have held office. Schroeder (1984a) has extensive information from Chimalpahin's writings concerning women of royal marriages and their roles.

20. See Offner (1983:202ff) for an extended discussion of succession to office. See Carrasco (1984) for information about royal marriages. The most famous case of a dynasty stressing links to females was the Mexica of Tenochtitlan who intermarried with the Culhua royal family and thereby claimed links to the Toltecs. Ever after, the Mexica called themselves the Culhua Mexica.

21. Previously (Cline, 1984b:50), I could not determine if doña Luisa Isabel's name was written by her, since at the time I was working from a transcription. With the original in front of me, I can state it is not her signature but is in the hand of the notary. However, all the signatures are in the same notarial hand as the text. Since all the documents seem to have

been copied, it is still unclear whether she signed it herself in the original. Documentation from Texcoco includes the name and possibly the signature of one noblewoman, but whether she signed it herself cannot be established (López y Magaña, 1980:80). Karttunen (1983:415) states flatly that there is no evidence of any Aztec woman being literate.

22. BNP–243–3v. See the discussion of "woman's land" in the next chapter.

23. Dowries were an important feature of European elites' wealth. See Lavrin and Couturier (1979).

24. The unmarked case in Spanish is masculine, and the passage in Motolinia does not specifically identify sisters and female cousins as sharing in the inheritance.

25. Widows in early modern Europe were often in a very good position to remarry since they controlled resources from their late husbands' estates (Faith, 1966:91; Goody, 1976:12; Hilton, 1975:99)

26. For women's role in courtroom situations, see Chapter 4.

27. There may have been regional variation in names, for the Matrícula de Huexotzinco (Prem, 1974) shows a greater variety of women's names.

28. This passage seems to refer only to boys.

29. We might speculate that she assumed the title doña at her marriage.

30. Some of the names sound as if the notary were making fun of the people, but the appellations seem to be genuine. My thanks to James Lockhart for help translating many of these names.

31. In the Culhuacan wills, names indicating birth order account for virtually all women's Nahuatl second names. The count is as follows: tiacapan, 80; tlaco, 16; teicuh, 37; xoco, 25; mocel, 6. Only three women have Nahuatl second names other than birth order names, two from the Motecuhçoma family, and one the daughter of a Culhuacan noblewoman, doña Ana Cihuanenequi. Census data for the Cuernavaca area around 1535 identify most females solely by their birth-order names (MNA–AH 549,550,551).

32. As noted previously Angelina's second name, "only," strongly suggests that she was not a daughter by Pablo Huitznahuatl's wife Bárbara Tlaco, since Bárbara had two daughters, Elena and Mónica.

33. The will of Miguel García, notary and executor, does have such goods.

34. The name of Pedro de Suero occurs in the Xochimilco area in 1548 as the name of a Spanish judge (Carrasco, 1977:234). The Culhuacan testator named don Pedro de Suero does not identify himself as a tlatoani in his testament. Since most tlatoque did state their status, likely don Pedro was not a tlatoani.

35. The types of women's names mentioned in the testaments are as

follows: single Spanish given name, 70; two Spanish given names, 37; Spanish given name, Nahuatl second name, 167; Spanish surnames, 4.

36. Saints names as surnames included San Agustín, 2; Santa Ana, 1; San Bartolomé, 1; San Gerónimo, 1; San Juan, 1; San Lázaro, 1; San Marcos, 2; Santa María, 1; San Martín, 1; San Miguel, 2; San Nicolás, 1; San Pablo, 5; San Pedro, 2 or 3. It is unclear what influenced the choice of saint's names. Elaborate religious symbolism was connected with saints (Williams, 1980). Culhuacan was under Augustinian jurisdiction, but only two men were named after Saint Augustine. Perhaps significantly, both were prominent. One was the testator Gregorio de San Agustín (TC 258ff) and the other was an alcalde, Pedro de San Agustín (TC 222,223). Sometimes the saint's name seems to have been in honor of the ward saint. The notary Juan de San Pedro was resident in the ward of San Pedro Çacaapan. In the prehispanic era, names were often names of calendar days, but we have no data on Culhuacan testators' birthdays, so it is impossible to say if the choice of saint coincided with the day someone was born.

37. Doña María de Motecuçoma is also called doña María Tiacapantzin (AGN–T–58–4–1r,5v).

38. *The Tlaxcalan Actas* have several cases of nobles doing this (Lockhart et al., n.d.).

39. Ortiz is identified as a Spaniard in AGN–T–1739–5.

Chapter 8

1. Much of this discussion of land tenure appeared in an article, "Land Tenure and Land Inheritance in late Sixteenth-century Culhuacan" (Cline, 1984a).

2. Faith (1966:89) notes that in medieval England when there was rapid turnover of ownership of land, parcels were identified by their previous owners.

3. AGN–T–58–4–3v.

4. AGN–T–58–4–9r.

5. BNP 110–5r. James Lockhart believes that the Spanish translation of this will was done by a native Nahuatl speaker. Calnek (*in litt.*) gives 1.65 meters for the Culhuacan matl. I have taken the braza (1.67 meters) and the matl to be equivalent in Culhuacan.

6. A frequent occurence was the listing of the unit of measure, such as the matl, once or twice within a will, and elsewhere in it just the number of units. I have taken this to mean that the unit mentioned was being used throughout.

7. Although in *The Testaments of Culhuacan* we translated *cenyollotli* as "one yollotli," I prefer viewing it as one word, following Molina.

8. The mecate was the standard unit of measure in the Yucatecan Maya area (Thompson, 1978). Castillo F. (1972:222) indicates that a mecatl is a cord of determinate length. Harvey and Williams (1980:505 n.23) found that in Tepetlaoztoc a rope of standard length was kept in the town hall. Ancient Egyptian surveryors were called "rope stretchers" (Kline, 1972:20).

9. AGN-T-58-4.

10. My thanks to Della Sprager of the University of Texas Press for correspondence concerning the iconography on which this discussion is based.

11. In other places, chinamitl also at times refers to a unit of residence, a group living around a closed patio.

12. With the Nahuatl locative suffix *-pa[n]*.

13. Also in Spanish land sale records: AGN-T-1739-5-6v. *Chinantle* is what the translator of Cristina Tiacapan's will called chinampas (BNP-110-5r).

14. Sanders estimates one man can work one-half hectare of chinampa land (quoted in Parsons, 1976:244-245), while Parsons suggests three-quarters hectare (Parsons, 1976:245). The estimate of chinampas' productivity of fifteen to twenty people per hectare is due to Sanders (cited in Parsons, 1976:242).

15. Some (Parsons, 1976; Blanton, 1970) believe that prehispanic chinampa construction was state directed and linked to a system of water management in the southern lake system, but I tend to doubt such large-scale planning.

16. She bequeathed apparently nineteen chinampas from this large plot.

17. The meaning of this passage is somewhat ambiguous, with this as the most probable translation.

18. Whether or not the map is an accurate reflection of the situation is unimportant here.

19. Testators with house chinampas TC 32,33; 46,47; 108,109; 144,145; 166,167; 172,173; 200,201; 204,205; 260,261.

20. TC 46,47; 66,67; 156,157; 218, 219; 236, 237, BNP-110-6r. *Atentlalli* may have been a toponym. The Spanish translation of Cristina Tiacapan's will takes atentlalli to be a placename, Atentli (BNP-110-5r,6r).

21. BNP 110-2r.

22. By 1580 the basic term appears with Nahuatl affixes, e.g. isolaryo; solarpan.

23. AGN-T-58-4-8v.

24. AGN-T-58-4-8v.

25. In *The Testaments of Culhuacan* we have translated tlalmilli as "cultivated land."

26. AGN–T–1739–5–14r has the Nahuatl loanword *tlalmil* to describe a plot of land sold to a Spaniard.

27. H. R. Harvey (*in litt.*) pointed this out to me.

28. AGN–T–58–4–8v.

29. AGN–T–58–4–8v.

30. In modern agriculture, cultivation of maguey is still important. According to Palerm (1967:39), a family needs some sixty magueys at different stages of growth to maintain levels of domestic consumption.

31. Thompson (1978:183) indicates that in the Yucatecan Maya area in the eighteenth century, individual branches of some trees were bequeathed.

32. Other references to tlaltepoztli are TC 52,53; 74,75; 158,159; 244,-245.

33. Rojas (1984:181) describes a tool which she terms the *uictli de hoja* which I have taken to be the tepozhuictli.

34. Other owners of tepozhuictli are TC 52,52; 74,75; 116,117; 158,159.

35. See Chapter 6 on sex-roles.

36. Torquemada mainly discusses the area north and east of Mexico-Tenochtitlan. Torquemada may have taken some of his information from Alva Ixtlilxochitl of Texcoco.

37. Usually the tlatoani became the gobernador.

38. Tocititlan TC 50,51; 70,71; 104,105; 166,167.

39. *Justiciatica* is the word used, from the Spanish *justicia,* "justice," and the Nahuatl affix *-tica,* "by means of."

40. Perhaps there was a connection through the female line or a cadet branch of the family.

41. In Reyes's interpretation, calpullalli was also a type of land to support religion.

42. Torquemada, 1975:II, 164; Motolinia, 1971:294; Zorita, 1963b:193.

43. Collection of fees for masses was standard practice, as we have seen. I note in passing that there is no evidence of any masses having been said for the soul of doña María.

44. The debt was long-outstanding, since Visitador Ramírez died in 1555 (TC 247).

45. Torquemada, 1975:II, 545–46; Guzmán, 1938:95. Carrasco (1971: 359) has argued against classifying pillalli as private property, saying "the status of *pilli* implied the political function of attending the ruler's palace for the performance of various duties." He considers pillalli a type of office land, but I do not agree with his assessment.

46. AGN–T–58–4.

47. *Auh amo pillalli marques itlaltzin calpullalli.* This quotation is given by Reyes without the archival citation.

48. If Gibson is correct in saying that tlalmilli (which I have taken to be simply cultivated land) was an allotment in calpulli land, we can add eight to the number of identifiable plots of calpulli land.

49. If calpullalli were lands of the temple, we might speculate that the magueys might have produced aguamiel for pulque to be used in religious festivities.

50. Harvey (1984) notes variations in commoners' holdings for several places in the Valley of Mexico.

51. See V. G. Kiernan's (1976) discussion of private property as an institution.

52. BNP Mex. Man. 243–3v. My thanks to Jerome A. Offner for a copy of this.

53. AGN–V–279–1–82v,86v.

54. As we have seen, the term "woman's house," cihuacalli, also needs to be seen in more contexts.

55. He is citing AGN–T–24–3–title page, 119r.

56. AGN–V–279–1–82v,86v.

57. I previously interpreted the passage in a different way, stating that this piece of land was not specifically bequeathed, (Cline, 1984a:290) but I have changed my interpretation. The plot is not bequeathed in the same statement as the listing of the land, in contrast to the usual case, but at the end of some other listings the testator declares all of the land to be his son's. I now take that to mean this plot too.

58. Tequiti could mean either.

59. Slade (1976) has found the distinction in the present-day Central Highlands of Mexico as has Kellogg (1979:69) for sixteenth-century native property in Mexico City.

60. AGN–V–179–1–114r.

61. AGN–V–279–1–115r.

62. Molina (1971:sec.2,157) gives the gloss *patrimonio* [patrimony] for *ueuetlatquitl* [patrimonial property].

63. AGN–V–279–1–115r.

64. Carrasco and Monjarás-Ruiz (1978:210–11) have translated huehuetlalli simply as "land," ignoring the distinction that exists in Nahuatl. In Spanish land sales documents for Culhuacan, there is a reference to *tierras patrimoniales,* which may be a translation of huehuetlalli (AGN–T–1739–5–5r).

65. Seven men: TC 32,33; 34,35; 118,119; 138,139; 166,167; 214,215; 270, 271; three women: TC 126,127; 148,149; 232,233.

66. If quauhtlalli is a soil type, then this is another type of land huehuetlalli could be. If quauhtlalli is conquered land, then it is a special type of patrimonial land. The passage is ambiguous. "And [I have] wooded land/conquered land [quauhtlalli] 20 [units of measure] square ... and 20

in Santiago Tetla... Both of these said pieces of patrimonial land will [be sold]" (TC 144,145).

67. TC 144,145; 148,149; 126,127.

68. Tlalcohualli is listed somewhat strangely under soil terms. Sahagún is silent on most aspects of land tenure.

69. MNA–AH 550, e.g. f. 55r.

70. See discussion of sale of land to Spaniards, below.

71. Calpoltitlan: TC 122,123; 212,213; 264,265.

72. Women who owned purchased land: TC 122,123; 194,195; 224,225.

73. Both men who inherited tlalcohualli got it from their fathers TC 114,115; 138,139.

74. TC 114,115; 138,139; 144,145; 196,197; 264,265.

75. AGN–T–1739–5–10v.

76. He may have used profits from trade to buy more land.

77. Consuegros are one's child's parents-in-law. (Nahuatl: *huexiuhtli*). [The translation in *The Testaments of Culhuacan* mistakenly gives "father-in-law" (TC 230,231).]

78. In nearby Xochimilco in 1582, another noblewoman restricted Spaniards from buying property. AGN–V–279–1–83,87.

79. AGN–T–58–4–6r.

80. TC 112, 113; 144,145; 196,197; 228,229. He is identified as a Spaniard in AGN–T–1739–5.

81. AGN–T–1739–5. My thanks to Edward E. Calnek for the microfilm of this. Because the measurements of both the length and width are given in brazas, conversion to hectares is possible.

82. Gibson, 1964:406–8. See also Prem's (1978) detailed study of land sales in the Puebla-Tlaxcala region.

83. AGN–T–1739–5–16r. This land could have fed 2,100 people and would have needed about 180 people to work it.

84. AGN–T–1739–5–6v.

85. Bernadino's testament is unfortunately a fragment, so we do not know what proportion of his estate he sold (TC 262ff).

86. Doubtless she was related to the other Motecuhçomas in the area.

87. AGN–T–1759–5–15v. This is about 357 hectares, to which must be added the 140 hectare plot of chinampa land he also sold. Don Diego de Motecuhçoma's land is also discussed in AGN–T–58–4 in the documentation for doña Luisa Juana's estate.

88. Indians in the Tlaxcala region were cultivating cochineal for commercial gain (Lockhart et al., n.d.), but no such enterprise is known for colonial Culhuacan.

89. We might speculate that the land being held by a woman who was absent was more vulnerable to usurpation than land owned by an absent man.

90. These may simply have been tributes paid on land after death. *Micca-* is the combining form of *micqui,* "dead person." Miccatlacallaquilli also may be a form of death duties, to pay for masses and burial fees, however.
91. About three-quarters of a bushel.
92. This should be *canel ye,* "since already."
93. Land liable for tribute: TC 62,63; 68,69; 162,165; 212,213; 214,215.

Chapter 9

1. See Appendix 2 for loanword lists.
2. AGN–T–58–4–7r.

GLOSSARY

Albacea*—Executor
Alcaide*—Jailor
Alcalde*—Judge and cabildo member
Alguacil*—Constable
Alguacil mayor*—Chief constable
Altepetl—City
Barrio—Ward
Braza—Spanish unit of measure, 1.67 meter
Cabecera—Head town
Callalli—House land
Calli—House or room
Calnepanolli—Two-story house
Calpulli—Territorial or social unit; the exact meaning unclear at present
Calpullalli—Calpulli land
Capellanía—Chantry
Cenyollotli—Unit of measure, lit: one heart
Chinampa**—Long, narrow, manmade extensions of farmland into the lakes around Mexico City
Church attendant(s)—Gloss for *teopantlacatl* "church person" and *teopantlaca* "church people"

Cihuacalli—"Woman house," possibly a common room
Cihuapilli—Noblewoman
Cihuatepixqui—A female lower offical
Cihuatlalli—"Woman land"; possibly a type of dowry land
Cihuatlatquitl—Women's weaving equipment
Cohuatequitl—Public works duty
Cohuaçacatl—Zacate tribute
Compadrazgo—Ritual godparenthood
Compadre*—Ritual coparent
Compañía*—Partnership
Corotopile—Indian official in charge of the choir
Corregidor—Spanish official in charge of a district
Corregimiento—Civil jurisdiction of a corregidor
Diputado*—Deputy
Don*—Noble title held at this time only by men of highest rank
Doña*—Noble title held by women of highest rank
Encomendero—Holder of a grant of Indians

Encomienda—Grant of the labor of Indians

Fanega*—Unit of dry measure, about a bushel and a half

Fiscal*—Highest Indian church official, general steward of the church and supervisor of lower officials

Fray*—Spanish title for European friars

Gobernador*—Governor, often the same person as the tlatoani

Huehuecalli—Patrimonial house

Huehuetlalli—Patrimonial land, a special category of inherited land

Huipil**—Woman's blouse (Nahuatl: *huipilli*)

Jacal** —Hut (Nahuatl: *xacalli*)

Jícara**—A type of calabash vessel (Nahuatl: *xicalli*)

Juez-gobernador*—"Judge-governor" the highest office in a major Indian political unit (*altepetl*)

Macehual**—Indian commoner (Nahuatl: *macehualli*, sg. *macehualtin*, pl.)

Matl—Unit of measure, literally "hand, arm"; approximately 1.67 m.

Mayordomo*—Steward, here apparently always a church official

Mecate**—Measure of area, in most places twenty by twenty matl but in the Culhuacan wills seemingly twenty by two hundred; literally "cord" (Nahuatl: *mecatl*)

Metate**—Grinding stone (Nahuatl: *metlatl*)

Mexicatlalli—"Mexica land," a civil category of unclear status

Molcajete**—Small mortar for grinding chiles (Nahuatl: *molcaxitl*)

Peso*—Spanish monetary unit of eight reales

Petate**—Reed mat (Nahuatl: *petlatl*)

Pillalli—Private land of lords

Pipiltin—Nobles

Pochteca—Long-distance merchants

Quahuitl—Unit of measure, literally "stick" or "rod," often equivalent to the matl

Quappantli—A measure for an amount of stone

Quauhacalli—Unit of measure, presumed to be about half a fanega

Quauhtlalli—A type of land, possibly deriving from *quahuitl*, "tree(s)" meaning wooded land or woods or alternatively, deriving from *quauhtli*, "eagle"; a type of conquered land

Real—Spanish monetary unit, one-eighth of a peso

Regidor*—Councilman in the cabildo

Regidor mayor*—Chief councilman

Solar*—Houselot

Tecomate**—Clay (or sometimes gourd) vessel (Nahuatl: *tecomatl*)

Tecpan—Unit of social organization of high nobles; court; noble house

Tecpancalli—Palace or community house

Tecpantlalli—Land belonging to the tecpan
Tecuhtli—Indian noble title; lord
Telpochcalli—"Young man's house," in the Culhuacan wills meaning a house built before a man's marriage; in the traditional sources, a school for young commoner boys
Temazcalli—Sweatbath
Teopantlalli—Church land
Teotlalli—Prehispanic sacred lands
Tepixqui—Lower official
Tequitl—Tribute or work
Tezontle*—Type of porous stone (Nahuatl: *teçontli*)
Tlacamecoyotl—"Human cordage"; lineage
Tlalcohualli—Purchased land
Tlalmilli—Cultivated land, possibly calpulli land
Tlalnemactli—Inherited land
Tlatoani—Dynastic ruler (pl. *tlatoque*)
Tlatocatlalli—Ruler's office lands
Tlaxilacalleque—ward heads or ward people
Tlaxilacalli—(Residential) subdivision of an Indian town
Tomín*—Spanish unit of money and coin equal to a real, eight to a peso; came to mean "money" in Nahuatl
Topile—Official, literally "holder of a staff"
Topile of the church—*teopan topile*, a church official of some sort
Vara*—Spanish unit of measure, 0.84 meter.
Zacate**—Grass used for fodder (Nahuatl: *zacatl*)
Zaragüelles*—Trousers

*Loanword from Spanish into Nahuatl
**Loanword from Nahuatl into Mexican Spanish

BIBLIOGRAPHY

Archival Sources & Abbreviations

AGN	Archivo General de la Nación, Mexico
—T	ramo Tierras
—V	ramo Vínculos
BNP	Bibliothèque Nationale of Paris
MNA–AH	Museo Nacional de Antropología, Archivo Histórico (Mexico)
TC	The Testaments of Culhuacan (Cline and León-Portilla, 1984)

Printed Sources

Anales de Cuauhtitlan (Códice Chimalpopoca). 1975. Mexico: Universidad Nacional Autónoma de México.

Anawalt, Patricia. 1980. "Costume and Control: Aztec Sumptuary Laws," Archeology, Jan./Feb.:33–43.

Anderson, Arthur J. O., Frances F. Berdan and James Lockhart. 1976. Beyond the Codices. Berkeley: University of California Press.

Ariès, Philippe. 1981. The Hour of Our Death. New York: Knopf.

Armillas, Pedro. 1961. "Mesoamerica," *in* A History of Land Use in Arid Regions, L. Dudley Stamp, editor. Paris: UNESCO, 264–68.

Artiles, Jenaro. 1969. "The Office of Escribano in Sixteenth-Century Havana," Hispanic American Historical Review 49:489–502.

Baudot, Georges. 1976. Utopie et histoire au Mexique. Paris: Privat.

Berdan, Frances F. 1978. "Tres formas de intercambio en la economía azteca," *in* Política e ideología en el México prehispánico, Pedro Carrasco and Johanna Broda, editors. Mexico: Editorial Nuevo Imagen.

Berkner, Lutz K. 1976. "Inheritance, Land Tenure and Peasant Family Structure: A German Regional Comparison," *in* Family and Inheri-

tance, Jack Goody et al., editors. Cambridge: Cambridge University Press, 71–95.
Berlin, Heinrich. 1948. Anales de Tlatelolco. Mexico: Antigua Librería Robredo.
Blanton, Richard. 1970. Prehispanic Settlement Patterns of the Ixtapalapa Peninsula Region, Mexico. Ph.D. dissertation, University of Michigan.
Blanton, Richard. 1972. "Prehispanic Adaptation in the Ixtapalapa Region, Mexico." Science 175(4028):1317–26.
Borah, Woodrow. 1983. Justice by Insurance. Berkeley: University of California Press.
Borah, Woodrow. 1984. "Some Problems of Sources," *in* Explorations in Ethnohistory, H. R. Harvey and Hanns J. Prem, editors. Albuquerque: University of New Mexico Press, 23–39.
Boserup, Ester. 1970. Women's Role in Economic Development. London: George Allen and Unwin, Ltd.
Brenner, Anita. 1931. The Influence of Technique on the Decorative Style in the Domestic Pottery of Culhuacan. Mexico: Publicación de la Escuela Internacional de Arqueología y Etnología Americana.
Burton, Michael L. and Douglas R. White. 1984. "Sexual Division of Labor in Agriculture," American Anthropologist 86(3):568–83.
Cabrera, Luis. 1974. Diccionario de aztequismos. Mexico: Ediciones Oases.
Calnek, Edward E. 1972. "Settlement Pattern and Chinampa Agriculture," American Antiquity 37(1):104–15.
Calnek, Edward E. 1973. "The Localization of the 16th-Century Map Called the Maguey Plan," American Antiquity 38(1)190–95.
Calnek, Edward E. 1974a. "Conjunto urbano y modelo residencial en Tenochtitlan," *in* Ensayos sobre el desarrollo urbano de México. Mexico, 11–65.
Calnek, Edward E. 1974b. "The Sahagún Texts as a Source of Sociological Information," *in* Sixteenth-Century Mexico: The Work of Sahagún, Munro S. Edmonson, editor. Albuqueque: University of New Mexico Press, 189–204.
Calnek, Edward E. 1975. "The Organization of Urban Food Supply Systems: The Case of Tenochtitlan" [published in Spanish translation] *in* Las ciudades de América Latina y sus áreas de influencia a través de la historia. Jorge Hardoy and Richard P. Schaedel, editors. Buenos Aires: Sociedad Interamericana de Planificación.
Calnek, Edward E. 1976. "The Internal Structure of Tenochtitlan," *in* The Valley of Mexico, Eric R. Wolf, editor. Albuquerque: University of New Mexico Press, 287–302.
Calnek, Edward E. 1978. "El sistema de mercado de Tenochtitlan," *in* Política e ideología en el México prehispánico, Pedro Carrasco and Johanna Broda, editors. Mexico: Editorial Nueva Imagen, 97–114.

Calnek, Edward E. 1982. "Patterns of Empire Formation in the Valley of Mexico, Late Pre-Classic Period, 1200–1521," *in* The Inca and Aztec States, George Collier, Renato I. Rosaldo and John D. Wirth, editors. New York: Academic Press, 43–62.
Carrasco, Pedro. 1961. "El barrio y la regulación del matrimonio en un pueblo del valle de México en el siglo XVI," Revista Mexicana de Etnología y Antropología 17:7–26.
Carrasco, Pedro. 1964. "Family Structure of 16th Century Tepoztlán," *in* Process and Pattern in Culture, Robert A. Manners, editor. Chicago: Aldine, 185–210.
Carrasco, Pedro. 1969. "Más documentos sobre Tepeaca," Tlalocan 6(1)1–37.
Carrasco, Pedro. 1971. "Social Organization of Ancient Mexico," *in* Handbook of Middle American Indians 10:349–75. Austin: University of Texas Press.
Carrasco, Pedro. 1972. "La casa y la hacienda de un señor tlalhuica," Estudios de Cultura Náhuatl 10:225–44.
Carrasco, Pedro. 1973. "Los documentos sobre las tierras de los indios nobles de Tepeaca en el siglo XVI. Comunicaciones 7:89–91.
Carrasco, Pedro. 1974. "The Joint Family in Ancient Mexico: The Case of Molotla," *in* Essays on Mexican Kinship, Hugo Nutini, Pedro Carrasco, and James M. Taggart, editors. Pittsburgh: University of Pittsburgh Press, 45–64.
Carrasco, Pedro. 1975. "La transformación de la cultura indígena durante la colonia," Historia Mexicana 25(2)175–203.
Carrasco, Pedro. 1976. "La sociedad mexicana antes de la conquista," *in* Historia General de México. Mexico: El Colegio de México.
Carrasco, Pedro. 1977. "Los señores de Xochimilco en 1548," Tlalocan 7:229–64.
Carrasco, Pedro. 1978. "La economía del México prehispánico," *in* Economía política e ideología en el México prehispánico. Pedro Carrasco and Johanna Broda, editors. Mexico: Editorial Nueva Imagen, 13–76.
Carrasco, Pedro. 1984. "Royal Marriages in Ancient Mexico," *in* Explorations in Ethnohistory, H. R. Harvey and Hanns J. Prem, editors. Albuquerque: University of New Mexico Press, 41–81.
Carrasco, Pedro and Jesús Monjarás-Ruiz. 1978. Colección de documentos sobre Coyoacán, II. Mexico: Instituto Nacional de Historia e Antropología.
Castillo F., Victor M. 1972. "Unidades nahuas de medida," Estudios de Cultura Náhuatl 10:195–223.
Chevalier, François. 1952. La formacion des grands domaines au Mexique. Paris: Institut d'Ethnologie.
Chimalpahin Cuauhtlehuantzin, Domingo Francisco de San Antón Muñon.

1958. Das Memorial breve acerca de la fundación de la ciudad de Culhuacan, Walter Lehmann and Gerdt Kutscher translators. Stuttgart: W. Kohlhammer Verlag.
Cline, Howard F. 1966. "The Oztoticpac Lands Map of Texcoco, 1540," Quarterly Journal of the Library of Congress 23(2):77–116.
Cline, S. L. 1984a. "Land Tenure and Land Inheritance in Late Sixteenth-Century Culhuacan," *in* Explorations in Ethnohistory, H. R. Harvey and Hanns J. Prem, editors. Albuquerque, University of New Mexico Press, 277–309.
Cline, S. L. 1984b. "A Legal Process at the Local Level: Estate Division in Sixteenth-Century Mexico," *in* Five Centuries of Law and Politics in Central Mexico, Ronald Spores and Ross Hassig, editors. Nashville: Vanderbilt University Publications in Anthropology 30:39–53.
Cline, S. L. and Miguel León-Portilla. 1984. The Testaments of Culhuacan. UCLA Latin American Center, Nahuatl Studies Series, v. 1.
Cortés, Hernán. 1971. Letters from Mexico, A. R. Pagden, translator and editor. New York: Grossman.
Códice Mendoza. 1979. Mexico: Editorial Cosmos.
Cook, Sherburne F. and L. B. Simpson. 1948. The Population of Central Mexico in the Sixteenth Century. Ibero-Americana, 31.
Davies, Nigel. 1973. The Aztecs. Norman: University of Oklahoma Press.
Davies, Nigel. 1977. The Toltecs. Norman: University of Oklahoma Press.
Davies, Nigel. 1980. The Toltec Heritage. Norman: University of Oklahoma Press.
Díaz del Castillo, Bernal. 1966. The True History of the Conquest of Mexico. Ann Arbor: University Microfilms.
Dibble, Charles. 1971. "Writing in Central Mexico," *in* Handbook of Middle American Indians 10:322–32. Austin: University of Texas Press.
Diskin, Martin. 1979. "The Peasant Family Archive: Sources for an Ethnohistory of the Present," Ethnohistory 26:209–29.
Durán, Diego. 1967. Historia de las Indias de Nueva España. Mexico: Editorial Porrúa.
Durand-Forest, Jacqueline. 1962. "Testament d'une indienne de Tlatelolco," Journal de la Societé des Americanistes. n.s. t l.l:129–58.
Dyckerhoff, Ursula. 1984. "Mexican Toponyms as a Source in Regional Ethnohistory," *in* Explorations in Ethnohistory, H. R. Harvey and Hanns J. Prem. editors. Albuquerque: University of New Mexico Press, pp. 229–52.
Faith, Rosamund Jane. 1966. "Peasant Families and Inheritance Customs in Medieval England," Agricultural History Review XIV:77–95.
Farriss, Nancy M. 1984. Maya Society Under Colonial Rule. Princeton: Princeton University Press.
Febvre, Lucien. 1977. Life in Renaissance France. Cambridge: Harvard University Press.

Gallegos, Gonzalo. 1927. "Relación geográfica de Culhuacan," Revista Mexicana de Estudios Históricos 1(6):171–73.
García Pimentel, Luis. 1897. Descripción del arzobispado de México hecha en 1570. Mexico.
Gerhard, Peter. 1972. A Guide to the Historical Geography of New Spain. New York: Cambridge University Press.
Gibson, Charles. 1952. Tlaxcala in the Sixteenth Century. New Haven: Yale University Press.
Gibson, Charles. 1964. The Aztecs Under Spanish Rule. Stanford: Stanford University Press.
Ginzburg, Carlo. 1980. The Cheese and the Worms: The Cosmos of a Sixteenth-Century Miller. New York: Penguin.
González de Cosío, Francisco. 1952. El libro de las tasaciones de pueblos de la Nueva España, siglo XVI. Mexico: Archivo General de la Nación.
Goody, Jack. 1976. "Inheritance, Property and Women: Some Comparative Considerations," *in* Family and Inheritance, Jack Goody et al., editors. Cambridge: Cambridge University Press, 10–36.
Goody, Jack, Joan Thirsk, and E. P. Thompson, editors. 1976. Family and Inheritance: Rural Society in Western Europe, 1200–1800. Cambridge: Cambridge University Press.
Gorbea Trueba, José. n.d. "Primer libro de bautismos del ex-convento de Culhuacán, D. F." INAH Boletín 6:3.
Guzmán, Eulalia. 1938. "Un manuscrito de la colección Boturini que trata de los antiguos señores de Teotihuacan," Ethnos III(4–5)89–103.
Harvey, H. R. 1984. "Aspects of Land Tenure in Ancient Mexico," *in* Explorations in Ethnohistory, H. R. Harvey and Hanns J. Prem, editors. Albuquerque: University of New Mexico Press, 83–102.
Harvey, H. R., and Barbara J. Williams. 1980. "Aztec Arithmetic: Positional Notation and Area Calculation," Science 210:499–505.
Hassig, Ross. n.d. "One Hundred Years of Servitude: Tlamemes in Early New Spain" *in* Handbook of Middle American Indians supplement 2, forthcoming. Austin: University of Texas Press.
Hellbom, Anna-Britta. 1967. La participación cultural de las mujeres: indias y mestizas en el México precortesiano y postrevolucionario. Stockholm: Ethnographical Museum.
Hicks, Frederic. 1974. "Dependent Labor in Prehispanic Mexico," Estudios de Cultura Náhuatl XI:243–66.
Hicks, Frederic. 1984. "Rotational Labor and Urban Development in Prehispanic Tetzcoco," *in* Explorations in Ethnohistory, H. R. Harvey and Hanns J. Prem, editors. Albuquerque: University of New Mexico Press, 147–74.
Hilton, R. H. 1975. The English Peasantry in the Later Middle Ages. London: Oxford University Press.

Himmerich, Robert H. 1984. The Encomenderos of New Spain, 1521–1555. Ph.D. dissertation, UCLA.

Homans, George Caspar. 1960. English Villagers of the Thirteenth Century. New York: Russell & Russell.

Howell, Cicely. 1983. Land, Family and Inheritance in Transition. Cambridge: Cambridge University Press.

Ixtlilxochitl, Fernando de Alva. 1977. Obras históricas. Mexico: Universidad Nacional Autónoma de México.

Karttunen, Frances. 1982. "Nahuatl Literacy," *in* The Inca and Aztec States, George A. Collier, Renato I. Rosaldo, and John D. Wirth, editors. New York: Academic Press, 396–417.

Karttunen, Frances and James Lockhart. 1976. Nahuatl in the Middle Years: Language Contact Phenomena in Texts of the Colonial Period. University of California Publications in Linguistics, 85.

Karttunen, Frances and James Lockhart. 1978. "Textos en náhuatl del siglo XVIII: un documento de Amecameca, 1746," Estudios de Cultura Náhuatl 13:153–76.

Keen, Benjamin. 1971. The Aztec Image in Western Thought. New Brunswick: Rutgers University Press.

Kellogg, Susan. 1979. Social Organization in Early Colonial Tenochtitlan-Tlatelolco. Ph.D. dissertation, University of Rochester.

Kellogg, Susan. 1984. "Aztec Women in Early Colonial Courts: Structure and Strategy in a Legal Context," *in* Five Centuries of Law and Politics in Central Mexico, Ronald Spores and Ross Hassig, editors. Nashville: Vanderbilt University Publications in Anthropology 30:25–38.

Kiernan, V. G. 1976. "Private Property in History," *in* Family and Inheritance, Jack Goody et al, editors. Cambridge: Cambridge University Press, 361–98.

Kline, Morris. 1972. Mathematical Thought from Ancient to Modern Times. New York: Oxford University Press.

Klor de Alva, J. Jorge. 1982. "Spiritual Conflict and Accommodation in New Spain: Toward a Typology of Aztec Responses to Christianity," *in* The Inca and Aztec States, George A. Collier, Renato I. Rosaldo, and John D. Wirth, editors. New York: Academic Press, 345–66.

Lavrin, Asunción and Edith Couturier. 1979. "Dowries and Wills: A View of Women's Socioeconomic Role in Colonial Guadalajara and Puebla, 1640–1790," Hispanic American Historical Review 59:280–304.

Leacock, Eleanor and June Nash. 1977. "Ideologies of Sex: Archetypes and Stereotypes," Annals of the New York Academy of Sciences 285:618–45.

León-Portilla, Miguel. 1976. "El libro de testamentos indígenas de Culhuacan," Estudios de Cultura Náhuatl 12:11–31.

LeRoy Ladurie, Emmanuel. 1979a. Montaillou: The Promised Land of Error. New York: Vintage Books.

LeRoy Ladurie, Emmanuel. 1979b. The Territory of the Historian. Chicago: University of Chicago Press.
LeRoy Ladurie, Emmanuel. 1980. The Mind and Method of the Historian. Chicago: University of Chicago Press.
Lewis, Oscar. 1951. Life in a Mexican Village: Tepoztlán Restudied. Urbana: Universtiy of Illinois Press.
Linné, Sigvald. 1948. El valle y la ciudad de México en 1550. Relación histórica fundada sobre un mapa geográfico, que se conserva en la biblioteca de la Universidad de Uppsala, Suecia. Stockholm.
Lockhart, James. 1973–74. "Españoles entre indios: Toluca a fines del siglo XVI," Revista de Indias 131–38:435–91.
Lockhart, James. 1980. "Y la Ana lloró: Cesión de un sitio para casa, San Miguel Tocuilan, 1583," Estudios de Cultura Náhuatl 8:21–33.
Lockhart, James. 1981. "Some Nahua Concepts in Postconquest Guise," paper presented at the American Historical Association Convention.
Lockhart, James, Arthur J. O. Anderson, and Frances Berdan. n.d. The Tlaxcalan Actas. Salt Lake City: University of Utah Press (forthcoming).
Loera y Ch., Margarita. 1977. Calimaya y Tepemaxalco. Cuadernos de Trabajo del Departamento de Investigaciones Históricas. Mexico: Instituto Nacional de Antropología e Historia.
Lombardo de Ruiz, Sonia. 1973. Desarrollo urbano de Mexico-Tenochtitlan según las fuentes historicas. Mexico: Instituto Nacional de Antropología e Historia.
López de Gómara, Francisco. 1943. Historia de la conquista de México. Mexico: Robredo.
López y Magaña, Juan. 1980. Aspects of the Nahuatl Heritage of Juan Bautista Pomar. Master of Arts Paper in Latin American Studies, UCLA.
MacLeod, Murdo. 1973. Spanish Central America. Berkeley: University of California Press.
Madsen, William. 1960. The Virgin's Children. Austin: University of Texas Press.
Markov, Gretchen. 1983. The Legal Status of Indians Under Spanish Rule. Ph.D. dissertation, University of Rochester.
Molina, Alonso de. 1970. Vocabulario en lengua castellana y mexicana y mexicana y castellana. Mexico: Editorial Porrúa.
Monterrosa Prado, Mariano. 1970. El plano de Culhuacán. INAH Boletín 39:12–16.
Mörner, Magnus. 1967. Race Mixture in the History of Latin America. Boston: Little, Brown and Company.
Motolinia, Toribio de Benavente. 1950. History of the Indians of New Spain. Elizabeth Andros Foster, translator. Berkeley: The Cortés Society.
Motolinia, Toribio de Benavente. 1951. History of the Indians of New

Spain. W. Steck, translator. Washington: American Academy of Franciscan History.
Motolinia, Toribio de Benavente. 1971. Memoriales o libro de cosas de la Nueva España. Mexico: Universidad Nacional Autónoma de México.
Nash, June. 1978. "The Aztecs and the Ideology of Male Dominance," Signs 4(2):349–62.
Nutini, Hugo. 1965. "Polygyny in a Tlaxcalan Community," Ethnology 4:123–47.
Offner, Jerome A. 1980. "Archival Reports of Poor Crop Yields in the Early Postconquest Texcocan Heartland and their Implications for Studies of Aztec Period Population," American Antiquity 45(4)848–56.
Offner, Jerome A. 1983. Law and Politics in Aztec Texcoco. Cambridge: Cambridge University Press.
Offner, Jerome A. 1984. "Household Organization in the Texcocan Heartland," *in* Explorations in Ethnohistory, H. R. Harvey and Hanns J. Prem, editors. Albuquerque: University of New Mexico Press, 127–46.
Olivera, Mercedes. 1978. Pillis y macehuales. Mexico: Ediciones de la Casa de Chata.
Palerm, Angel. 1967. "Agricultural Systems and Food Patterns," Handbook of Middle American Indians 6:26–52. Austin: University of Texas Press.
Parry, J. H. 1953. The Sale of Public Office in the Spanish Indies Under the Hapsburgs. Iberoamericana 37, Berkeley: University of California Press.
Parsons, Jeffrey R. 1976. "The Role of Chinampa Agriculture in the Food Supply of Aztec Tenochtitlan," *in* Cultural Change and Continuity, Charles E. Cleland, editor. New York: Academic Press, 233–262.
Parsons, Jeffrey R., et al. 1982. Prehispanic Settlement Patterns in the Southern Valley of Mexico: The Chalco-Xochimilco Region. Memoirs of the Museum of Anthropology, University of Michigan, Number 14.
Paso y Troncoso, Francisco del. 1979. Relaciones geográficas de México. Mexico: Editorial Cosmos.
Piho, Virve. 1972. "Tlacatecuhtli, tlacochtecutli, tlacateccatl, y tlacochcalcatl," Estudios de Cultura Náhuatl 7:315–28.
Pollock, Sir Frederick and Frederic William Maitland. 1923. The History of English Law before the Time of Edward I. Cambridge: Cambridge University Press.
Prem, Hanns J. 1967. Die Namenshieroglyphen der Matricula von Huexotzinco. Ph.D. dissertation. Universität Hamburg.
Prem, Hanns J. 1974. Matrícula de Huexotzinco. Graz: Druck und Verlagsanstalt.
Prem, Hanns J. 1978. Milpa y hacienda: Tenencia de la tierra indígena y española en la cuenca de Alto Atoyac, Puebla, México 1520–1650. Wiesbaden: Franz Steiner Verlag GMBH.

Ravicz, Robert. 1967. "Compadrinazgo," Handbook of Middle American Indians 6:238–53. Austin: University of Texas Press.
Redfield, Robert. 1930. Tepoztlán: A Mexican Village. Chicago: University of Chicago Press.
Reyes García, Luis. 1975. "El término calpulli en los documentos del centro de México," presentation at the Seminario de Verano sobre Organización Social del México Antiguo. Mexico: CIS–INAH.
Reyes García, Luis. 1977. Cuauhtinchan del siglo XII al XVI: Formación y desarrollo histórico de un señorío prehispánico. Wiesbaden: Franz Steiner Verlag GMBH.
Reyes García, Luis. 1978. Documentos sobre Tierras y Señoríos en Cuauhtinchan. Mexico: Instituto Nacional de Antropología e Historia.
Reyes García, Luis. 1979. "El término calpulli en documentos del siglo XVI," paper presented at the International Congress of Americanists, Vancouver.
Ricard, Robert. 1966. The Spiritual Conquest of Mexico. Berkeley: University of California Press.
Riché, Pierre. 1978. Daily Life in the World of Charlemagne. Philadelphia: University of Pennsylvania Press.
Rojas Rabiela, Teresa. 1984. "Agricultural Implements in Mesoamerica," *in* Explorations in Ethnohistory, H. R. Harvey and Hanns J. Prem, editors. Albuquerque: University of New Mexico Press, 175–204.
Rounds, J. 1977. "The Role of the Tecuhtli in Ancient Aztec Society." Ethnohistory 24(4)343–61.
Sabean, David. 1976. "Aspects of Kinship Behaviour and Property in Rural Western Europe before 1800," *in* Family and Inheritance, Jack Goody, et al., editors. Cambridge: Cambridge University Press, 96–111.
Sahagún, Bernardino de. 1950–1983. The Florentine Codex, Arthur J. O. Anderson and Charles Dibble, translators. Salt Lake City: University of Utah Press.
Sanders, William T., Jeffrey Parsons, and Robert S. Santley. 1979. The Basin of Mexico: Ecological Processes in the Evolution of a Civilization. New York: Academic Press.
Schroeder, Susan. 1984a. "Chimalpahin and the Role of *Cihuatl*," paper presented at the American Society for Ethnohistory.
Schroeder, Susan. 1984b. Chalco and Sociopolitical Concepts in Chimalpahin. UCLA Ph.D. dissertation.
Séjourné, Laurette. 1970. Culhuacan. Mexico: Instituto Nacional de Antropología e Historia.
Siméon, Rémi. 1977. Diccionario de la lengua náhuatl o mexicana. Mexico: Siglo Veintiuno.
Slade, Doren L. 1976. "Kinship in the Social Organization of a Nahuat-speaking Community of the Central Highlands," *in* Essays in Mexican

Kinship, Hugo Nutini et al., editors. Pittsburgh: University of Pittsburgh Press, 155–86.

Spufford, Margaret. 1976. "Peasant Inheritance Customs in the Midlands, 1280–1700," *in* Family and Inheritance, Jack Goody et al., editors. Cambridge: Cambridge University Press.

Sullivan, Thelma. 1976. Compendio de la gramática náhuatl. Mexico: Universidad Nacional Autónoma de México.

Taggart, James M. 1983. Nahuat Myth and Social Structure. Austin: University of Texas Press.

Tawney, R. H. 1967. The Agrarian Problem in the Sixteenth Century. New York: Harper & Row, Publishers.

Taylor, William B. 1979. Drinking, Homicide and Rebellion in Colonial Mexican Villages. Stanford: Stanford University Press.

Tezozomoc, Fernando Alvarado de. 1975. Crónica mexicayotl. Mexico: Universidad Nacional Autónoma de México.

Thompson, Philip C. 1978. Tekanto in the Eighteenth Century. Ph.D. dissertation, Tulane University.

Torquemada, Juan de. 1975. Monarquía indiana. Mexico: Editorial Porrúa.

Vargas Rea, Luis. 1957. "Relación geográfica de Ixtapalapa." Mexico: Biblioteca Aportación Histórica.

Vetacurt, Agustín de. 1971. Teatro mexicano. Mexico: Editorial Porrúa.

Vovelle, Michel. 1978. Piété baroque et déchristianisation en provence au XVIIIe siècle. Paris: Editions du Seuil.

Weber, Eugen. 1976. Peasants into Frenchmen. Stanford: Stanford University Press.

West, Robert C. and Pedro Armillas. 1950. "Las chinampas de México," Cuadernos Americanos 40:165–82.

Whorf, Benjamin. 1937. "The Origin of the Aztec tl," American Anthropologist 39:265–74.

Williams, Barbara J. 1976. "Aztec Soil Science," Boletín: Instituto de Geografía 6:115–20.

Williams, Barbara J. 1984. "Mexican Pictorial Registers," *in* Explorations in Ethnohistory, H. R. Harvey and Hanns J. Prem, editors. Albuquerque: University of New Mexico Press, 103–25.

Williams, Caroline. 1980. Saints. New York: St. Martin's Press.

Zorita, Alonso de. 1963a. Breve y sumaria relación de los señores de la Nueva España. Mexico: Universidad Nacional Autónoma de México.

Zorita, Alonso de. 1963b. Life and Labor in Ancient Mexico. Benjamin Keen, translator. New Brunswick: Rutgers University Press.

INDEX

Acatzintitlan, 126
Acatl, Pedro Cano, 55, 154
Acol, Gabriel, 64
Acolhua, 4
Acolhuaque, 3, 4
Acolnahuacatl, Marcos Hernández, 69
agriculture, 132–35; *chinampas,* 132–35; crops cultivated, 138–40; dry land, 132; fruit trees, 139–40; level land, 132; native tools, 140; soil in Culhuacan, 132–33, 137, 138; surpluses, 104, 140; upland, 132; zones of cultivation, 132. *See also* land
Aguilar, don Juan de, 153
Agurto, Cristóbal de, 21
albaceas, 43, 44, 45. *See also* executors
alcaide, 39, 42, 46
alcalde, 39, 41, 47, 48–49, 62, 63, 74, 109, 116
alguacil, 37, 39, 41, 42, 45, 48, 49, 51, 126–27
altepetl, 36, 38, 58, 115
Amantlan, 100
Amaro, Baltasar, 33
Amaxac, 57, 145
Amecameca, 53
Ana, María, 120
Anales de Cuauhtitlan, 4, 5
Andrés, Felipe, 29
Aquino, Tomás de, 27, 81, 134
artisans, 89–90
Aticpac (Santa María Asunción), 54
Atlixocan, 138, 150
Atzcapolzalco, 134
audencia, 37

Augustinians, 15, 20–21, 27, 47, 49. *See also* Núñez, fray Juan
aunts. *See* Aztec kinship, uncles and aunts
axalli. See land, wet and sandy
Ayahualco, 76
Ayauhtonco, 125, 126
Aztec, use of the term, xvi
Aztec Empire, 4; relationship with Toltecs, 4
Aztec kinship, 59–85; bilateral, 66; children, 69–70; classificatory system, 66; father's role, 66; ideal mother, 69; grandparents, 71; joint family, 78–79; multiple wives, 78; nuclear family, 164; parent-child relationships, 68–70, 78; prehispanic, 74; siblings, 74–77, 80, 81; surrogate parents, 70–75; uncles and aunts, 73–74. *See also compadrazgo;* women, and daughters
Aztecs, xii, xiii; colonial, xiii; conversion to Christianity, 6; gender differences, 79–82; inheritance, 77–85; prehispanic, xiii, 91, 100, 118, 127, 144; regional differences, xiv. *See also* Nahua-speaking Indians
Aztlan, 4

bail, 55, 92
barrios, 37
Bautista, Juan, 46, 59, 70, 73, 74, 80, 120, 126, 135
bequests: overall patterns of, 83–84. *See also* inheritance
blacks, 43

250 / INDEX

blankets, 104
boats, 97
books, 27–28, 96
braza, 129
brothers. *See* Aztec kinship, siblings
burial, 21–24, 27; expenses, 21–23
Bueno, Juan, 76, 94

cabecera, 37
cabecera towns, 58
cabeza, 37
cabildo, 39, 41, 43, 44, 48, 50–51, 53, 58, 113, 115, 119, 162
Çacaapan, San Pedro, 143
Cacama, Tomás, 75
cacao beans, 97
cadastrals, 127, 128, 130–31
calendars. *See* timekeeping
callalli, 135–36
calli, 97–98, 102
calnepanolli, 99
calpoltlaxilacalli, 53. *See also* wards
calpullalli, 141. *See also* land, *calpulli* land
calpulleque, 53
calpulli, 36, 53, 87, 141, 147. *See also* wards
calpulli heads, 127
calpulli land. *See* land, *calpulli* land
Caltenco (Santa Ana), 55, 146
camellones. See chinampas
canals, 2, 131, 135
candles, 24
Cano, Martín, 94
canoes, 2, 96, 97
capellanía, 26
carpentry, 101
Castañeda, don Miguel de, 92
Castro, Sebastián de, 21
causeways, 2
Central Mexico, 1
Cerón, Miguel, 30, 141–42
Cerro de la Estrella, 2, 3, 36, 137
cemacolli, 130
cemmitl, 130
cenyollotli, 129, 130
Cervantes, Gonzalo Gómez de, 62
cetos de cañas, 99
chahuanantli, 70. *See also* marriage, stepkin
Chalca, 3

Chalcas, 4
Chalco, 6
Chapultepec, 4
charitable donations, 26
Chichimecatl, Gaspar, 78
Chichimecs, 4
children, bequests to, 65–66; legitimacy of, 65–66. *See also* kinship
Chimalpahin, 4
chimaltecuhtli, 119
Chimaltecuhtli, Miguel, 22, 119
chinamitl. See chinampas
chinampas, 2–3, 55, 71, 73, 75, 88, 89, 110, 125, 132–35, 140, 142, 143, 145, 146, 148, 150, 151; accompanying houses, 134–36; cultivation of, 132–33; sale of, 22
Chinampa Towns, 2–3, 4, 5
Christian Church, 161–62; and crown, 6; and Indians, 6, 13–34, 143–44; and land, 143–44; involvement in Indians' lives, 47–50; native officials in, 15. *See also* Augustinians; ecclesiastics; Franciscans; Núñez, Fray Juan
cihuacalli. See "woman's house"
cihuapilli, 109
Cihuatecpan, 119
cihuatecpanecatl, 119
Cihuatecpanecatl, Francisco, 119
cihuatepixque, 54
cihuatl, 60
cihuatlalli. See "woman's land"
cihuatlatquitl, 113. *See also* women's equipment
cioatlatole, 117
Cipriano, Baltasar, 80
cities: after Conquest, 38; names of, 38; hierarchy, 38–39. *See also* municipal government; *names of specific cities*
city council. *See cabildo*
ciudad, 38
class, xv, 107; and wealth, 110–12
clothing, 102, 112, 113, 114–15
Coatequitzin, Miguel, 31
Coatlan, 12, 54, 145, 148
cocoliloc, 118
cocoliste, 14
codices, 4
cohuaçacatl, 42. *See also* tribute

cohuatequitl, 42. *See also* tribute
commerce, 87, 92–97, 100, 104–105, 167. *See also pochteca* (long-distance merchants); merchants
commoners, 107, 108, 110, 116
compadrazgo, 71–72, 81, 82, 85
compañía, 95
Conquest, 6–7, 58, 161; chronicles of, 6–7; impact on Aztecs, xiv
constable. *See alguacil*
Constantina, doña Elena, 11, 31, 70, 74, 110, 118, 120, 132
cooking ware, 102
Coronado, doña Ana de, 94
corotopile, 47
corregidor, 7, 13–14, 37, 41, 42, 58, 101
corregimiento, 37
Cortés, Hernando, 6
Coyoacan, 4, 122, 127
crops: bequests of, 89. *See also* agriculture
Cuauhtemoc, xiii, xiv
Cuauhtinchan area, 141
Cuernavaca area, 54, 74–75, 78, 105, 116
Cuitlahuac, 3, 4, 80
Cuitlatetelco, 94
Culhua-Mexica, 5, 6
Culhuacan, xi, xiv, 36, 61; and Cortés, 6; and encomienda, 6, 7; and Spanish Conquest chronicles, 6–7; becomes San Juan Evangelista Culhuacan, 38; boundaries of, 6; Christianization of, 7, 10–11, 13–14; corregidor of, 7, 13–14, 37; defeat of in 1253, 4; encomendero of, 6–7, 36, 37; founding of, 1; geography of, 1–2; historical importance of, 3–7; in hierarchy of cities, 38; Indian population in 1580, 7; map of, 40; medicine in, 27; post-Conquest layout, 39; relationship with Toltecs, 3–4, 36; rulers of, 4–6

Day of the Dead (Christian), 25
Day of the Holy Cross, 25
death: causes of, 19–20; prehispanic practices concerning, 24–25; religious practices concerning, xiv. *See also* burial, inheritance, wills

debts, 111, 113
defense, 36
demography, 104
diet, 2–3
digging stick, 103, 140
directions (cardinal), 127, 129
disputes, 41. *See also* property, disputes over
disinheritance, 82–83
divorce, 60, 116
don, doña, 108, 109, 120, 121
doors. *See* houses, doors
dowries. *See* marriage, dowries
Durán, Diego, 54, 60

Ecatl, Melchor de Santiago, 31
ecclesiastics, 50, 54, 111. *See also* Christian Church, involvement in Indians' lives
economy, 87; prehispanic, 87, 91; sixteenth century Culhuacan, xv. *See also* diet; wealth
Eitlatocan, 12, 38
elites. *See* native hierarchies; Spanish hierarchies
Elías, Diego, 13, 120
enclosure, 98
encomendero, 42, 58
encomienda, 6–7, 36
escribano. See notary
estancias, 37
executors, 35, 44–45, 46, 95, 103, 104, 114

family. *See* Aztec kinship
Feast of St. Catherine, 25
feasts, 25
fiscal, 15, 35, 47, 111
Flores, don Francisco, 63, 71–72, 74
food, 133; storage of, 103; surpluses of, 87. *See also* agriculture; diet
Franciscans, 15, 74
Francisco, Juan, 70, 102
Francisco, Lorenzo de, 48
frezadas. See blankets
furniture, 102–104

Gallegos, Gonzalo, 7, 37, 41
gambling, 152
García, don Juan, 49, 121
García, Hernando, 77

252 / INDEX

García, Miguel, 16, 25, 32, 45, 46–47, 95–97, 104, 143
gender, xv; and division of work, 112–13; and language, 117; and status, 115. See also Aztecs, gender differences; women
godparents. See compadrazgo
Gómara, Francisco López de, 16
González, Francisco, 143
government, post-Conquest, 58; prehispanic Valley of Mexico, 36. See also local government; municipal government
grandparents. See Aztec kinship, grandparents
great hall, 99, 100
Guadalajara area, 7
Guzmán, Nuño de, 7

Hernández, Marcos, 20, 136
Hernández, Miguel, 64, 95
hierarchy. See cities, hierarchy; native hierarchy
horses, 93, 94, 95, 96
house land, 135–36
houselot, 136–37
houses, 49, 52, 64, 68, 73, 74, 76, 77, 78, 79–81, 87, 105–107; and accompanying *chinampas,* 134–35; as a type of wealth, 97; compounds, 97; dismantling of, 101–102; doors, 101; great halls, 99; relative values of, 97–98; types of, 97–101
Hualmoquetza, Lázaro, 93
Huantli, Miguel, 57, 58, 75, 76, 80
Huapalcalco, 92
huehuetlalli. See land, inherited land
Huelihuitl, Miguel, 42, 91–92
huexotl (willow), 140
Huexotzinco, 6
Huitzilcoatl, Martín, 55
Huitzilopochco, 6, 20
huitznahuatl, 119
Huitznahuatl, Pablo, xvi, 14, 25, 38, 59, 61, 64, 68, 69, 80, 83, 87, 88, 101, 107, 109, 110, 119, 120, 121, 129, 132, 135, 138, 142
Huitznahuatocatl, Miguel, 51, 53
huitzoctli, 140. See digging stick
Huixachtecatl, 2, 137
Huixachtlan, 137
hut. See *xacalli*

ichpochtli, 68
Icnocihuatl, María (of Cihuatecpan), 55, 63, 89, 111, 135
Ilpitoc, Andrés, 139
Inés, Bárbara, 111
Inés, María, 74, 89, 110
inheritance, xv, 53. See also wills
Inquisition, xi
interprete. See interpreter
interpreter, 37
Isabel, doña Luisa, 48–49, 115, 120
Itzic, Miguel, 24
Itzmalli, Gabriel, 60, 65, 70
Itzpancalqui, Juan, 29
Iuhcatlatzin, Miguel, 31
Ixlilxochitl, Alva, 141, 145
Ixtapalapa, 6, 37, 93
Ixtapalapa peninsula, 1, 2
Iyauhtenco (Santa Ana), 54, 55
Iztic, Miguel, 76

jacal, 100
Jacobo, Antón, 45
Jacobo, Miguel, 21, 35, 46
jail, 42, 55
Jiménez, Agustín, 49
Jiménez, Alonso, 45
Jiménez, Fabián, 32
Josef, Miguel, 13, 35, 45, 144
Juana, Ana, 60, 63, 64–65, 70, 71, 98, 102, 120, 136, 169
Juana, doña Luisa, 11, 18–19, 20, 24, 29, 31, 42, 47, 50, 88, 99, 118, 120, 128, 138, 146, 189–211
Juárez, Andrés, 121
Juárez, doña María, 26, 55, 69, 99, 116, 118, 126, 139, 144, 145, 146, 152, 169
Juárez, Mateo, 22, 31, 110, 118
judge-governor. See *juez-gobernador*
judicial system, 51, 53; jurisdiction, 53–54; Spanish, 73, 84–85, 123, 142, 165. See also legal system
juez-gobernador, 41, 47–48, 58, 126–27, 161
Justina, María, 113

kinship. See Aztec kinship; Spanish kinship

Lake Chalco-Xochimilco, 1, 2–3
Lake Texcoco, 1, 5

Lake Xaltocan-Zumpango, 1
Lake Xochimilco, 96
lakes, in Valley of Mexico, 1–2. *See also specific lake names.*
land, 95, 96, 107, 111, 125–59; adjacent to the house, 135–36; alienation of, 145, 146, 147, 152; and Christian Church, 143–44; and nobles, 146, 147; and Spanish courts, 142; and subsistence, 88; as source of wealth, 87, 104–105; bequests of, 79–80, 82, 88, 113, 125, 148; bequests of usufruct rights, 78; boundaries of, 126–27, 140; *calpulli* land, 137, 149; changes in ownership of, 26–27, 48–49, 83–84; church land, 143–44; civil categories of, 82; commoners and, 87; cultivated, 127, 145; dry, 137, 141, 148; for support of nobles, 145; houselots, 136–37; individual nobles', 146–47, 149; inherited, 141, 151–52; kinds of, 125, 134, 135–38; "land of the Mexica," 150; level, 151; locations of, 126; mandated cultivation of, 142; measurement of, 129–30, 134; nobility and, 87; ownership of, 127; patrimonial, 145, 148, 150–51; post-Conquest changes in tenure, 144, 152–59; prehispanic distribution, 87; purchased, 141, 148, 152–58; redistribution of, 82, 83, 125; rental of, 26; rulers' office land, 141–42, 146; schematic plans of parcels (cadastrals), 127, 130–31; small landowners', 89; soil, 138; Spanish-Indian transactions, 155–58, 168–69; surpluses, 87, 88, 89; temple (lands), 144; usufruct rights, 78, 82, 104; wet and sandy, 145, "woman land," 141, 145, 149–50; workers of, 90. *See also* land sales; land tenure; land values
land sales, xiii; land, purchases
land tenure, xv, 127, 140–59, 168–69; erosion of relevant prehispanic categories, 140–41; prehispanic, 146–47; rental, 143, 144; taxation, 158
land values, 156–57
law: about wills, 16–17; of property transfer, 152; Spanish, xv
Laws of Toro, 29
Lázaro, Martín, 143

legal system, Aztec, 65; post-Conquest, 43
level land, 135–37
Libro de Bautismos, 37, 56–57
lieutenant. *See teniente*
literacy, 16; and women, 122; in Nahuatl, 115
local government, 35. *See also* municipal government
Los Angleles, Juan de, 146
Luna, Joaquín de, 22, 24, 75–76, 94

macehual, 118
maguey, 138–39
Maguey Plan, 134, 135
Maldonado, Gabriel, 35, 45
Maldonado, Miguel Jacobo de, 9, 13–14, 18, 19, 21, 33, 35, 41, 46, 55, 68, 96
Malinalco, 4
market economy, 90–91
marriage, 60–66, 105; and fidelity, 65; dowries, 116, 122–23; financial aspects of, 63–64; polygyny, 78; prehispanic, 60, 61, 116; remarriage, 70–71; Spanish-Indian intermarriage, 115, 122, 165; stepkin, 70–71; women's roles in, 62–65, 81. *See also* divorce
Martín (of the ward of San Andrés), 111–12
Martina, Juana, 28, 120, 144
masses. *See* memorial masses; wills, as religious acts
matl, 88, 129, 130
Matlalacan, Joaquín, 30, 32 83
mats. *See petates*
measurement, 134; glyphic representations of units of, 130; units of, 129–30
mecate, 130
mecatl, 129
medium of exchange, 97, 113
memorial masses, 48, 49, 50, 64, 68, 76, 77, 79, 80, 82, 84, 95, 96, 112, 126, 144, 164
Mendoza, don Antonio de, 7
merchants: local, 90–91. *See also pochteca* (long-distance merchants)
merchants: long-distance. *See pochteca*
Mesa Central, 1
Mexica, xvi, 3, 4; and Culhuacan, 4–7

254 / INDEX

Mexicatlalli. See land, "land of the Mexica"
Mexicatzinco, 2, 6, 37, 140
Mexico City, 6, 7, 36, 37, 38, 51, 53, 72, 73, 77i, 75, 78, 81, 84, 89, 94, 96–97, 98, 105, 127, 129, 135, 147, 150
Michoacan, 103
mictlampa, 127
Mixquic, 4
Mixton War, 7
Mocel, Angelina, 11, 21, 23, 25–26, 27, 32, 59, 61, 64, 68, 69, 73, 89, 100, 107, 135, 138; deathbed of, 13, 30, 59, 125; will of, 18, 21, 23, 25, 26, 28, 29–30, 33, 38, 45, 47, 73
Molina, Alonso de, 17, 18, 28
money-lending, 87, 91–93, 153
Morelos, Marcos, 81
Motecuhçoma, xiii, xiv, 6, 11
Motecuhçoma, don Diego de, 65, 118
Motecuhçoma, doña Juana, 118
Motecuhçoma, doña María de, 11, 118
Motecuhçoma family, xii, 65, 118
Motecuhçoma Ilhuicamina, 150
Motecuhçoma Xocoyotzin, 118
Motolinia, Toribio de Benavente, 16, 23, 25
Motolinia, Tomás, 73, 74, 76, 97, 110, 116
movable goods, 102–104, 105, 111, 113
Moxixicoa, Simón, 19, 22, 27, 29, 33, 113
mud, 101
mulattoes, 43
municipal government, 35–37, 58, 161–62; functions of, 41–58; officials of, 28, 39, 41–47. *See also* wards

Nahua: use of term, xvi
Nahua-speaking Indians, xiii. *See also* Aztecs
Nahuatl, xi, xii
Nahuatl language, 17–18; kinship terms, 65, 70, 72, 73, 75; personal names and status, 121–22; land tenure terms, 140, 141, 142, 143; written, 96, 138
namictli, 60
naming patterns, 117–22; prehispanic, 118
nantli, 70

native hierarchy, 15, 35, 36, 37, 103, 107, 146; and women, 122; in municipal government, 39–41; nahuatl-language titles, 39, 42; nobility in, 41, 62, 87, 93, 97, 98, 99–100, 107, 108; prehispanic, 41, 43, 107, 115–16; relationship to Spanish hierarchy, 35–36. *See also* nobility
Nentequitl, Baltasar, 20, 100
Nentlamati, Gabriel, 143
New Fire ceremony, 2
Nezahualcoyotl, 149
nitrous land, 137
nobility, 109, 111, 122, 126; and land, 139, 141; lesser, 108; marriages between, 115; titles, 108, 119; *tlatoque* (high nobles), 108, 118, 120–21. *See also* native hierarchy, nobility in
noble houses, 145, 151
nochpoch, 68
nonamictzin, 60
nopilhuan, 68
norte, 129
notaries, 13–14, 17, 18, 20, 25, 28, 29–30, 32, 33, 35, 37, 41, 68, 95, 104, 115, 120, 121, 143; native compared to Spanish, 46; general functions of, 43–44, 45–47. *See also* Maldonado, Miguel Jacobo de
notatzin, 68
nuclear family, 78
numbers, 130–31
Núñez, Elvira, 49
Núñez, fray Juan, 21, 27, 47, 50, 122

Oçoma, Miguel, 19, 22, 25, 31, 96, 99
Ocuilan, 4
Oñate, Cristóbal de, 6, 36
Oñate, Hernando, 7, 36
Oñate family, 36
Opan, Mateo, 24, 77, 93–94
oquichpan. See great hall
oquichtlatole, 117
oquichtli, 60
order (public), 36, 42. *See also* alguacil
Ortiz, Pedro, 122
Otomí, 3
Otumpan, 4

palaces, 87, 145. *See also* tecpancalli
pantli, 130

Index / 255

pawning, 94
petates, 102
petlatolli, 138
Petronila, Marta, 51, 66, 71
physicians, 27
pillalli. See land, individual nobles'
pipiltin, 108, 109, 127
plague, 13–14, 20
plaza, 39
pochteca (long-distance merchants), 87, 90, 95, 107. See also commerce
polygyny, 61, 78
pottery, "Culhuacan style," 3
prehispanic Aztecs. See Aztecs, prehispanic
prenda, 94
priesthood: of Indians, 15
prior (Spanish), 41, 47. See also ecclesiastics: Núñez, fray Juan
prison, 42
property: disputes, 164; prehispanic settlements over, 116; prices of, 173–75; Spanish concepts, 167; transfer of, 41, 48–49, 77–78, 152; types of, 79. See also houses; land
Puebla-Tlaxcala region, xiv, 1, 53
pueblo, 38
puerta. See houses, doors
pillalli, 141
public works, 41, 42
pulque, 139

quahuitl, 129, 131, 132
quauhtlalli (conquered land?), 138
Quauhtlalpan, 91, 92
Quauhtli, Francisco, 55, 63
Quechol, Pablo, 22, 27, 69, 80, 97, 103, 104, 115
quenitoloc, 118
Quenitoloc, Juan Bautista, 49

Ramírez, Diego, 145
Ramírez, don Juan, 49
reeds, 138
regidor, 39, 41, 45, 109, 110, 119
regions, xiv
Relación Geográfica, xii, 5, 37, 38, 39, 40, 41, 56–57, 98, 100, 139–40
religion, post-Conquest Aztec, xiv, 18, 36. See also Christian Church; Christianization of; wills, as a religious act

residence, 54, 55, 78–79
retirement, 78

Sahagún, Bernardino de, xv, 66, 91, 99, 150, 152
saints' names, 119
Salomé, María, 13, 59, 120
San Agustín, Pedro de, 49
San Francisco Tlemachica, Antonio, 20
San Gabriel, doña Juana de, 47, 154
San Juan Evangelista Culhuacan, 10, 15, 39, 76
San Marcos, Josef de, 118
San Miguel, Andrés de, 33, 63, 118, 121
San Miguel, Juan de, 31, 42, 48, 49, 50, 70, 145
San Pablo, Lázaro de, 54
San Pedro, Juan de, 18, 20, 61, 100, 121
San Román, Diego de, 49, 50
Sánchez, Diego, 20, 21, 27, 43, 55, 77–78, 81, 83, 169
Sánchez, Miguel, 76
Santa María, Antonio de, 91–93, 96, 122, 153
Santa María Cihuatecpan, 12
Santa María Madalena, 28
Santa María Tezcacoac, 12, 19. See also Santa María Cihuatecpan
Santiago, Alonso Dávila de, 20
Santiago Ecatl, Melchor de, 31, 80, 134, 140, 145
Santiago, Martín de, 45
schools, 100
"shield lord," 119
siblings. See Aztec kinship, siblings
Siete Partidas, 28, 29, 30
sisters. See Aztec kinship, siblings
solar. See houselot
space: Indian conceptions of, 127, 129
Spanish, 93; and Aztec government, 58; and land, 155–58; impact on estate administration, 162; impact on Indian culture, 114–15, 162, 165–68; judicial system, 51, 55. See also Conquest
Spanish inheritance, 84
Spanish kinship, 71–72
Spanish loanwords, 28, 37, 39, 44, 94, 102, 129, 177–81

256 / INDEX

Spanish naming patterns, 117–18; and status, 120–21
status, 107–23; and names, 117–22; and Spanish names, 120–21; and wealth, 107, 108, 109, 110–12, 123; leveling after Conquest, 108. *See also* commoners; native hierarchy; nobles
stone (for construction), 22, 101
stonemasons, 32, 101
storage rooms, 99
subsistence, 87
Suero, don Pedro de, 62, 88, 99, 121, 129, 131–32, 134, 146
sujeto, 37, 38
surveyor, 41, 49
sweatbath, 100, 102
swords, 104

tatli, 72
taxation, 36, 158
Tecali, 109
teccalli, 145
tecomate, 103
tecpan, 141, 145, 151
tecpancalli, 99, 141
Tecpanecatl, Mateo Juárez, 30
tecpanpouhqui, 145
tecpantlalli, 145
tecuhtli, 109, 110
teicuh, 119, 120
Teicuh, Ana, 121
Teicuh, doña María, 121
Teicuh, Lucía, 77, 80, 113, 139
Teicuh, María (of Cihuatecpan), 77, 78, 80, 99, 119, 134, 152
Teicuh, María (of Tezcacoac), 64, 82, 121
teilpiloyan. See jail
Téllez, Baltasar, 13, 59, 61, 62, 80, 113
Téllez, don Juan, 47, 102, 104
telpochcalli. See "young men's house"
temazcalli. See sweatbath
temples, 87, 147; and land, 141, 142–43
teniente, 37
Tenochtitlan, xvi, 2, 5, 6, 133
Teotihuacan: contacts with Culhuacan, 3
teniente, 58

teotlalli, 141, 142–43
tepancalli, 87. *See also* enclosure; palace
Tepaneca, 3, 4
tequiticatepixqui, 41
tequitopile, 41
tequixquiçacatl, 138
tequixquitlalli. See nitrous land
testaments, xi, xii. *See also Testaments of Culhuacan, The;* wills
Testaments of Culhuacan, The, xi, xii, xiv, xvi, 9–12, 169
testigos, 29. *See also* wills, witnesses to
Tetla, 25, 36, 37, 38, 94, 126
Teuhccho, Marta, 77
Teuhcihuatl, Gerónimo, 69, 147–48
teuhtlalli. See land, dry
Texalpan, 25
Texcoco, 129, 141, 149
Texcoco region, 139
textiles, 87, 103–104, 114. *See also* weaving
Tezca, Juan, 20, 22, 60
Tezcacoac, 54, 145
Tezozomoc of Texcoco, 5
tlacapan, 119, 120
Tiacapan, Ana, 19, 77
Tiacapan, Ana (of Amantlan), 99–100, 139
Tiacapan, Ana (of Santa Cruz), 55, 99
Tiacapan, Ana (of Tepanecapan), 20, 27, 30, 31–32, 45, 63, 69, 89, 97, 100, 102
Tiacapan, Ana (of Tezcacoac), 31
Tiacapan, Cristina, 33, 51, 183–87
Tiacapan, Juana, 18, 54
Tiacapan, Juana (of Atempan), 77, 89, 103, 114
Tiacapan, Juana (of Aticpac), 22, 23, 27, 55, 61, 77, 134
Tiacapan, Juana (of Coatlan), 140
Tiacapan, Juana (of Mexico City), 92, 94
Tiacapan, Francisco, 80
Tiacapan, Magdalena, 121
Tiacapan, María, 11, 14, 19, 59, 62, 63, 64, 80, 89–90, 94, 119, 127
Tiacapan, María (of Cihuatecpan), 73, 129
Tiacapan, María (of Coatlan), 71, 72, 80, 89

Tiacapan, María (of Tianquizçolco), 24, 64, 76, 77, 80, 82, 91, 93, 94
Tiacapantzin, doña Ana, 121
timekeeping, 43–44
titles, 39–41. *See also* native hierarchy; nobles
tlacamecayotl, 66–69. *See also* Aztec kinship
Tlacatecpan (San Francisco), 54
tlacatecuhtli, 119
Tlacatecuhtli, Miguel Sánchez, 119
tlaco, 119
Tlaco, Agustina, 119
Tlaco, Ana, 22, 61–62, 94
Tlaco, Ana (of Yecapixtla), 76, 96
Tlaco, Bárbara, 13, 14, 64, 69, 73, 80, 119
Tlaco, María, 69
tlacochcalcatl, 109, 119
Tlacochcalcatl, Juan Rafael, 23, 30, 54, 98, 119, 134, 138, 143, 148
Tlacuilocan Xallah (Santa Ana), 53–54
tlalcacutle, 101
tlalcohualli. See land, purchased
Tlallachco, 127
tlalmantli. See land, level
tlalmilli, 137–38. *See also* land, cultivated
tlalnemactli. See land, inherited
tlalpouhqui, 49. *See* surveyor
tlalpoztli, 140
tlaltopile, 41, 49
Tlamacazco, 143
tlamecayotl, 70–71
tlapancalli, 99
Tlatecco, 125, 126
Tlatelolco, 91
tlatli, 72
tlatoani, 36, 39, 49, 140–41, 142, 153, 161; separated from *juez-gobernador,* 39
tlatocatlalli, 39, 141, 142. *See also* land, ruler's office land
tlatoque, 87, 142
Tlauhpotonqui, Luis, 19, 26–27, 30, 33, 74, 76, 77, 91, 92, 94, 122, 134, 153, 169
Tlaxcala, 6, 38, 39, 41, 122, 141
tlaxicaleque, 53
tlaxicalli, 36, 53. *See also* wards
tlaxilacalleh, 54

Tlaxoxiuhco, 95
Tleçannen, Melchor, 73–74
tlecopatl, 99
tlemachica, 118
Tlemachica, Antonio, 11, 14, 23–24, 27, 28, 59, 73, 103, 110, 118, 120–21, 144
tliltic, 43
Toca, Antonio, 112
tochomitl, 113
Tocititlan, 142
Tollan, 4
Toltecs, xi, xiv, 1, 3, 5, 36; relationship with Culhuacan, 3–4
tonatiuh ycalaquiyanpa ytzicac, 127
tonatiuh yquiçayanpa ytzticac, 127
tools, 103, 104; native agricultural, 140
topile, 45, 57, 61, 109
topileque, 92
Torquemada, Juan de, 133, 141
Tototl, Juan, 78
town councillor. *See regidor*
towns, post-conquest, 39; segregation of, 49. *See also* cities; *names of specific towns*
Transfiguración (ward of), 96
transportation, 96–97; lakes, 2
Tres Reyes. *See* Eitatlocan
tribute, 42, 58, 87, 108, 111, 133, 140, 145, 158
Tzapotla, 62
-tzin, 60
tzontli, 130, 131

uncles. *See* Aztec kinship, uncles and aunts

Valley of Mexico, xiii, 1–3, 13, 96, 101, 140
Valley of Toluca, 1
vara, 129
Vázquez, Agustín, 13, 30, 35, 111
Vázquez, Bernardino, 11, 99, 129, 134, 136–37
Vazquez, Francisco, 46
Velasco, don Juan Marcos de, 48
Velazquez, Juan, xv–xvi, 11, 14, 23, 26, 32, 53, 54, 59, 61, 68, 89, 98, 110, 114, 120, 140
villa, 38

258 / INDEX

village life, 2–3
violence, 19

wage labor, xv, 89–90, 104; agricultural, 90
ward heads, 53, 55, 63, 115, 149; and *tecpan,* 146; and land, 158
wards, 53–58, 61; and elders, 54–55; and residence, 54–55; and tribute, 58
wealth, 87–105; and land, 87–89; and status, 107, 108, 109, 110–12, 123; defined, 87; movable goods as, 102; prehispanic, 87; sources of, 87, 90; types of, 102, 104–105
weavers, 87, 89
weaving, 112, 113, 114
widowhood, 116
willow, 140
wills, xi–xii, 163–64; and Church; and kinship, 77–85; as religious acts, 14, 18, 19, 21, 26, 27–28; before Conquest, 16; bequests of crops, 89; bequests for charity to poor, 26–27; bequests of land, 88, 89; bequests to offspring, 78; bequests to siblings, 75; bequests to spouses, 64; disputes over inheritance, 44, 50–51, 53; laws regarding, 16–17, 29–30; multiple heirs, 79; procedure, 19–21; repository for, 33; types of, 28–29; use of *et cetera* in, 19; uses of, xii, 170; witnesses to, 28–31. *See also* executors, inheritance, notaries, witnesses
witnesses, 28–32, 44, 47
"woman land," 141, 149
"woman's house," 100–101
women, 122–23, 164–66; and agricultural work, 140; and daughters, 80; and hierarchies, 122–23; and inheritance, 165; and land, 145, 164–65; and offices, 115; and property ownership, 115–16; and Spanish surnames, 121; bequests of houses by, 79–80; commoner, 116; control of property by, 184, 122–23; elite, 116; hygiene of, 100; names of, 117; nobility, 126; roles in marriage, 62, 81; status of, 116–17. *See also* marriage
women's equipment, 113
women's speech, 117, 122
writing: Aztec, 16

xacalli, 100, 102
xochiamatl, 118
Xochiamatl, Vicente, 32, 55, 71, 72, 90, 101, 139
Xochicuetzin, Martín Tlacochcalcatl, 23, 31
Xochimilco, 3, 4, 5, 38, 74, 76, 81, 98, 100, 127, 128, 133
xoco, 119
Xoco, Ana, 21, 74, 111
Xoco, Juana, 63
Xoco, Luisa, 121
Xoco, María, 32, 119
Xomiltepec, 92, 93

Yaochihualoc, Agustín, 95
yaotl, 118
Yaotl, Domingo, 22, 89, 139
Yecapixtla, 54, 62, 76, 94, 95, 105
"young men's house," 100

zacate, 138
Zacatecas, 7
Zimbrón, fray Juan, 21, 35, 111
Zorita, Alonso de, 53, 55, 62, 65, 69, 141